CHARLES DICKENS

CHARLES DICKENS

THE MAKING OF A LITERARY GIANT

BY

Christopher Hibbert

First published as *The Making of Charles Dickens* in 1967 by Harper and Row
Publishers, Inc.

This edition, first published in paperback in 2009 by PALGRAVE
MACMILLAN® in the United States – a division of St. Martin's Press LLC,
175 Fifth Avenue, New York, NY 10010.

Where this book is distributed in the UK, Europe and the rest of the world,
this is by Palgrave Macmillan, a division of Macmillan Publishers Limited,
registered in England, company number 785998, of Houndmills, Basingstoke,
Hampshire RG21 6XS.

Palgrave Macmillan is the global academic imprint of the above companies and
has companies and representatives throughout the world.

Palgrave® and Macmillan® are registered trademarks in the United States, the
United Kingdom, Europe and other countries.

ISBN-13: 978-0-230-61426-0
ISBN-10: 0-230-61426-4

Library of Congress Cataloging-in-Publication Data is available from the
Library of Congress.

A catalogue record of the book is available from the British Library.

Design by Macmillan Publishing Solutions

First PALGRAVE MACMILLAN paperback edition: May 2009

10 9 8 7 6 5 4 3 2 1

Printed in the United States of America.

For Godfrey and Jane

When my thoughts go back now to that slow agony of my youth, I wonder how much of the histories I invented hangs like a mist of fancy over well-remembered facts! When I tread the old ground, I do not wonder that I seem to see and pity, going on before me, an innocent romantic boy, making his imaginative world out of such strange experiences and sordid things.

The Personal History of
David Copperfield

CONTENTS

FOREWORD

I was lucky enough to read *Charles Dickens* when it was first published forty years ago. It was one of the books that convinced me as a young scholar that devoting my career to Victorian fiction would be a professional life well spent.

In the larger sphere, Christopher Hibbert's admirably jargonless biography played a role in one of the necessary corrections of English literary history. For a century after his death, Dickens had been depreciated along the lines of Fitzjames Stephen's jaundiced verdict on *Oliver Twist*—'all very well, but damned low'. In his dictatorial work on English fiction, *The Great Tradition* (1948), F. R. Leavis cast Dickens among the irredeemably less than great—at least as an artist. He was, at best, a 'great entertainer'. Nothing more.

The rehabilitation of Dickens as a writer of Shakespearian achievement was the work of many critical hands. Edmund Wilson played a pioneer's part with his essay, 'Dickens: the Two Scrooges'. Wilson was American and psychoanalytically inclined. Humphry House, an Oxford don, took a more social historical line in *The Dickens World* (1950). House portrayed the novelist as a child of his age—an age which had been slashed, as by a knife, by the industrial revolution. House noted Dickens's practice of nostalgically 'antedating' the action of his fiction to a period before the railways thundered across the Victorian landscape. He inhabited two worlds—and always yearned for the one which was forever lost.

Other critics were instrumental in Dickens's critical rehabilitation and Christopher Hibbert deserves a place in their roll of honour. He was not a career Dickensian. He was what John Gross (another distinguished Dickensian in one of his many parts) called 'the English man of letters'.

Hibbert founds his book on a question that must fascinate all admirers of the novelist. How did Dickens happen? The key lay, of course, in the child and young man. But the formative experience was not merely those traumatic months in Warren's Blacking Factory. Hibbert locates the core of Dickens's genius years earlier in the 'grisly fables' his nurse told him:

> All his life he was to be fascinated by the sinister and the grotesque, the fanciful, the morbid and the occult, those dark corners of the

mind that he felt irresistibly drawn to explore. His work—even his *Child's History of England*—is full of the strange fruits of this festering imagination, this disquieting, insatiable curiosity which was to lead him, almost against his will—'dragged by invisible forces', as he put it himself—to wander at night into the slum quarters of London and into the morgues of Paris, fearful, as so many of his characters are, not only *for* himself but *of* himself. (p. 19)

These phobic terrors would have destroyed others. Mysteriously, they made Dickens. No critic has used more intelligently than Hibbert the typically little read and fugitive pieces of Dickens's work (the 'Uncommercial Traveller' essays, for example). Nor has any commentator more skilfully knit his conclusions around his subject's own words, which are made, by apt citation, to glow on the page. Dickens is not merely discussed: he is vividly present everywhere in this book.

The portrait which emerges is complex. The medical term was not current when Hibbert wrote, but his diagnosis irresistibly recalls bipolar disorder—manic bursts of energy alternating with black, paralysing, gloom.

Admiring as the study is, Hibbert never flinches from less sympathetic aspects about his subject. The Dickens, for example, who dismissed publishers like Macrone, Bentley, and Bradbury & Evans, who had helped him on his way. Equally unflinching is Hibbert's depiction of Dickens the husband, chronically impatient with Mrs Dickens and her perpetual 'uninteresting condition'—that is, the ten children she laboriously bore him. To those children, whom he could never see as worthy of himself, he was often a poor father: even before he cast off his wife in favour of a young partner, Ellen Ternan, scarcely older than some of them were.

Hibbert wrote his study of Dickens at a time when to write well and to be well read was not automatically decried as dilettantism: when scholarship did not mean dragging a vast trail of footnotes behind the text like Marley's chain. There have been hundreds of books and thousands of articles on the novelist since 1967. This remains one of the handful it is essential to read.

—John Sutherland

AUTHOR'S NOTE

'There is no need to emphasise any more', Humphry House wrote in *The Dickens World*, that Dickens 'used the years of his youth with a persistence and confident exactness unequalled by any other writer whose youth was not, like Proust's, his one chosen subject. . . . The years between 1816, when he was four, and 1836, when he began to be successful, could bring his imagination to a state of such intense creative excitement that he was sometimes tempted to draw on that time mechanically when other capital failed; or else in a moment of hesitation a scrap would shoot up from his memory and bring a whole dull page to life.'

In this book I have tried to record all that can be discovered about Dickens's childhood, to tell the story of the early years of his success, and, at the same time, to show how he interpreted his youthful experiences both to his readers and to himself. I have also attempted to show how these experiences affected him as a writer and as a man.

Although I had been reading and re-reading his novels with increasing admiration for nearly thirty years, I cannot pretend to be a Dickens scholar. And my debt to those who can is naturally very great. I must express particular gratitude to Professor Edgar Johnson whose excellent two-volume biography has perhaps as strong a claim to be considered definitive as any life could have—at least until the Clarendon edition of the novels and the Pilgrim edition of *The Letters* are completed.

I want also to thank Mrs Madeline House whose editorship of the letters (with Graham Storey) has been so skilfully begun. Mrs House, in addition to her other generous help and advice, has been good enough to answer my questions about any of the so far unpublished letters which might have had a bearing on my theme.

For their great kindness in having read the manuscript I am most grateful to Lady Pansy Pakenham and Professor K. J. Fielding, both of whom have given me much helpful advice.

I am most grateful, also, to Mr William J. Carlton, the leading authority on Dickens's early years, who has found time to give me some useful information.

For their help in a variety of other ways I want to thank Mr Cedric

C. Dickens, Mr Leslie C. Staples (Editor of *The Dickensian*), Miss D. L. Minards (Assistant Secretary of the Dickens Fellowship), the late Lord Brain, Dr J. F. Foster, Dr Francis Sheppard, Mr Hamish Francis, Mr Anthony Rubinstein, the partners of Messrs Wood, Nash & Co., the staffs of the Records Department of the Law Society and of the London Library, Mrs Joan St George Saunders, Mr Timothy Toswill, Mr Maurice Richardson, Mr Jonathan Owen, Mrs Maurice Hill and my father.

I am very grateful also to my wife for having read the proofs and prepared the index.

Quotations from Dickens's letters written between 1820 and 1839 are taken from the Pilgrim Edition and are reproduced by permission of the Clarendon Press, Oxford. Passages from letters written after 1839 are taken with permission from the Nonesuch Edition published by the Nonesuch Press. In quoting extracts from Dickens's speeches I have followed the texts given in K. J. Fielding's edition published by the Oxford University Press.

C. H.

A NOTE ON THE REFERENCES

The sources of quotations from Dickens's novels, short stories and articles are given at the foot of the page. All other sources and notes are at the end of the book and start on p. 271. Numbers not enclosed in brackets refer to sources only; numbers enclosed in brackets refer to additional information or critical comment.

I

THE BETTER WORLD
1812-1822
aet. 1-10

2 ORDNANCE TERRACE AND 18 ST MARY'S PLACE
CHATHAM KENT

*All my early readings and early imaginations dated
from this place, and I took them away so full of
innocent construction and guileless belief, and I
brought them back so worn and torn, so much the
wiser and so much the worse.*

The Uncommercial Traveller

1

Soon after the death of Lord Crewe's old butler in 1785, his widow, Mrs Elizabeth Dickens, was appointed housekeeper at Crewe Hall, Cheshire, at a salary of eight guineas a year. She was a talkative, warm-hearted, though outwardly rather formidable woman in her early forties, who derived great pleasure from telling a story; and Lord Crewe's children could well remember in later years how, on winter evenings, they used to sit round the fire in Mrs Dickens's neat little room, and listen to her retailing her eccentric versions of fairy stories, historical legends, and tales from her own past, suitably exaggerated and embellished for the benefit of young listeners.

In her old age she lived in retirement in Oxford Street, and here her grandson Charles, her younger son John's little boy, was taken to see her. Charles seems to have been a little frightened of his grandmother, faintly intimidated by that gracious severity of deportment, the acquired manner of women who have been employed as upper servants in the houses of the rich. And there were those who thought that they recognised in Mrs Rouncewell, the elderly housekeeper at Chesney Wold, a good deal of the character of old Mrs Dickens:

'Mrs Rouncewell is rather deaf, which nothing will induce her to believe. She is a fine old lady, handsome, stately, wonderfully neat, and has such a back, and such a stomacher, that if her stays should turn out when she dies to have been a broad old-fashioned family fire-grate, nobody who knows her would have cause to be surprised.'*

Mrs Dickens died in April 1824; and although the pension she received from Lord Crewe died with her, she was able to leave her two sons £950 from her accumulated savings. Her elder son William, to whom she had already given £750, received £500. But John (who had been born the year her husband died at the age of sixty-six) was left only £450.

For John had been a disappointment to her. He was, she said, a 'lazy fellow', and one of Lord Crewe's daughters recalled how Mrs Dickens 'never tired of inveighing against his idleness and general incapacity'. She had been obliged, so she often complained, to give her son 'many a

* *Bleak House*, ch. VII.

sound cuff on the ear', and had made him many a loan which was never repaid.

John was not really a lazy fellow. But he was certainly an improvident one, most of whose life had been spent, and was always to be spent, in the midst of financial difficulties. Generous, extravagant, socially pretentious and gregarious, he found it quite impossible to manage on the money he received as a clerk in the Navy Pay Office.

He had entered the Office in 1805, on the recommendation of Lord Crewe, who was a close friend of George Canning, Treasurer of the Navy. His salary was five shillings a day. It had risen, after four years' satisfactory service, to rather more than £100 a year; and on this income he had married, renting a small but genteel house on the outskirts of Portsmouth where he had been posted by the Office to pay off ships in the Dockyard.

His bride was Elizabeth Barrow, a small, gay, pretty girl of nineteen whose family were in far better circumstances, both socially and financially, than his own. Her father, Charles Barrow, was also in the Navy Pay Office, but in a much more exalted position than his son-in-law. Elizabeth's mother was the daughter of a retired manufacturer of musical instruments who had been in a fair way of business at Bristol and Cheapside and who proudly numbered amongst his ancestors several of the more distinguished worthies of Buckinghamshire.[1]

It came as a fearful shock to the family, therefore, when, eight months after his daughter's marriage, Charles Barrow was accused of extensive and prolonged embezzlement, and fled abroad leaving his ten children in the care of his distracted wife. They soon recovered from their disgrace, however, and two at least of the sons became well enough off to be frequently subjected to their prodigal brother-in-law's urgent importunities.

At his house near Portsmouth—387 Mile End Terrace, Landport[2]—this tiresomely irrepressible brother-in-law still lived well beyond his means. The rent of £35 a year was a good deal more than he could afford; and after a daughter, Fanny, was born, in the autumn of 1810, he was in tighter straits than ever. For although a family had been started, a nursemaid employed, and a second child soon conceived, neither he nor his lively and sociable wife was prepared to forgo the pleasures to which she had always been used and he had always aspired.

On the evening of 6 February 1812 Mrs Dickens, in the last stages of her pregnancy, went to a dance at the Beneficial Societies Hall. She arrived home in the early morning of the 7th, and a few hours later the new baby was born. It was a boy. He was christened Charles (after her father) John (after her husband) Huffam (after his godfather, Christopher Huffam, a well-to-do 'Rigger to His Majesty's Navy', whom John Dickens had met in the course of his duties).

By midsummer the family's finances had reached such a low ebb that they were compelled to make the first of the moves that were to become a regular feature of Charles's childhood. Their new home, in Hawke Street, was a poor place compared with the one that they had left. It was in a respectable neighbourhood which contained several villas advertising rooms to let to 'superior naval persons'. But it was a small cheap house with wooden steps up to the front door, and a box-like parlour whose window faced out directly on to the street. (3)

Charles's first memories appear to have been of life in this house. They were misty and muddled memories; but they came to him as happy ones. He had dream-like recollections of crawling about in the tiny back garden with his sister, Fanny, at his side and with something to eat in his hand, a piece of bread and jam perhaps or a bun with currants in the middle. He seemed to remember the nursemaid looking at him through the basement window, her face on a level with the gravel path. He had vague memories, too, of being carried up to see the soldiers of the garrison marching about on parade, and of being taken down to the dockyard to watch the sailors coming off the ships, and then, on a cold winter's day, of leaving Portsmouth and going by coach to London.

He did not remember this time in London, though. The house where they had lodgings was at 10 Norfolk Street (now Cleveland Street) which runs from Euston Road to Goodge Street between the Middlesex Hospital and Tottenham Court Road. But he could not call it to mind.

When in 1817 the family moved to Chatham, however, the world in which he lived took on a sharp, clear reality which was never to be forgotten.

John Dickens had had his income raised to over £200 a year and had been offered a more responsible job in the enormous Chatham dockyard. (4) It seemed to him that his financial difficulties might at last be over, and he left to take up his new appointment in cheerful spirits.

There were three children at the time of the move to Chatham: Fanny who was seven, Charles who was five, and a new baby, Letitia, who was one. There had been a baby brother, Alfred, but he had died when only a few months old.

John was still only thirty-two himself; Elizabeth was twenty-eight. Also part of the family now was Elizabeth's eldest sister, Mary, who had come to live with them after her husband, a lieutenant in the Royal Navy, had been drowned off the coast of Brazil. And, as well as the nursemaid, Mary Weller, there was a kitchen maid, Jane Bonny. They all got on very well together, Charles thought; and they were happy.

2

The sun was shining when John Dickens and his family arrived in Chatham on a hot midsummer's day. The coach was driven through the town and up the hill to a row of neat, three-storied houses in Ordnance Terrace, where it stopped outside Number 2.[5] The big hayfield opposite was covered with daisies and buttercups.

The pleasant, spacious house stood back from the street behind tall iron railings. The site was high and healthy and the wide sash windows of the bedrooms looked down upon the roofs of the lower town and the River Medway winding its sluggish way through the marshes. The neighbourhood was respectably and firmly middle class.

Three doors away lived an old lady, Mrs Newnham, a widow whose son lived in India and whose house was an ideal of neatness and gentility. She sometimes came to tea at Number 2, and when she did so her maid Sarah would come out first to knock on the door so that the old lady did not have to wait outside in the cold. When the invitations were returned, Mrs Newnham and Sarah dusted and polished the room, got out the best china tea-service and the Pope Joan board, and the visitors were 'received in the drawing-room in great state'.

Dickens's later descriptions of Mrs Newnham's behaviour and way of life are coloured, of course, by his inventive imagination. But the picture he presents of her, and of her neighbours, is a true and revealing one of the kind of people amongst whom these early years at Chatham were spent:

> The little front parlour, which is the old lady's ordinary sitting-room, is a perfect picture of quiet neatness: the carpet is covered with brown Holland, the glass and picture-frames are carefully enveloped in yellow muslin; the table-covers are never taken off, except when the leaves are turpentined and bees'-waxed, an operation which is regularly commenced every other morning at half-past nine o'clock—and the little knick-knacks are always arranged in precisely the same manner. The greater part of these are presents from little girls whose parents live in the same row. . . .

Here the old lady sits with her spectacles on, busily engaged in needlework—near the window in summer-time; and if she sees you coming up the steps, and you happen to be a favourite, she trots out to open the street-door for you before you knock. . . .

Her name always heads the list of any benevolent subscriptions, and hers are always the most liberal donations to the Winter Coal and Soup Distribution Society. She subscribed £20 towards the creation of an organ in our Parish Church, and was so overcome the first Sunday the children sang to it, that she was obliged to be carried out by the pew-opener.*

Next door to Mrs Newnham lived an old naval officer on half-pay who was, so Dickens said, often to be seen smoking cigars in his front garden or lifting up his neighbour's door-knocker with his walking-stick and asking her maid to be kind enough to pass him a glass of table ale over the railings.

Fancying himself as something of an odd-job man he seems to have been a severe trial to the old lady, taking her eight-day clock to pieces in order to clean it and then finding himself unable to put it together again, cleaning her brass door plate with aqua-fortis so that her name was completely effaced from it, filling her garden with unwanted marigolds, and dropping the silk-worms he bred on to her carpet.

But all this is nothing to his seditious conduct in public life. He attends every vestry meeting that is held; always opposes the constituted authorities of the parish, denounces the profligacy of the church-wardens, contests legal points against the vestry-clerk, *will* make the tax-gatherer call for his money till he won't call any longer, and then he sends it: finds fault with the sermon every Sunday, says that the organist ought to be ashamed of himself, offers to back himself for any amount to sing the psalms better than all the children put together, male and female; and, in short, conducts himself in the most turbulent and uproarious manner.

The worst of it all is, that having a high regard for the old lady, he wants to make her a convert to his views, and therefore walks into her little parlour with his newspaper in his hand, and talks violent politics by the hour.†

Immediately next door to the Dickenses, at Number 1, the last house of the terrace, lived a little girl of Charles's own age, Lucy Stroughill, and her elder brother George, nicknamed 'Struggles'.(6) Charles confessed that he fell in love with Lucy, a 'peach-faced creature in a blue sash, and shoes to correspond', who frequently asked him to tea. It always

* *Sketches by Boz*, 'Our Parish'.   † *Ibid.*

seemed to be her birthday and he could never think about her afterwards
without surrounding her with seed cake, sweet wine and shining presents.
George had a magic lantern.

'Sometimes Charles would come downstairs,' his nurse, Mary Weller
recalled, 'and say to me, "Now, Mary, clear the kitchen, we are going
to have such a game", and then George Stroughill would come in with
his magic lantern and they would sing, recite, and perform parts of
plays.'⁷

Once Charles and another girl, whom he called Olympia, were taken
to an orrery, where, so he said:

> A low-spirited gentleman with a wand said, 'Ladies and Gentlemen'
> meaning particularly Olympia and me, 'the lights are about to be
> put out, but there is not the slightest cause for alarm.' It was very
> alarming. Then the planets and stars began. Sometimes they wouldn't
> come on, sometimes they wouldn't go off, sometimes they had holes
> in them, and mostly they didn't seem to be good likenesses. All this
> time the gentleman with the wand was going on in the dark tapping
> away at the heavenly bodies, between whiles, like a wearisome wood-
> pecker, about a sphere revolving on its own axis eight hundred and
> ninety-seven thousand millions of times—or miles—in two hundred and
> sixty-three thousand five hundred and twenty-four millions of some-
> thing elses. . . .
>   Olympia, also, became much depressed, and we both slumbered and
> woke cross, and still the gentleman was going on in the dark, cyphering
> away about planes of orbits to such an infamous extent that Olympia,
> stung to madness, actually kicked me.*

Usually, however, such excursions ended less unhappily, for Charles was
a contented, friendly child, easy to like and easy to entertain. He did not
yet go to school. It was his mother who taught him to read, using alphabet
books 'with deliciously smooth covers of bright red or green', and it was
she who gave him his first lessons in English, and even in Latin. She
taught him, he was convinced, 'thoroughly well'. She was 'a dear good
mother', Mary Weller thought, 'and a fine woman'.

Her son, however, even at this age and before his experiences in
London had aroused such bitterness in his heart, seems to have felt
closer to his father than to her.

Indulgent, good-natured and expansive, John Dickens, preferring to
entertain his children, or be entertained by them, rather than to instruct
them, was not a responsible parent. Yet he was indeed a lovable one. He

---

* *The Uncommercial Traveller*, 'Birthday Celebrations'.

was 'a chatty, pleasant companion', a man who knew him in later years remembered, 'possessing a varied fund of anecdotes and a genuine vein of humour. He was a well-built man, rather stout, of very active habits, a little pompous. . . . He dressed well, and wore a goodly bunch of seals suspended across his waistcoat from his watch chain.'[8]

He loved telling stories and in Charles and Fanny he had an admiring, captive audience. He often took them out for walks and for trips on the river, for visits to Rochester and down to the local inn.

When he went to Sheerness on business, he would take them with him. They went in the *Chatham*, an old yacht belonging to the Navy Pay Office, and it was 'a grand treat' to sail in her, past the muddy-looking islands in the Medway and the flocks of sheep pasturing on the marshes and the little craft that bobbed about in the silvery grey water, towards the great ships standing out to sea.

Often Charles and his dearly loved father would go for walks alone together, and when he was old enough they got as far as Frindsbury, Chequers Street and Chalk. A favourite walk of theirs was to make for Cobham, as Pickwick, Snodgrass and Winkle do—and

a delightful walk it was . . . through a deep and shady wood, cooled by the light wind which gently rustled the thick foliage, and enlivened by the songs of the birds that perched upon the boughs. The ivy and the moss crept in thick clusters over the old trees, and the soft green turf overspread the ground like a silken mat. They emerged upon an open park, with an ancient hall [Cobham Hall, seat of the Earl of Darnley], displaying the quaint and picturesque architecture of Elizabeth's time. Long vistas of stately oaks and elm trees appeared on every side: large herds of deer were cropping the fresh grass; and occasionally a startled hare scoured along the ground, with the speed of the shadows thrown by the light clouds which sweep across a sunny landscape like a passing breath of summer.*

Charles and his father would call at The Leather Bottle opposite the church, 'a clean and commodious village ale-house' whose low-roofed parlour was 'furnished with a large number of high-backed leather-cushioned chairs, of fantastic shapes, and embellished with a great variety of old portraits and roughly-coloured prints of some antiquity'.† Then they would go home by way of Gad's Hill where Falstaff robbed the travellers.

There was a house at Gad's Hill which Charles much admired, an imposing red brick house with big bay windows, a white-painted portico

* *Pickwick Papers*, ch. XI.　　　† *Ibid.*

and a charming little belltower on the slated mansard roof. It was called Gad's Hill Place, and noticing how much his son was impressed by it, John Dickens said to him one day, 'If you were to be very persevering, Charles, and were to work hard, you might some day come to live in it.' Oh, thought Charles, but that's impossible. He always remembered, though, what his father had said.

They went home along the Canterbury-Dover road, past the cherry orchards, and the corn fields and the hop gardens. If they were lucky, the Dover mail would come rattling down the hill behind them into Snorridge Bottom. On their way back through Rochester they might stop for a moment on the bridge, and, leaning on the parapet, contemplate the scene as Mr Pickwick did when he was waiting for breakfast before his ride to Dingley Dell:

> On either side, the banks of the Medway, covered with cornfields and pastures, with here and there a windmill, or a distant church, stretched away as far as the eye could see, presenting a rich and varied landscape, rendered more beautiful by the changing shadows which passed swiftly across it, as the thin and half-formed clouds skimmed away in the light of the morning sun. The river, reflecting the clear blue of the sky, glistened and sparkled as it flowed noiselessly on; and the oars of the fishermen dipped into the water with a clear and liquid sound. . . .*

It is an idyllic scene. It is the setting for the first adventures in Dickens's first novel, and, overcast by a deepening gloom, it is the setting for the enduring mysteries of his last. It is the background of an early childhood which remained precious to him for ever, and to which he felt repeatedly drawn to return. 'Ah! fine place,' as Alfred Jingle, the strolling actor in *Pickwick*, jauntily describes it, 'glorious pile—frowning walls—tottering arches—dark nooks—crumbling staircases—old Cathedral too—earthy smell—pilgrims' feet worn away the old steps—little Saxon doors—confessionals like money-takers' boxes at theatres—queer customers those monks . . . fine place—old legends too—strange stories: capital.'†

When it reappears for the last time the sparkle and freshness have gone, and there remains only the drowsy antiquity, shadowed now by a sombre atmosphere of decay and sad nostalgia, and such an 'oppressive respectability' that the tramps, who pass through the narrow streets of the town, quicken their limp a little.

It is a 'monotonous, silent city, deriving an earthy flavour throughout

---

* *Pickwick Papers*, ch. v. † *Pickwick Papers*, ch. II.

from its Cathedral crypt . . . a drowsy city whose inhabitants seem to suppose, with an inconsistency more strange than rare, that all its changes lie behind it . . . a city of another time with its hoarse Cathedral bell, its hoarser and less distinct rooks. . . . All things in it are of the past.'*

3

When he was six, Charles was sent to school with Fanny. It was a very small dame-school, upstairs over a dyer's shop, in Rome Lane; and he hated going there. In a room at the back there lived a woman who was always sniffing and who never appeared outside her room without a brown beaver bonnet on her head. She owned a fearful puppy, 'a puffy pug-dog', which ran barking down 'an eternal entry long and narrow' whenever the children approached. It snapped at Charles's legs and, in his anxiety to escape, the frightened little boy would fall over the steps and sometimes bang his ankle as he nervously and hastily cleaned his shoes on the mud-scraper. 'The bark of that baleful Pug, a certain radiating way' he had of snapping at his legs, 'the ghastly grinning of his moist black muzzle and white teeth, and the insolence of his crisp tail curled like a pastoral crook' lived in Charles's memory for ever.†

Even more formidable than the dog, was the vinegary old woman who kept the school, 'a grim and unsympathetic old personage, flavoured with musty dry lavender and dressed in black crape', who frightened and muddled the children by knocking them on the head with a hard knuckle in a perverse attempt to force out the right answers, and by pointing out the words in their reading books with a mesmerising pin.

In a speech given shortly before his death he referred to this old lady, who, to his mind, had 'ruled the world with the birch'. Mentioning her reading lessons, he continued, 'I thought the letters were printed and sent there to plague me, and I looked upon the printer as an enemy. When I was taught to say my prayers I was told to pray for my enemies, and I distinctly remember praying for the printer as my greatest enemy. I never now see a row of large, black, fat, staring Roman capitals, but this reminiscence rises up before me.'[9]

Some of the more forbidding aspects of Charles's grim teacher were later represented by her intimidated pupil in the character of Mrs Pipchin, the owner of that 'infantine boarding-house of a very select description' to which Paul Dombey is sent at Brighton.

---

* *Edwin Drood*, chs. III, XIV.   † *Reprinted Pieces*, 'Our School'.

[Mrs Pipchin was] a marvellous, ill-favoured, ill-conditioned old lady, of a stooping figure, with a mottled face like bad marble, a hook nose, and a hard grey eye, that looked as if it might have been hammered at on an anvil without sustaining any injury. Forty years at least had elapsed since the Peruvian mines had been the death of Mr Pipchin; but his relict still wore black bombazeen, of such a lustreless, deep, dead, sombre shade, that gas itself couldn't light her up after dark, and her presence was a quencher to any number of candles. . . .

She was held to be an old lady of remarkable firmness, who was quite scientific in the knowledge of the childish character. . . . It being a part of Mrs Pipchin's system not to encourage a child's mind to develop and expand itself like a young flower, but to open it by force like an oyster, the moral of [her Early Readings] was usually of a violent and stunning character—the hero (a naughty boy) seldom, in the mildest catastrophe, being finished off by anything less than a lion or a bear.

Such was life at Mrs Pipchin's.*

And something such, we may suppose, was life at the dame-school in Rome Lane, Chatham. For in a letter Dickens wrote to a friend when this passage appeared in one of the early instalments of *Dombey and Son*, he said, 'I hope you will like Mrs Pipchin's establishment. It is from the life, and I was there—I don't suppose I was eight years old; but I remember it all as well, and certainly understood it as well, as I do now.'[10]

Life had its compensations, though. Chatham was a wonderful place for a curious-minded little boy. Its principal productions, Mr Pickwick recorded, were

soldiers, sailors, Jews, chalk, shrimps, officers, and dockyard men. The commodities chiefly exposed for sale in the public streets, are marine stores, hard-bake, apples, flat-fish, and oysters. The streets present a lively and animated appearance, occasioned chiefly by the conviviality of the military. It is truly delightful to a philanthropic mind, to see these gallant men, staggering along under the influence of an overthrow, both of animal, and ardent spirits; more especially when we remember that the following them about, and jesting with them, affords a cheap and innocent amusement for the boy population. . . .

The consumption of tobacco must be very great; and the smell which pervades the streets must be exceedingly delicious to those who are extremely fond of smoking. A superficial traveller might object to the dirt which is their leading characteristic; but to those who view it as an indication of traffic, and commercial prosperity, it is truly gratifying.† [11]

* *Dombey and Son*, ch. VIII. 'New Year's Day', *All the Year Round* (January 1859).
† *Pickwick Papers*, ch. II.

'It being part of Mrs Pipchin's system not to encourage a child's mind to develop and expand itself like a young flower, but to open it by force like an oyster'

The Dockyard was not far from the Dickenses' house, and sometimes his father would take Charles down with him to the office, a staid, red-brick building with heavily barred windows and strong-rooms lined throughout with iron. On the white stone steps his father would kiss him and leave him to wander off, to stare in the windows of the marine store shops, to peer at the rough blue jackets with their mother-of-pearl buttons, the oilskin hats and the enormous canvas trousers, the models of ships in bottles, prints of naval battles, compasses, silver watches in thick leather cases, tobacco boxes with anchors on the lids, cases full of rusty guns, and trays full of rusty keys.

Often Charles would go down to the gun-wharf to see the huge stores of cannon and shot guarded by a single red-coated soldier who marched up and down in front of them, 'a mere toy figure, with a clockwork movement'. Or he would go to see the reservoirs where the timber was steeped and seasoned, and watch the travelling crane on its overhead railway lifting the immense logs out of the water and carrying them away dripping to the stacks—and he would think how much he would like to work that crane himself. He would sit for hours with the smell of oakum and tarred rope in his nostrils, watching the workmen hammering in the empty hulls of the half-built ships, the joiners planing the blades of oars, the anchor-smiths and block-makers, and the rope-makers working in a ring, the storekeepers rolling great coils of hemp, and making lists of sails and spars and rigging and rowlocks and those curious twisted shapes of metal so precious in the eyes of shipwrights.

The best day in the year to go down to the yard was 23 November, St Clement's Day. For then the blacksmiths held a pageant in honour of their patron saint, made their traditional speeches, and collected money from the officers of the dockyard before parading round the streets of the town.

The senior apprentice, chosen to play the part of Old Clem in an oakum wig, a mask and a long white beard, was carried at the head of the procession in a chair with a crown and anchor on the top. Surrounded by attendants carrying torches, banners and flags, and marching to the music of a drum and fife, he stopped at the various public houses of the town and took his companions in for a drink. And whenever the smiths moved off to the next inn they sang the song, in imitation of the measure of a hammer beating on an anvil, that Joe Gargery sings at his forge:

> 'Beat it out, beat it out—old Clem!
> With a clink for the stout—old Clem!

Blow the fire, blow the fire—old Clem!
Roaring dryer, soaring higher—old Clem!'*

Some of the work in the dockyard was done by convicts under the eyes of soldiers who marched them up and down from the great prison hulk that was anchored in the dock like a wicked Noah's ark, 'cribbed and barred and moored by massive rusty chains'. Newly sentenced convicts were brought down from London by stage-coach, handcuffed together, two by two, with irons on their legs and 'with great numbers on their backs as if they were street doors'. They carried with them, 'that curious flavour of bread-poultice, baize, rope-yarn, and hearthstone which attends the convict presence'.† Then they were rowed out to the hulk, and were only seen again when they were let out to work in the yard.

And from the yard, behind the tall chimneys smoking above the ceaseless clangour 'with a quiet—almost a lazy—air, like giants smoking tobacco', only a little way beyond the immensely formidable gates, the convicts could see the open country of cornfields, hop-gardens and orchards.

There Charles could forget the looks that the convicts gave him when they caught his eye, and he could play with his sisters and his friends. Years later he remembered how, in the haymaking time, he had been delivered from the dungeons of Seringapatam (an immense haycock) by his own brave countrymen (the boy next door and his two cousins), how he had been recognised with ecstasy by his fiancée (the little girl from Number 1) who had come all the way from England (the second house in the Terrace) to ransom him and marry him. Here, too, he had heard 'from someone whose father was greatly connected, being under Government, of the existence of a terrible banditti called "The Radicals" whose principles were, that the Prince Regent wore stays, and that nobody had a right to any salary, and that the army and navy ought to be put down—horrors at which I trembled in my bed, after supplicating that the Radicals might be speedily taken and hanged'.‡

It was not only these dangerous brigands, 'The Radicals', who made Charles tremble in his bed. For at night-time in his darkened room, Mary Weller used to tell him stories. And Mary, so her charge later suggested, had a wildly extravagant imagination and was compulsively fascinated by the occult, the ghoulish, and the secrets of the midwife's and undertaker's crafts.

---

* *Great Expectations*, ch. XII. † *Great Expectations*, ch. V, XXVIII.
‡ *The Uncommercial Traveller*, 'Dullborough Town'.

One of the most vivid of Dickens's recollections of his childhood is of being taken by Mary to a 'great number of lying-ins'. Once she took him to a greengrocer's shop where a lodger had had quadruplets (he was 'afraid to write five' though he fully believed it was five) at a birth. Their little dead bodies were laid out, side by side, on a clean cloth on a chest of drawers, and they reminded Charles of pigs' trotters 'as they are usually displayed at a neat tripe shop'.

After singing the evening hymn as she put him to bed, Mary Weller would settle down to tell him a story which left him so utterly terrified that he could not move, except to shudder, for the fear that gripped him, and he could not sleep for the horrendous images that continued to swarm in his brain.

He never forgot—he never could forget—these stories and the fears which they evoked; and he never underestimated their effect on his future development. 'If we all knew our own minds,' he wrote, 'I suspect we should find our nurses responsible for most of the dark corners we are forced to go back to against our wills.' There were many dark corners to which he was to feel forced unwillingly to return in his later life, and it was Mary Weller who made him first aware of them. Years afterwards he related her stories as though they had contained a marvellously grotesque humour, but at the time he was not conscious of the humour, only of the terror and the cold sweat as the nurse acted out her themes, clawing the air and uttering long hollow groans in the dark room.

There was the story of 'The Black Cat', a weird animal that prowled about at night in search of the blood of children, and with a special and burning thirst for the blood of Master Dickens. There was the story of Chips, the shipwright down in the dockyard, who had sold his soul to the Devil for an iron pot, a bushel of tenpenny nails, half a ton of copper and a rat that could speak. He hadn't wanted the rat, but the Devil, his huge squinting eyes shooting out sparks of blue fire through his clattering eyelashes, said that Chips couldn't have 'the metal without him, and he's a curiosity'. So Chips gave way and took the rat and could never afterwards get rid of it. He tried to kill it, but it wouldn't die; he poured boiling pitch over it, but it did not mind the pitch a bit. And when Chips said to himself he feared the rat would stick to him for ever, the rat, who could read his thoughts, said, 'Yes, I will—like pitch'.

Soon the rat was joined by other rats that filled Chips's pockets and got into his hat and into the sleeves of his coat. 'And they could all speak to one another, and he understood what they said. And they got into his lodging, and into his bed, and into his teapot, and into his beer, and into his boots. And he was going to be married to a corn-chandler's daughter; and when he gave her a workbox he had himself made for her, a rat jumped out of it; and when he put his arm round her waist a rat clung about him, so the marriage was broken off.'

Chips always knew what the rats were doing; and he was voted mad; and lost his job, and was pressed for a sailor. On his ship the rats told him they would eat the planks and drown the crew and then eat them, too. But when he warned the Admiral, the Admiral merely said, 'My dear fellow, you are a case for the doctor'.

So the ship sank, the crew were drowned and eaten, and Chips floated to shore with an immense overgrown rat sitting on his corpse and laughing. And 'ever since,' so Dickens said, 'I have been morbidly afraid of my own pocket lest my exploring hand should find a specimen or two of those vermin in it'.

Then there was the story of the animal foreboding death that appeared to a parlour-maid who was sent out to fetch the beer for supper. It seemed at first to be a black dog, but gradually swelled and swelled 'into the semblance of some quadruped greatly surpassing a hippopotamus'.

The first time he heard this story Charles found it scarcely credible and found the courage to report his disbelief to Mary who was extremely touchy on this point, since she insisted that one or other of her relatives had either witnessed the events described or had actually taken part in them. Why, Mary protested indignantly, the parlour-maid who had seen the dreaded monster in the street was none other than her own sister-in-law! 'I perceived then,' commented Dickens, 'that there was no hope, and resigned myself to this zoological specimen as one of my many pursuers.'

Mary's most inspired tale—or the one that inspired Dickens to add his own most imaginative embellishments—was the famous history of Captain Murderer, a full-blooded villain whose tastes are those of the Robber Bridegroom of the brothers Grimm.

Captain Murderer's 'warning name would seem to have awakened no general prejudice against him', Dickens remarks when recalling this particular bedtime story, 'for he was admitted into the best society and possessed immense wealth'.

Captain Murderer's mission was matrimony, and the gratification of a cannibal appetite with tender brides.

On his marriage morning, he always caused both sides of the way to church to be planted with curious flowers, and when his bride said,

'Dear Captain Murderer, I never saw flowers like these before; what are they called?' he answered, 'They are called Garnish for house-lamb,' and laughed at his ferocious practical joke in a horrid manner, disquieting the minds of the noble bridal company, with a very sharp show of teeth, then displayed for the first time.

He made love in a coach and six, and married in a coach and twelve, and all his horses were milk-white horses with one red spot on the back which he caused to be hidden by the harness. For, the spot *would* come there, though every horse was milk-white when Captain Murderer bought him. And the spot was young bride's blood. . . .

When Captain Murderer had made an end of feasting and revelry, and had dismissed the noble guests, and was alone with his wife it was his whimsical custom to produce a golden rolling-pin and a silver pie-board. Now, there was this special feature in the Captain's court-ships, that he always asked if the young lady could make pie-crust; and if she couldn't by nature or education, she was taught. Well. When the bride saw Captain Murderer produce the golden rolling-pin and silver pie-board, she remembered this, and turned up her laced-silk sleeves to make a pie.

The Captain brought out a silver pie dish of immense capacity, and the Captain brought out flour and butter and eggs and all things needful, except the inside of the pie; of materials for the staple of the pie itself the Captain brought out none.

Then said the lovely bride, 'Dear Captain Murderer, what pie is this to be?' He replied, 'A meat pie.' Then said the lovely bride, 'Dear Captain Murderer, I see no meat.' The Captain humorously retorted, 'Look in the glass.'

She looked in the glass, but still she saw no meat, and then the Captain roared with laughter, and suddenly frowning and drawing his sword, bade her roll out the crust.

So she rolled out the crust, dropping large tears upon it all the time because he was so cross, and when she had lined the dish with crust and had cut the crust all ready to fit the top, the Captain called out, '*I* see the meat in the glass!'

And the bride looked up at the glass, just in time to see the Captain cutting her head off; and he chopped her in pieces, and peppered her, salted her, and put her in the pie, and sent it to the baker's, and ate it all, and picked the bones.

Well, Captain Murderer goes on like this, eating his way through a succession of beautiful brides and picking their bones, with teeth filed exceedingly sharp by the family blacksmith, until he marries the dark-haired twin of a bride who has formed the staple of his most recent pie. The new bride knows his terrible secret and is determined to be revenged upon him for the death of her sister. She pretends that she loves him and on their wedding night, just as she is making the pie crust, he comes up behind her with his great sword as is his usual practice—and then he cuts her head off, chops her in pieces, peppers her, salts her, puts her in the pie, sends it to the baker, eats it all, and picks the bones.

But before she began to roll out the paste she had taken a deadly poison of a most awful character, distilled from toads' eyes and spiders' knees; and Captain Murderer had hardly picked her last bone, when he began to swell, and to turn blue, and to be all over spots, and to scream. And he went on swelling and turning bluer, and being more all over spots and screaming, until he reached from floor to ceiling, and from wall to wall; and then, at one o'clock in the morning, he blew up with a loud explosion.★

Night after night the nurse related this grisly fable, or something like it, to the impressionable and terrified child, groaning and wailing, clutching at the air in simulated fright, while he, 'rigid with terror', lay in bed listening in silence, imagining even worse horrors when Mary had gone and left him alone in the darkness, unwillingly going over the story again in his mind in wonderment and fear.

All his life he was to be fascinated by the sinister and the grotesque, the fanciful, the morbid and the occult, those dark corners of the mind that he felt irresistibly drawn to explore. His work—even his *Child's History of England*—is full of the strange fruits of this festering imagination, this disquieting, insatiable curiosity which was to lead him, almost against his will—'dragged by invisible forces', as he put it himself—to wander at night into the slum quarters of London and into the morgues of Paris, fearful, as so many of his characters are, not only *for* himself but *of* himself.

In *Bleak House*, for example, when Dickens wants to symbolise the just fate of a corrupt legal system and of a whole social structure rotten and diseased to its very heart—'engendered in the corrupted humours of the vicious body itself'—he chooses to depict an old half-demented rag-and-bone dealer, the self-styled 'Lord Chancellor' Krook, 'short, cadaverous and withered, like some old root in a fall of snow', meeting an end as gruesome as Captain Murderer's, and dying of 'Spontaneous Combustion' amongst his jumbled collection of mouldy law books, bits of cracked parchment, ink bottles and skinned cats.†

Indeed, in all his novels—even in *Hard Times* and *Our Mutual Friend*—there is an atmosphere, more or less pervasive, of the Gothic fairy tale.

★ *The Uncommercial Traveller*, 'Nurse's Stories'.   † *Bleak House*, ch. XXXII.

The plots of several of them resemble those of the traditional fairy story from beginning to end, while the terrifying appearance of Magwitch in the graveyard, the luring of Florence Dombey by good Mrs Brown, and the wild flights of Quilp's imagination—'I'll beat you with an iron rod, I'll scratch you with a rusty nail, I'll pinch your eyes if you talk to me'— are the very stuff of which nurses' tales are made.

4

Soon there was another influence at work on the childish imagination, less persistent and less awesome than Mary Weller, but no less lastingly impressive: the Theatre Royal at the bottom of Star Hill, Rochester.

It was a small theatre whose pretentious portico, supported by two columns over the pavement, failed to impress the worldly-wise; but to the excited, stage-struck boy it seemed more thrilling than a palace, a whole new world in miniature. Like Maggy in *Little Dorrit* he thought it 'a Ev'nly place'. The melodramas, the farces, the tragedies, the pantomimes, all delighted him alike. He thought that 'to marry a Columbine would be to attain the highest pitch of all human felicity', that to paint your face like a clown and to have an endless supply of sausages stored in your red pantaloons would be to achieve the highest ambition.

It is some years now since we first conceived a strong veneration for Clowns [he wrote later, remembering these visits to the Theatre Royal], and an intense anxiety to know what they did with themselves out of pantomime time and off the stage. As a child, we were accustomed to pester our relations and friends with questions out of number concerning these gentry;—whether their appetite for sausages and such like wares was always the same, and if so at whose expense they were maintained; whether they were ever taken up for pilfering other people's goods, or were forgiven by everybody because it was only done in fun; how it was they got such beautiful complexions, and where they lived; and whether they were born Clowns, or gradually turned into Clowns as they grew up. On these and a thousand other points our curiosity was insatiable. . . .

The delights—the ten thousand million delights—of a pantomime come streaming upon us now, even of the pantomime which came lumbering down in Richardson's waggons at fair time to the dull little town in which we had the honour to be brought up, and which a long row of small boys, with frills as white as they could be washed, and hands as clean as they would come, were taken to behold the glories of in fair daylight.*

* Introduction to *Memoirs of Joseph Grimaldi*.

Yet Shakespeare delighted him as much as Grimaldi, and after seeing Richard III backing up towards the stage-box while struggling for his life against the virtuous Richmond, and Macbeth's eyes starting at the sight of the ghost, he could not decide whether he did not prefer a tragedy to even such a wonderful farcical melodrama as the one in which he had seen 'the funny countryman, but countryman of noble principles, in a flowered waistcoat, crunch up his little hat and throw it on the ground, and pull off his coat, saying, 'Dom thee, squire, coom on with thy fistes then!'' At which the lovely young woman who kept company with him was so frightened for his sake that she fainted away.'

It mattered nothing to Charles that the company of actors was decidedly understaffed, that the witches in *Macbeth* 'bore an awful resemblance to

'Sitting in that little warm theatre pervaded with the smell of paint and orange-peel and lamp-oil, with an undercurrent of sawdust, he was capable of the most demanding suspensions of disbelief'

the Thanes and other respectable male inhabitants of Scotland', that good King Duncan 'couldn't rest in his grave, but was constantly coming out of it and calling himself somebody else'. Sitting in that little warm theatre pervaded with the smell of paint and orange-peel and lamp-oil, with an undercurrent of sawdust, he was capable of the most demanding suspensions of disbelief; and like most impressionable children he dismissed with anger the cynical objections of the disenchanted.

He recalled a schoolmaster, whom he called 'Mr Barlow'—in acknowledgment of an earlier model of the 'instructive monomaniac' in Thomas Day's *Sandford and Merton*—and he hated him for his prosaic and disapproving attitude towards the splendours of an unbridled imagination.

What right had he [Charles protested] to bore his way into my Arabian Nights? Yet he did. He was always hinting doubts of the veracity of Sinbad the Sailor. If he could have got hold of the Wonderful Lamp, I knew he would have trimmed it and lighted it, and delivered a lecture over it on the qualities of sperm oil, with a glance at the whale fisheries. . . . He would have proved, by map and compass, that there was no such kingdom of Casgar, on the frontiers of Tartary.

'Mr Barlow', that unsparing caricature of the ponderous prude, could even sully Charles's enjoyment of the pantomime.

I recall the chilling air that ran across my frame and cooled my hot delight, as the thought occurred to me, 'This would never do for Mr Barlow!' After the curtain drew up, dreadful doubts of Mr Barlow's considering the costumes of the Nymphs of the Nebula as being sufficiently opaque obtruded themselves on my enjoyment. In the clown I perceived two persons: one a fascinating unaccountable creature of a hectic complexion, joyous in spirits though feeble in intellect, with flashes of brilliancy; the other a pupil of Mr Barlow. I thought how Mr Barlow would secretly rise early in the morning, and butter the pavement for *him*, and, when he had brought him down, would look severely out of his study window and ask him how *he* enjoyed the fun.*

But not even the shadow of Mr Barlow could darken the stage for long; and Charles abandoned himself to that intoxicating lure which was always to remain one of the deepest passions of his life, and one of the fundamental mainsprings of his art.

One of those who took Charles to the Theatre Royal was Dr Mathew Lamert, an Army surgeon who worked in the Ordnance Hospital at Chatham, and who had developed a deep attachment to Elizabeth Dickens's sister Mary, whom the children now called Aunt Fanny. A

---

* *The Uncommercial Traveller*, 'Mr Barlow'.

kindly, busy, ebullient middle-aged widower, Dr Lamert had a 'short, odd way of expressing himself' which still survived in the recollection of a few old people in Chatham seventy years later. It survived, too, in the memory of Charles Dickens who represented it in the character of Dr Slammer, surgeon to the 97th, 'a little fat man, with a ring of upright black hair round his head, and an extensive bald plain on the top of it'.*

Dr Lamert had a passionate enthusiasm for the theatre, and he and his son James, a former Sandhurst cadet who was awaiting his commission, took Charles not only to the professional performances at the Theatre Royal, but also to the amateur productions which the doctor himself organised in the rambling Ordnance Hospital. Just before Christmas 1821 Dr Lamert and Aunt Fanny were married, and soon afterwards they went to live in Ireland. But James and Charles continued to make their regular visits to the theatre.

Dickens's fascination with the theatre was to lead him, as soon as he was old enough, to become an enthusiastic and highly talented actor himself; and this, in turn, left its unmistakable imprint on his work. But even now at Chatham, he was encouraged to display a precocious gift for recitation and mimicry.

He could recite Dr Watts's 'The Voice of the Sluggard' with 'great effect', Mary Weller said, 'and with *such* action and *such* attitudes!' He could sing well, too, and (with Fanny, who was learning to play the piano) he delighted his father with 'The Cat's Meat Man' and a repertoire of other comic songs which he sang without a trace of that embarrassment he afterwards claimed to feel when recalling what a nuisance he must have been to visitors whom his father prevailed upon to listen to his performances.

For John Dickens was extremely proud of his son's accomplishments; and needed as little inducement to lift his son up on to a chair to entertain his guests, as the son required to lead off into his favourite song:

> Long time I've courted you, miss
> And now I've come from sea;
> We'll make no more ado, miss,
> But quickly married be. . . .

Sometimes his father would take him down to the Red Lion Inn, on the corner of High Street and Military Road, or to the Mitre and Clarence, a hotel in Chatham High Street kept by his friends the Tribes.(12) And

---

* *Pickwick Papers*, ch. II.

in these places, too, standing on a table or a chair, he sang that song in his clear treble, Fanny contributing each alternate verse; and afterwards he would have 'salmon and fowls and be tipped'. He performed, also, at picnics in the summer and at Twelfth Night parties in the winter, at birthday parties and at tea parties, at supper parties and punch parties. And whether or not it was politely dutiful, there was always loud applause.

5

There were many parties, for John Dickens was so very gregarious, so compulsively convivial, 'a fellow of infinite humour', according to one of his colleagues at the dockyard, 'chatty, lively and agreeable'.[13]

He was a good deal more than chatty, thought others who knew him— he was extravagantly prolix. He would never say, 'I do not think he will live long', preferring to observe, 'I must express my tendency to believe that his longevity is (to say the least of it) extremely problematical'. And Charles recognised this well enough himself. 'We are very sorry to lose the benefit of his advice,' he wrote to a friend years later when regretting the departure of a good doctor—'or, as my father would say, to be deprived, to a certain extent, of the concomitant advantages, whatever they may be, resulting from his medical skill, such as it is, and his professional attendance, in so far as it may be so considered.'[14]

This taste for involved, meandering sentences, many of which never found their way to a close, was one of John Dickens's idiosyncrasies which his son parodied in the conversations of Mr Micawber:

'My dear young friend,' said Mr Micawber, 'I am older than you; a man of some experience in life, and—and of some experience, in short, in difficulties, generally speaking. At present, and until something turns up, which I am, I may say, hourly expecting, I have nothing to bestow but advice. Still my advice is so far worth taking that—in short, that I have never taken it myself, and am the'—here Mr Micawber, who had been beaming and smiling, all over his head and face, up to the present moment, checked himself and frowned—'the miserable wretch you behold.'
'My dear, Micawber!' urged his wife.
'I say,' returned Mr Micawber quite forgetting himself, and smiling again, 'the miserable wretch you behold. My advice is never to do to-morrow what you can do to-day. Procrastination is the thief of time. Collar him!'
'My poor dear papa's maxim,' Mrs Micawber observed.

'My dear,' said Mr Micawber, 'your papa was very well in his way and heaven forbid that I should disparage him. Take him for all in all, we ne'er shall—in short, make the acquaintance probably, of anybody else possessing, at his time of life, the same legs for gaiters, and able to read the same description of print, without spectacles. But he applied that maxim to our marriage, my dear; and that was so far prematurely entered into, in consequence, that I never recovered the expense.'*

As well as being verbose, Mr Micawber suffered more or less permanently from what he chose to call 'some temporary embarrassments of a pecuniary nature'. So still did John Dickens. And in the spring of 1821, soon after the birth of his sixth child (Frederick William),(15) John Dickens was compelled to give up the house in Ordnance Terrace and move to a smaller, cheaper, less comfortable house in the lower part of the town, 18 St Mary's Place, known as The Brook.

Number 18 was a poor, cramped, white-washed house; and Mary Weller, who stayed with the family, remembered that after moving here there were no such parties as she had seen at the Terrace.

But Charles remained a cheerful, contented child. He was still rather pale and sickly and his 'attacks of violent spasm', as his friend John Forster termed them, prevented him from joining in the more lively games of his friends.(16) But he derived pleasure from watching the others at play; and he derived even greater pleasure from reading. 'Little Charles was a terrible boy to read,' Mary Weller recalled, 'and his custom was to sit with his book in his left hand, holding his wrist with his right hand, and constantly moving it up and down, and at the same time sucking his thumb.'17

He had gone beyond fairy stories and chap-books now, and in a little room next to his attic bedroom he pored over the novels that his father kept there. Here he discovered *Roderick Random* and *Peregrine Pickle*, *Humphry Clinker* and *Tom Jones*, *The Vicar of Wakefield*, *Don Quixote* and *Gil Blas*. Here he found *Robinson Crusoe* 'with dog and hatchet, goat-skin cap and fowling pieces; and Persian tales, with flying chests and students of enchanted books shut up for years in caverns; and there too was Abudah, the merchant, with the terrible little old woman hobbling out of the box in his bedroom; and there the mighty talisman, the rare *Arabian Nights*, with Cassim Baba, divided by four, like the ghost of a dreadful sum, hanging up, all gory, in the robbers' cave'.† (18)

These books 'kept alive my fancy', he wrote when his own name was as

* *David Copperfield*, ch. XII.   † *Martin Chuzzlewitt*, ch. V.

well known as any of their authors, 'and did me no harm, for, whatever harm was in some of them, was not there for me; *I* knew nothing of it'.

He read them avidly, and the characters in them became real for him, just as the characters in his own stories were later to become real for him, with a life of their own outside the pages of his books. Looking through the little attic window he could see the spire of St Mary's Church, and beneath it, the clustered headstones of the graves in the churchyard where sometimes at night he and Fanny would walk, looking up at the stars; and he imagined, as he was to make David Copperfield imagine, Tom Pipes climbing up the spire, and Strap, with his knapsack on his back, resting by the wicket gate.

He identified himself with these characters, too:

I have been Tom Jones (a child's Tom Jones, a harmless creature) for a week together. I have sustained my own idea of Roderick Random for a month at a stretch, I verily believe. I had a greedy relish for a few volumes of Voyages and Travels—I forget what, now—that were on those shelves; and for days and days I can remember to have gone about my region of our house, armed with the centrepiece out of an old set of boot-trees—the perfect realisation of Captain Somebody, of the royal British navy, in danger of being beset by savages, and resolved to sell his life at a great price. [19]

The extraordinary imaginative perception, which enabled Dickens to portray a world as though it had been seen by an artist with an abnormally heightened vision, induced Dickens, the young schoolboy, to fill the real world around him with a strange, unpredictable, exciting life of his own making. All boys of his age do this to some extent; but Charles did it in an acute and highly personal way.

In those walks round the town and down by the river which he loved to make, he was carried far away from the real world around him. Wandering down the High Street, which he thought must be 'at least as wide as Regent-Street, London, or the Italian Boulevard at Paris', he would look up at the Town Hall clock and think that it must surely be the finest clock in the world. The Town Hall itself, where he had once seen an Indian swallow a sword, was so glorious a structure that he set it up in his mind 'as the model on which the Genie of the Lamp built the palace for Aladdin'.

Passing the marine store shops and the secondhand clothes stalls he would study the wares on display, form pictures in his mind of the people to whom they had formerly belonged, and invent stories to suit them. 'Whole rows of coats have started from their pegs,' he wrote of a

'Whole rows of coats have started from their pegs, and shoes suddenly found feet to fit them'

later time, 'and shoes suddenly found feet to fit them.' At Simpson's
coach office he would stop to stare through the window and to gaze at
the oval transparency, which was even more beautiful at dusk when the
light from inside the office shone through it, and to wonder about the
little coach depicted on it—a coach rattling past a milestone very fast,
'completely full inside and out, and all the passengers dressed in the first
style of fashion, and enjoying themselves tremendously'.*

And sometimes he would walk down by the river, the best place of all
for day-dreams, and watch the brown and russet sails of the barges flap-
ping in the wind, the slender yachts with their small hulls and huge white
sheets of canvas, the heavy colliers floundering down before the tide.
He would look at the figureheads of the old ships with 'their excessively
wide-awake aspect, and air of somewhat obtrusive politeness',† and listen
to the splash and plop of the water, the clinking of a distant windlass, the
cry of the gulls as they swooped over the flat, monotonous marshes
towards the dim horizon. Here it was, in this same marsh country,
'down by the river, within, as the river wound, twenty miles of the sea',
that Pip gained his 'first most vivid and broad impression of the identity
of things' one memorable raw afternoon towards evening. At such a time
he found out for certain that the 'dark flat wilderness beyond the churchyard, intersected by dykes and mounds and gates, with scattered cattle
feeding on it, was the marshes; and that the low leaden line beyond was
the river; and that the distant savage lair from which the wind was
rushing, was the sea'.‡

Before Dickens settled down to write *Great Expectations* he came back
to Chatham to revisit the scenes of his childhood. Only the river and
the marshes remained the same. The South Eastern Railway had swallowed up the playing-field and turned it into a wilderness of rusty iron;
the Theatre Royal was to let and a dealer in wine and bottled beer had
taken over its box office; Pickford's had taken the place of Simpson's—
and worse than that:

> Pickford had not only knocked [Simpson's] down, but had knocked
> two or three houses down on each side of [Simpson's], and then had
> knocked the whole into one great establishment with a pair of big
> gates, in and out of which, his (Pickford's) waggons are, in these days,
> always rattling, with their drivers sitting up so high, that they look in at
> the second-floor windows of the old-fashioned houses in the High

---

* *The Uncommercial Traveller*, 'Dullborough Town'.
† *The Old Curiosity Shop*, ch. LXII.   ‡ *Great Expectations*, ch. I.

Street as they shake the town. I have not the honour of Pickford's acquaintance, but I felt that he had done me an injury, not to say committed an act of boyslaughter, in running over my childhood in this rough manner; and if ever I meet Pickford driving one of his own monsters, and smoking a pipe the while (which is the custom of his men), he shall know by the expression of my eye, if it catches his, that there is something wrong between us.*

The splendid Town Hall turned out to be no more than 'a mean little brick heap, like a demented chapel, with a few yawning persons in leather gaiters, and in the last extremity for something to do, lounging at the door with their hands in their pockets, and calling themselves a Corn Exchange'. Its clock, the finest clock in the world, had as sadly degenerated into a paltry thing, 'inexpressive, moon-faced and weak'.

The greengrocer, whose lodger had had all those babies, was leaning against the doorpost of his shop, looking strangely shrunken. Dickens went over to tell him that he was the little boy whose nurse had taken him to see them. But the greengrocer was not in the least surprised or gratified by the accuracy of the recollection:

Yes, summut out of the common—he didn't remember how many it was (as if half-a-dozen babies either way made no difference)—had happened to a Mrs What's-her-name, as once lodged there, but he didn't call it to mind particular.

Nettled by this phlegmatic conduct I informed him that I had left the town when I was a child. He slowly returned, quite unsoftened, and not without a sarcastic kind of complacency. *Had* I? Ah! And did I find it had got on tolerably well without me?

Such is the difference (I thought, when I had left him a hundred yards behind, and was by so much in a better temper) between going away from a place and remaining in it. I had no right, I reflected, to be angry with the greengrocer for his want of interest, I was nothing to him: whereas he was the town, the cathedral, the bridge, the river, my childhood, and a large slice of my life to me.†

The same thought occurred to Dickens that evening when he had dinner with Lucy Stroughill, who had married a doctor. She had grown fat, and her face was so altered from the little face that had looked down upon him as he lay in the fragrant dungeons of Seringapatam that 'if all the hay in the world had been heaped upon her' it could not have altered it more. They talked about those far-off, happy days in the playing-field, and it seemed to Dickens as though they were talking about other people who were now dead. And so, indeed, he decided, they *were* dead and gone,

* *The Uncommercial Traveller*, 'Dullborough Town'.　　　† *Ibid.*

just as the playing-field itself was dead and gone. Then Lucy's youngest child came into the room, and the little girl looked so much like that dead little girl in the hay that she quite touched his 'foolish heart'.

'Ah, who was I,' he wrote as though there were tears in his eyes, 'who was I to quarrel with the town for having changed to me, when I myself had come back, so changed, to it! All my early readings and early imaginations dated from this place, and I took them away so full of innocent construction and guileless belief, and I brought them back so worn and torn, so much the wiser and so much the worse.'

He was always to remember the Chatham of the early 1820s with this deep, almost despairing nostalgia. He was for ever to surround it, and the whole lost world of childhood that it evoked, with a romantic, mystical light. For childhood was a dream of perfect life when 'everything was happy, when there was no distance and no time', and he felt a constant need to return to it in his memory, 'the best and purest link between this world and a better'. The fascination, as he said himself, was one he 'did not care to resist', and he went back again and again to 'the old green field with its gently waving trees, where the birds sang as he has never heard since—where the butterfly fluttered far more gaily than he ever sees him now, in all his ramblings—when the sky seemed bluer, and the sun shone more brightly—when the air blew more freshly over greener grass, and sweeter-smelling flowers—where everything wore a richer and more brilliant hue than it is ever dressed in now'.*

The 'better world' of childhood occurs at its most idealistic—though transferred to Suffolk—in the early pages of *David Copperfield* where David decides that he has never known anything in his life half so green as the grass outside his bedroom window, half so shady as the trees he remembers growing in the churchyard, half so quiet as the tombstones, and that the fruit which clusters on the trees in the garden at the back is 'riper and richer than fruit has ever been since, in any other garden'.

The scene is The Rookery, Blunderstone, but Dickens is thinking of St Mary's Place, Chatham.

6

Next door to the house in St Mary's Place was the Providence Baptist Chapel; and not far away was the Zion Baptist Chapel. The Baptist

* *Christmas Stories*, 'A Christmas Tree'; *Sketches*, 'The First of May'; *Reprinted Pieces*, 'A Child's Dream of a Star'.

Minister was the Rev. William Giles and, although John and Elizabeth Dickens had both been brought up in the Church of England, they were not in the least conscientious in their Anglican observances and, being on friendly terms with Mr Giles, they quite often attended the nonconformist chapel instead of the Anglican services at St Mary's, taking their children with them.

Charles detested these services, and ever afterwards when he was to write a scene showing children in church or chapel it was nearly always with the hint that it would have been better if they had not been made to go. The Minister would sometimes preach for a full two hours, and the bored, impatient, restless, uncomfortable boy soon began to hate him, and to detest his 'big round face', and the infuriating habit he had of 'looking up the inside of his outstretched coat-sleeve as if it were a telescope with the stopper on'. On warm Sunday evenings in the summer, when he longed to stay outside, he was scrubbed and washed and brushed 'as a purification for the Temple', and carried off to be 'steamed like a potato in the unventilated breath' of this hated Minister and his congregation, until what small mind he had was quite steamed out of him, and he felt himself slowly, slowly falling asleep, only to wake up with a jerk to a new awareness of the Minister's doom-laden prophecies alternating with a lumbering jocularity.

He was left with a permanent distaste for Nonconformism, and an enduring determination to associate its more earnest and narrow devotees —and, indeed, any extravagantly and self-consciously religious character —with selfishness, spite and ill-temper.

There is Mrs Clennam, for instance, who, 'stern of face and unrelenting of heart, would sit all day behind a bible—bound, like her own construction of it, in the hardest, barest and straitest boards, with one dinted ornament on the cover like the drag of a chain, and a wrathful sprinkling of red upon the edges of the leaves', while her poor adoptive son, Arthur, 'sat with his hands before him, scared out of his senses by a horrible tract which commenced business with the poor child by asking him in its title, why he was going to Perdition?—a piece of curiosity that he really in a frock and drawers was not in a condition to satisfy—and which, for the further attraction of his infant mind, had a parenthesis in every other line with some such hiccupping reference as 2 Ep. Thess. c. iii. v. 6 & 7'.*

There is Mrs Varden who was 'most devout when most ill-tempered' and who, after quarrelling with her long-suffering husband, was in the

* *Little Dorrit*, Bk. i, ch. iii.

habit of retiring to bed and sending down 'to be immediately accom-
modated with the little black tea-pot of strong mixed tea, a couple of
rounds of buttered toast, a middling-sized dish of beef and ham cut thin,
and the Protestant Manual in two volumes post octavo'.*

There is Miss Murdstone, 'and a gloomy-looking lady she was . . .
with very heavy eyebrows, nearly meeting over her large nose, as if,
being disabled by the wrongs of her sex from wearing whiskers, she had
carried them to that account'. Miss Murdstone's religion is austere and
wrathful and when, of a Sunday, she sits in her pew, wearing a black
velvet gown that looks as if it had been made out of a pall, she mumbles
the responses, emphasising all the dread words with a cruel relish and
rolling her dark eyes round 'when she says "miserable sinners", as if she
were calling all the congregation names'.†

And there are many more. The nonconformist preachers who minister
to such frightful creatures, are even less attractive than these specimens of
their flock. While an Anglican clergyman is rarely worse than an amiable
fool—and more often such a man as the 'simple-hearted old gentleman, of
a shrinking, subdued spirit' who is the incumbent of the parish where
Little Nell dies, or like the 'good old' Vicar of Blunderstone, or the mild-
looking young curate (obviously afraid of the baby) who christens Paul
Dombey, or the Rev. Septimus Crisparkle, the muscular Christian of
Edwin Drood whose 'radiant features teemed with innocence'—a nonconformist Minister is more likely to resemble the Rev. Melchisedech
Howler, Minister of the Ranting Persuasion. Mr Howler's preachings,
given in a front parlour, opened for this purpose, produce so powerful an
effect on his congregation that they are driven to a 'rapturous performance of a sacred jig' which results in the floor breaking 'through into a
kitchen below, and disabling a mangle belonging to one of the fold'.‡

Mr Chadband, the lay preacher in *Bleak House*, is 'a large yellow man
with a fat smile, and a general appearance of having a good deal of train
oil in his system', who 'never speaks without first putting up his great
hand, as delivering a token to his hearers that he is going to edify them'.

'My friends,' [he says on the doorstep of the Snagsbys' house to which
he has been invited for the evening] 'Peace be on this house! On the
master thereof, on the mistress thereof, on the young maidens and on
the young men! My friends, why do I wish for peace? What is peace?
Is it war? No. Is it strife? No. Is it lovely, and gentle, and beautiful, and

* *Barnaby Rudge*, ch. IV.   † *David Copperfield*, ch. IV.
‡ *Dombey and Son*, ch. XV.

pleasant, and serene, and joyful? O yes! Therefore, my friends, I wish for peace, upon you and upon yours.'

In consequence of Mrs Snagsby looking deeply edified, Mr Snagsby thinks it expedient on the whole to say Amen, which is well received.

'Now my friends,' says Mr Chadband, 'since I am upon this theme . . .'*

It is a theme—and a style—which he rarely abandons.

The Minister of Little Bethel, which Mrs Nubbles attends, is, however, more inclined to dwell, and to dwell at inordinate length in a very loud voice, upon the difficulties of reaching Paradise (which he compares to the difficulties of reaching his out-of-the-way chapel as opposed to the broad thoroughfare leading to the parish church), upon the terrible dangers of disbelieving in the inexorable wrath of God, and upon the evil of going to the theatre.†

Kit Nubble's detestation of the Little Bethel Chapel and its Minister is an exact reflection of Charles's hatred of the Chatham Chapel and the preacher who officiated there, boring remorselessly into his congregation with his 'fifthly, his sixthly, and his seventhly' until Charles 'regarded that reverend person in the light of a most dismal and oppressive Charade'.[20]

The Minister of the Zion Baptist Chapel, however, had a son, William Giles, whose influence on Charles was much more benign.

The young William Giles kept a school on the corner of Rhode Street and Best Street. And to this school, the 'Classical, Mathematical and Commercial School', Charles and his sister Fanny, having outgrown the dame-school in Rome Lane, were now sent.

Charles was far happier here than he had been at the dame-school. William Giles was a kindly, intelligent Oxford graduate of twenty-three who took great care with his pupils, and recognised in Charles one of the most promising amongst them. Giles's sister remembered that Charles was already a very handsome boy, cheerful and friendly, with long, curly, light brown hair. 'He was quite at home at all sorts of parties, junketings and birthday celebrations . . . he took a great delight in 5th November festivities round the bonfire.'[21]

With other children from the school, wearing the distinctive white beaver hat which was part of the uniform, he would go down to the dockyard and over to Rochester, past the Cathedral and up to the ruined Castle, talking gibberish and telling jokes. Sometimes he and his sister and

* *Bleak House*, ch. XIX.   † *The Old Curiosity Shop*, chs. XXII, XLI.

their friends would go up to Chatham Lines to watch the soldiers drilling and carrying out their fire-practice. Occasionally there was an inspection of the troops by the commander-in-chief, and this would bring out huge crowds of adults as well as boys:

> A few moments of eager expectation, and colours were seen fluttering gaily in the air, arms glistened brightly in the sun: column after column poured onto the plain. The troops halted and formed; the word of command ran through the line, there was a general clash of muskets, as arms were presented; and the commander-in-chief, attended by Colonel Bulder and numerous officers, cantered to the front. The military bands struck up altogether: the horses stood upon two legs each, cantered backwards, and whisked their tails about in all directions: the dogs barked, the mob screamed, the troops recovered, and nothing was to be seen on either side, as far as the eye could reach, but a long perspective of red coats and white trousers, fixed and motionless.*[22]

7

Towards the end of 1822 John Dickens was transferred to London. His finances were peculiarly strained, and he was obliged to sell the household furniture. As the pieces were removed from the house—an exodus with which his family was to become only too familiar—it seemed that the bright sunshine days of Charles's childhood were gone for ever.

* *Pickwick Papers*, ch. IV.

2

WARREN'S BLACKING
1823-1824
aet. 11-12

30 HUNGERFORD STAIRS STRAND LONDON

In the little world in which children have their existence, whosoever brings them up, there is nothing so finely perceived and so finely felt, as injustice. It may be only a small injustice that the child can be exposed to; but the child is small, and its world is small.

Great Expectations

2

Charles stayed behind in Chatham to finish the school term, and then, just before Christmas, in one of Simpson's coaches, with a book of Goldsmith's essays that Mr Giles had come 'flitting in among the packing-cases' to give him as a leaving present, he went to join his family. It was a damp and dreary morning and he never forgot the smell of the wet straw inside the coach where he was the only passenger. He ate his sandwiches in silence and alone, and it rained all the way to London.

He arrived in London at the Cross Keys, Wood Street, Cheapside; and from there he was taken to Camden Town, a quiet, dreary, 'shabby-genteel' satellite, not yet part of the capital but having no real identity of its own. The family were living at 16 Bayham Street, a small, plain house, rented for £22 a year, in a row of forty which had been built about ten years before.[1] There was an open meadow at the back, but it seemed to Charles a poor, gloomy wasteland of rank grass and rubbish dumps compared with the fresh fields at Chatham. 'It looked rather like a barbarous place of execution, with its poles and cross-poles erected for the beating of carpets; and it was overrun with nettles and dockweed'.[2]

> There were frowzy fields, and cow-houses, and dung hills, and dust-heaps, and ditches, and gardens, and summer-houses, and carpet-beating grounds . . . little tumuli of oyster shells in the oyster season, and of lobster shells in the lobster season, and of broken crockery and faded cabbage leaves in all seasons . . . posts, and rails, and old cautions to trespassers, and backs of mean houses, and patches of wretched vegetation.*

The neighbours seemed a far cry from Mrs Newnham and the half-pay officer, the Stroughills and the Gileses. Next door lived a washerwoman, and opposite a Bow Street runner. At the northern end of the street there was a cheap-looking roadside house, kept by a widow and her two daughters who made a modest living out of the local inhabitants—mostly tradesmen, clerks and labourers—and those who passed that way to take the lonely road to Kentish Town. Near this house the watchman had his box, and as soon as it was dark he would walk down the street to light

* Dombey and Son, ch. VI.

the little oil lamps that threw a fitful, flickering glimmer between the houses. At the other end of the street was a terrace of gloomy almshouses, backing on to a burial ground. Charles would often go up to look beyond them over the dust-heaps and the fields full of dock-leaves, towards the cupola of St Paul's looming through the smoke, a treat, so he said, 'that served him for hours of vague reflection afterwards'.

Life at Number 16, which comprised only four rooms, a basement and a garret, was very cramped. The Dickenses had six children now, for as well as Charles, who was eleven, and Fanny who was twelve, Letitia, six, Harriet, three, and Frederick, two, there was a new baby, Alfred, who had been born in Chatham in the spring of the year before. James Lamert, still waiting for his commission, had come with them too. And although Mary Weller had married a dockyard worker and stayed behind there was a little orphan from the Chatham workhouse who had come to take her place, a sharp and worldly creature with a kind heart, the model for Sally Brass's downtrodden maid, described by Dick Swiveller as a 'very extraordinary person—surrounded by mysteries, ignorant of the taste of beer, unacquainted with her own name (which is less remarkable), and taking a limited view of society through the key-holes of doors'.*

Soon the little house was slightly less crowded for Fanny won a scholarship to the Royal Academy of Music and went there as a boarder for thirty-eight guineas a year.

Charles was distressed beyond measure to see Fanny go. It was not only that he was deprived of a beloved companion at a time when he had found no new friends to take the place of those he had left behind in Chatham. What wounded him more deeply than this was that Fanny was being given her chance in life, while he was being utterly neglected, taken away from one school without any thought, so it seemed, of being sent to another.

> As I thought in the little back garret in Bayham Street, of all I had lost in Chatham [he confided to a friend years later, when the memory of the loss was scarcely less bitter than it had been at the time], what would I have given, if I had had anything to give, to have been sent back to any other school, to have been taught something anywhere. . . .
>
> I know my father to be as kind-hearted and generous a man as ever lived in the world. Everything that I can remember of his conduct to his wife, or children, or friends, in sickness or affliction, is beyond all

* *The Old Curiosity Shop*, ch. LVIII.

praise. By me, as a sick child, he has watched night and day, unweariedly and patiently many nights and days. . . . He was proud of me, in his way, and had a great admiration of the comic singing. But, in the ease of his temper, and the straitness of his means, he appeared to have utterly lost at this time the idea of educating me at all, and to have utterly put from him the notion that I had any claim upon him, in that regard whatever. So I degenerated into cleaning his boots of a morning, and my own; and making myself useful in the work of the little house; and looking after my younger brothers and sisters; and going on such poor errands as arose out of our poor way of living.[3]

James Lamert did his best to comfort him, and built him a small puppet theatre to take the place of the Theatre Royal at Rochester; but Charles found a deeper solace in wandering about in Camden Town and Kentish Town and Somers Town, staring at houses and factories, taverns and bakeries, old-clothes shops and eating-rooms, living in a strange world of his own imagining, and finding in that world an escape and release from the real world he could no longer like nor fully understand.

Sometimes he strayed further south through Holborn and into the City where there was a poor demented woman who used to roam about 'dressed all in black with cheeks staringly painted, and hence popularly known as *Rouge et Noire*'. He remembered, too, another woman, 'dressed entirely in white, with a ghastly white plating round her head and face, inside her white bonnet. . . . This is her bridal dress. She is always walking up here, on her way to church.'[*]

Once he was taken to the Bazaar in Soho Square to have a present bought for him 'to the value of half a crown'. He chose a 'Harlequin's wand—painted particoloured, like Harlequin himself'.[†] And once, so he said, he got lost in the Strand on an expedition to St Giles's Church. He had one and fourpence in his pocket (a present from his godfather, Christopher Huffam), and a pewter ring with a bit of red glass in it on his little finger (a present from Lucy Stroughill). At first he cried, but then, feeling hungry, he went to buy a penny roll in a baker's shop:

> But I looked into a number of cook-shops before I could muster courage to go into one. At last I saw a pile of cooked sausages in a window with the label, 'Small Germans, A Penny'. Emboldened by knowing what to ask for, I went in and said, 'If you please, will you sell me a small German?' which they did, and I took it, wrapped in paper in my pocket, to Guildhall. . . .

* *Household Words* (January 1853), 'Where We Stopped Growing'.
† *All the Year Round* (January 1859), 'New Year's Day'.

'They used to say I was an odd child, and I suppose I was'

Thus I wandered about the City, like a child in a dream, staring at the British merchants, and inspired by a mighty faith in the marvellousness of everything. Up courts and down courts—in and out of yards and little squares—peeping into counting-house passages and running away.★

He peered into Austin Friars and into South Sea House, and on Royal Exchange he stared at the shabby men munching biscuits as they stood about under the posters advertising the sailing of ships. He

★ *Household Words* (August 1853), 'Gone Astray'.

decided that these men were misers who had invested all their money in some sailing expedition and were waiting there for the captains to come and tell them it was time to leave—the biscuits were to keep off seasickness.

He looked in at the grated kitchen window of the Mansion House, and watched the cooks at work in their white caps, until one of them with black whiskers, called out, 'Cut away, you sir!' He went to the India House, and asked a boy what it was, and the boy made faces and pulled his hair before he told him; other boys chased him down turnings and brought him to bay in doorways where they treated him 'quite savagely'. He seemed to remember that he was wearing fine white cord breeches, a green coat with bright buttons, a monstrous shirt collar, and a white hat, which naturally attracted their attention; one of the boys wrote his address on the hat with the stump of a black-lead pencil.

Although he was lost and far from home, he could not resist going to a theatre in Goodman's Fields where the audience in the gallery was composed of sailors and 'others of the lowest description, and their conversation was not improving'.

But I understood little or nothing of what was bad in it then, and it had no depraving influence on me. I have wondered since how long it would take, by means of such association, to corrupt a child nurtured as I had been, and innocent as I was. . . .

It was late when I got out into the streets, and there was no moon, and there were no stars, and the rain fell heavily. . . . I felt unspeakably forlorn; and now, for the first time, my little bed and the dear familiar faces came before me, and touched my heart. By daylight I had never thought of the [worry] at home. I had never thought of my mother. . . .

I found a watchman in his box. . . . He had a dreadful cough, and was obliged to lean against a wall, whenever it came on. We got at last to the watch-house, a warm and drowsy sort of place embellished with great coats and rattles hanging up. When a paralytic messenger had been sent to make enquiries about me, I fell asleep by the fire, and awoke no more until my eyes opened on my father's face.

This is literally and exactly how I went astray. They used to say I was an odd child, and I suppose I was.*

As well as the streets of London, books still stimulated Charles's imagination—not just his father's books, but books that belonged to his uncle's landlady. This uncle, Thomas Barrow, a colleague of John Dickens's in the Navy Pay Office, was confined to his rooms in Gerard

* *Ibid.*

Street, Soho, by a broken leg, and his nephew Charles was a frequent visitor there, acting as 'his little companion and nurse'. His landlady's husband—a man named Manson, father to the partner in the firm of auctioneers now known as Christie, Manson and Woods—had been a bookseller and she herself still carried on the business in a little shop on the ground floor. Sometimes she would take Charles into the shop and lend him a book.

One of the most vividly remembered of these books was George Colman's *Broad Grins*, which as Dickens later told a friend, seized his fancy very much. Colman's story, 'The Elder Brother', which describes in verse the adventures of an *accoucheur* who specialises in unmarried mothers, made an understandable impression on the eleven-year-old boy whose own mother was so often pregnant. One of the *accoucheur's* patients is a spinster whose nephew fears that he will lose his long-hoped-for inheritance when he learns that his '*maiden* Aunt is *big* with *child*'. 'Your fortune will continue much the same,' he is comforted, 'For,—keep the secret—you're his elder brother.' Charles was so excited by the description of Covent Garden in this story that he ran down to the market to see it for himself, and there inhaled 'the flavour of the faded cabbage-leaves as if it were the very breath of comic fiction'.[4]

One of the smells in Uncle Thomas's rooms that lingered most strongly in his memory was that of shaving-soap. A barber came in regularly to shave his uncle, and this barber was a highly memorable character who had an obsessive interest in the Napoleonic wars and loved to expatiate to his customers on the Emperor's mistakes and to demonstrate how his career could have ended in triumph.[5] Charles wrote a sketch of him— as a companion piece to a sketch of a deaf old woman in Bayham Street 'who made delicate hashes with walnut-ketchup'—but he was too shy to show it to anyone. Years afterwards he made use of it in describing Poll Sweedlepipe with whom Mrs Gamp lodges in Kingsgate Street.

Sweedlepipe is a friendly, talkative, inquisitive man with a kind heart, a 'very small, shrill, treble voice' and a bald head which 'lost itself in a wig of curly black ringlets, parted on one side, and cut away almost to the crown, to indicate immense capacity of intellect'. His hands are cold and clammy and smell strongly of shaving-soap. He shaves a man for a penny, and cuts his hair for twopence and while employing these skills wears 'an apron not over-clean, a flannel jacket, and corduroy knee-shorts'.*

As well as visiting his uncle in Soho, Charles would sometimes go to

* *Martin Chuzzlewit*, ch. XXVI.

see his godfather, Christopher Huffam, the rigger, who lived 'in a substantial handsome sort of way' in Limehouse, where, behind the rich merchants' houses of the old village, the warehouses and dockers' tenements, shipwrights' sheds, ferry houses, and sailors' cabins were jumbled side by side between the jetties and wharfs along the river front. It was a place which fascinated Charles, and for ever afterwards the whole of the London river and the warrens of ramshackle buildings that crowded down beside the water's edge, filled his mind with wonder, curiosity and fear.

Ship-breakers' yards and dry docks, rope walks and timber sheds, stranded boats and old hulks half-knocked to pieces in the mud, ooze and slime and dregs of tide and floating coal scum, rusty anchors, and chain cables, steam boilers, diving bells and windmill sails, oyster boats and colliers, tenders and lighters, the Rotterdam steamer and the *Betsy of Yarmouth*, figureheads 'with a firm formality of bosom and knobby eyes starting two inches out of their heads', floating broken baskets and frayed hempen hawsers, creaking piers and rotting wharfs, all teem in his brain and tumble out in his books, which are alive, too, not only with the sights but with the noises of the river—steamships impatiently beating the water with their paddles as though they wanted room to breathe, barges bumping up against other craft and making crunching sounds like breaking walnuts, dogs barking as they run up and down on the long black tiers of colliers, hammers clanking in the shipbuilding yards, saws cutting through timber planks, engines pumping in leaky ships, capstans clanking as they wind in dripping cables.

But the river, as well as a source of excitement and restless energy, is a place of death. Here the grotesque dwarf Quilp is drowned and the water toys with his corpse, bruising it against slimy piles that stick out of the mud, hiding it in the long grass, dragging it over stones and gravel and, at last, flinging it on to a swamp, and leaving it there to bleach head downwards in the night wind.* Here Bill Sikes's mistress, Nancy, thinks that she will come in the end to drown herself; and so does Little Emily. Here Martha Endell does, in fact, try to drown herself, knowing like all Dickens's prostitutes, that she is like the river, crying passionately over and over again,

'Oh, the river! The river! . . . I know it's like me. I know that I belong to it. I know that it's the natural company of such as I am. It

* *The Old Curiosity Shop*, ch. LXVII.

comes from country places, where there was once no harm in it—and it creeps through the dismal streets, defiled and miserable . . . . I can't keep away from it. I can't forget it. It haunts me day and night. It's the only thing in all the world that I am fit for, or that's fit for me. Oh, the dreadful river.'*

The river is dreadful, too, for Esther Summerson. It has 'a fearful look, so overcast and secret, creeping away so fast between the low flat lines of shore: so heavy with indistinct and awful shapes, both of substance and shadow: so deathlike and mysterious'.† And for Lizzie Hexham—whose father searches the riverside for bodies and is himself dragged out of the water, a corpse with hailstones in his hair—the river is a fearful, cruel place which she looks into at night, trying to see there the vast blank misery of life, 'knowing it lay there dim before her, stretching away to the great ocean, Death'. And for old Betty Higden, too, the river is an invitation to death as it calls, 'whispering to many like herself, "Come to me, come to me! . . . I am Relieving Officer appointed by eternal ordinance to do my work. . . . Death in my arms is peacefuller than among the pauper-wards. Come to me!" '‡

In *Our Mutual Friend*, indeed, the misery and corruption of the London riverside permeate the whole atmosphere of the book. And when Charlie Hexham tries to persuade his sister to marry Bradley Headstone, he impresses upon her the importance of getting away from its corrupting influence, 'You would at length get quit of the river side and the old disagreeables belonging to it'.

'Even the upper reach of the river, the idyllic Berkshire valley, takes on a sinister colour when the inhabitants of the corrupted lower river, Riderhood and Headstone, invade it.'[6]

To little Paul Dombey the river seems to be carrying him away to death. 'His fancy had a strange tendency to wander to the river, which he knew was flowing through the great city; and now he thought how black it was, and how deep it would look . . . and more than all, how steadily it rolled away to meet the sea.' Why will it never stop, he asks his sister as he lies dying. 'Why will it never stop, Floy? It is bearing me away, I think.'§

This 'strange tendency to wander to the river' was as much Paul's creator's as it is Paul's own. But Dickens's fascination with the river, or

---

* *David Copperfield*, ch. XLVII.   † *Bleak House*, ch. LVII.
‡ *Our Mutual Friend*, Bk. I, chs. I, VI, Bk. II, ch. XV, Bk. III, ch. VIII.
§ *Dombey and Son*, ch. XVI.

more exactly with the river at night, was one almost of repulsion. He was drawn to it, and to crumbling buildings decaying by its shores, to places like Jacob's Island and to Quilp's wharf, as he was drawn to the Paris morgue—he never wanted to go there, but he was always pulled there, 'dragged by invisible forces'. The riverside at Limehouse, below his godfather's house at 5 Church Row, was an early and significant stage in a reluctantly yet compulsively repeated journey.

The journeys home to Camden Town from Limehouse were at once a relief and a new excitement. Through a London, 'strange in its glooms and flaring lights', the coach rattled,

> through the noisy, bustling, crowded streets, now displaying long double rows of brightly-burning lamps, dotted here and there with the chemists' glaring lights, and illuminated besides with the brilliant flood that streamed from the windows of the shops . . . streams of people apparently without end poured on and on, jostling each other in the crowd and hurrying forward, while vehicles of all shapes and makes, mingled up together in one moving mass like running water, lent their ceaseless roar to swell the noise and tumult. . . .
>
> The rags of the squalid ballad-singer fluttered in the rich light that showed the goldsmith's treasures, pale and pinched-up faces hovered about the windows where was tempting food, hungry eyes wandered over the profusion guarded by one thin sheet of brittle glass—an iron wall to them; half-naked shivering figures stopped to gaze at Chinese shawls and golden stuffs of India.*

Down Commercial Road and Cheapside, Charles went, past St Paul's and Fleet Street, then turning up through Covent Garden into the swarming district of St Giles and Seven Dials; and all the way he looked out spellbound at the flickering lamps and the lighted shops, the muffin-boy ringing his way down the streets, the beer-man going his rounds with a lantern in front of his tray, the sudden flare of a gaslight over a kidney-pie stand or a portable oven, the men calling flat fish or oysters, fruit and baked potatoes, a waterman going home with a dim and dirty lamp in his hand and a big brass plate on his chest, an apprentice running up the steps of a playhouse, a chimney-sweep sauntering into a drink shop for a 'go' of gin or brandy or a pint of stout. It was all so exciting and curious and wonderful. But sometimes, in the frightening slums north of the Oxford road, 'wild visions of wickedness, want and beggary' arose in the boy's anxious mind.

* *Nicholas Nickleby*, ch. XXXII.

'In the frightening slums north of the Oxford Road, "wild visions of wickedness, want and beggary"'

For want, as well as deprivation and exclusion, seemed a part of his own life now. There were strange, adult, conversations overheard in Bayham Street which he could not follow, but which filled him with apprehension. The words 'the Deed' were frequently spoken and he began to fear that his father had committed some unmentionable crime for which punishment would soon be inflicted. More and more economies were practised in the household; more pieces of furniture were sold; and sometimes there was 'not too much for dinner'. But still 'the Deed' and all the dark mysteries which the term implied loomed menacingly over the family.[7]

Charles's suppressed anxiety reacted on his health. He became subject to repeated attacks of fever and spasms, and for days he lay ill in bed in his little garret wondering how much longer the consequences of 'the Deed' would be delayed.

John Dickens, it seems, was less concerned about his predicament than was his son. Expecting, perhaps, like Mr Micawber that something would soon turn up, he appears to have largely ignored the problem and rested his hopes for its solution on providence, his friends and his relations. He had contracted in 'the Deed' to make a composition with his creditors and there were those who could help him meet the payments if the worst came to the worst—there were the Barrows, there was Christopher Huffam, there was his mother.

In the event it was his wife who decided to make some sort of effort to get them out of their difficulties. She decided she would open a school. With energy, enthusiasm and high hopes she set about to find suitable premises, to draw up an inviting prospectus, to design a brass plate. And thus far she succeeded. Premises were found at 4 Gower Street North, a rather larger and certainly more imposing place than the dingy house in Bayham Street;[(8)] a short prospectus was printed and pushed through likely looking letter-boxes by Charles and the little orphan maid; a handsome brass plate was inscribed, 'Mrs Dickens's Establishment' and prominently displayed beside the front door.

All that was now wanting were the pupils. And no pupils came.

'Nobody ever came to the school,' Dickens told his friend, John Forster, 'nor do I recollect that anybody ever proposed to come, or that the least preparation was made to receive anybody.'

He described the response to the brass plate engraved, 'Mrs Micawber's Boarding Establishment for Young Ladies' in almost identical words; and in a continuation of this autobiographical passage recorded:

The only visitors I ever saw or heard of, were creditors. *They* used to come at all hours, and some of them were quite ferocious. One dirty-faced man, I think he was a boot-maker, used to edge himself into the passage as early as seven o'clock in the morning, and call up the stairs to Mr Micawber—'Come! You ain't out yet, you know. Pay us, will you? Don't hide, you know; that's mean. I wouldn't be mean if I was you. Pay us, will you? You just pay us, d'ye hear? Come!' Receiving no answer to these taunts, he would mount in his wrath to the words 'swindlers' and 'robbers'; and these being ineffectual too, would sometimes go to the extremity of crossing the street, and roaring up at the windows of the second floor, where he knew Mr Micawber was. At these times Mr Micawber would be transported with grief and mortification, even to the length, as I was once made aware by a scream from his wife, of making motions at himself with a razor; but within half-an-hour afterwards, he would polish up his shoes with extraordinary pains, and go out, humming a tune with a greater air of gentility than ever. Mrs Micawber was quite as elastic.* (9)

2

Mrs Dickens certainly had need to be elastic. Her son scorned this quixotic attempt of hers 'to restore' the family fortunes. And to take a new house at £50 a year when they could not afford the rent of £23 for a smaller one, to set up a school without the least experience of running one or teaching in one, to trust to luck and to Christopher Huffam to find her pupils (believing that Huffam would induce his business friends in the East Indies to send their children to school in Gower Street), to suppose that the maid could cope with all the housework and the babies while she was instructing these pupils, is without doubt to behave in a way which invites both disaster and ridicule. But, at least an effort *had* been made; and John Dickens and his children were no doubt happier with a woman who acted foolishly than they would have been with one who stayed sulkily at home and nagged her husband for not acting at all.

Charles, however, thought she was silly, and he seems to have continued to think so for the rest of his life. And when writing *Nicholas Nickleby* (at a time when he was on particularly bad terms with her, for she had protested against certain ' "sneering" passages' in his letters)⁻ he introduced into the character of Nicholas's mother some of the stupidities and vanities he confessed he had discovered in his own.

Mrs Nickleby, a silly, clumsy, susceptible woman, 'who had at no

* *David Copperfield*, ch. XI.

time been remarkable for the possession of a very clear understanding', has a habit of pouring forth 'a perfectly wonderful train of disjointed expressions'. She is likely to entertain her guests 'with a lament over her fallen fortunes, and a picturesque account of her old house in the country, comprising a full description of the different apartments, not forgetting the little store-room, and lively recollection of how many steps you went down to get into the garden, and which way you turned when you came out at the parlour-door, and what capital fixtures there were in the kitchen'.

Proud of her past and her family connections, she is always anxious to impress upon her acquaintances that her present straitened circumstances are not at all like her glittering past—

'We used to keep such hours! Twelve, one, two, three o'clock was nothing to us. Balls, dinners, card-parties—never were such rakes as the people about where we used to live. I often think now, I am sure, that how we ever could go through with it is quite astonishing—and that is just the evil of having a large connexion and being a great deal sought after . . . there was one family in particular, that used to live about a mile from us—not straight down the road, but turning sharp off to the left by the turnpike where the Plymouth mail ran over the donkey—that were quite extraordinary people for giving the most extravagant parties, with artificial flowers and champagne, and variegated lamps, and, in short, every delicacy of eating and drinking that the most singular epicure could possibly require.'

She affects to believe that this sort of life is a shared experience, and asks poor, simple-minded Smike, the runaway boy from Dotheboys Hall, whether he has ever dined with the Grimbles of Grimble Hall.

'My dear mother,' reasoned Nicholas. 'Do you suppose that the unfortunate outcast of a Yorkshire school was likely to receive many cards of invitation from the nobility and gentry in the neighbourhood?'

'Really, my dear, I don't know why it should be so very extraordinary,' said Mrs Nickleby. 'I know when *I* was at school, I went at least twice every half-year to the Hawkinses at Taunton Vale, and they are much richer than the Grimbles; so you see it's not so very unlikely, after all.'

Having put down Nicholas in this triumphant manner, Mrs Nickleby was suddenly seized with a forgetfulness of Smike's real name, and an irresistible tendency to call him Mr Slamms. . . .

It is a common form of forgetfulness—' "There was a lady in our neighbourhood,' said Mrs Nickleby, 'speaking of sons put me in mind of it—a lady, in our neighbourhood when we lived near Dawlish, I think her name was Rogers; indeed I am sure it was if it wasn't Murphy, which is the only doubt I have. . . ." '

She will also as readily forget the advice she has given her children. When her rapacious brother-in-law Ralph finds Kate a job with Madame Mantalini, a buxom milliner, her first thoughts are of 'certain wicker baskets lined with black oilskin, which she remembered to have seen carried to and fro in the streets, but as Ralph proceeded these disappeared, and were replaced by visions of large houses at the West End, neat private carriages and a banker's book, all of which images succeeded each other with such rapidity, that he had no sooner finished speaking than she nodded her head and said, "Very true," with great appearance of satisfaction.'

She assures Kate that she will make her fortune, and calls to mind two authentic cases of milliners who had been possessed of considerable property, 'though whether they had acquired it all in business, or had had a capital to start with, or had been lucky and married to advantage, she could not exactly remember'.

When the Mantalinis' business fails, however, and Kate loses her job, her mother declares that she had expected it all along.

> 'And I say again,' remarked Mrs Nickleby (who, it is scarcely necessary to observe, had never said so before), 'I say again, that a milliner's and dress-maker's is the very last description of business, Kate, that you should have thought of attaching yourself to. I don't make it a reproach to you, my love; but still I will say, that if you had consulted your own mother . . .'*

After she had read *Nicholas Nickleby*, Elizabeth Dickens asked her son whether he *really* thought that anyone as silly as Mrs Nickleby could possibly have existed. Perhaps she had recognised something of herself in the caricature, and wished to be reassured. Her son's reply is not recorded, but he told a friend that Mrs Nickleby herself had asked him the question.

Of course, it *is* a caricature. His mother, according to one witness, was indeed vain and incoherent; but another found that she had 'a good stock of common sense, and a matter of fact manner'; and her son-in-law thought that she was 'as thoroughly good-natured, easy-going, companionable a body as one could wish to meet with'. Certainly, as was generally agreed, she did have a sense of humour, which Mrs Nickleby conspicuously lacks, and she was a kind mother to her children.

* *Nicholas Nickleby*, chs. XXVII, XLV, XXV, XXXVII, X.

3

After the failure of 'Mrs Dickens's Establishment', there was nothing to do but pawn all the household effects which could conceivably be spared and which had not found their way to the broker already. Charles was given the unpleasant and unwelcome task of getting rid of the books.[10] He took them, a few at a time, to a bookseller in Hampstead Road who was usually in bed and invariably drunk. Sometimes the bookseller, his face cut and his eyes bruised black, could scarcely manage to get the money out of his pocket because his hand shook so badly; at other times he could not find any money at all, and his wife, holding their baby in her arms, would shout insults at him. On these occasions he told Charles to call another day; but his wife had always got some money (she had taken her husband's, Charles supposed, when he was drunk) and she completed the bargain secretly on the stairs.

With his books gone, his education quite forgotten while Fanny was delighting her parents with her progress in hers, without friends, even, so it seemed to him, without love, Charles sank ever deeper into the dark, unfathomable miseries of childish despair. And at this time, when the happiness of Chatham appeared like some other brighter world to which he longed to return, he was thrown sharply farther away from it into a new, quite different world which seemed like the end of hope.

4

The way to this new misery had been opened up for him by James Lamert who, grown tired of waiting for his commission, had left the Dickenses before the move to Gower Street North to manage a small business for his cousin.

This business had recently been bought from Jonathan Warren, a relation of the famous Robert Warren whose boot-blacking—'Warren's Jet Blacking, the pride of mankind'—was at that time one of the best known of the thirty-odd brands on the market, due mainly to the employment of men who chalked on the pavement 'WARREN'S BLACKING IS THE BEST', and to a series of advertisements in verse, widely read and widely parodied, which were regularly displayed in the newspapers above the bold legend: 'WARREN'S BLACKING, 30, STRAND.'

Jonathan Warren had quarrelled with his family, maintaining that it was he who had discovered the formula for the blacking which Robert had then exploited. To revenge himself Jonathan had set up his own business from which he sold bottles of blacking labelled WARREN'S BLACKING, 30, Hungerford Stairs, STRAND, with the Hungerford Stairs in very small type to confuse the public and to profit by Robert's advertising. He also— since there was no Trade Marks Act to prevent his doing so—used the same designs.

This was the business which James Lamert managed and in which he now offered Charles Dickens a job at six shillings a week for a twelve-hour day from eight in the morning till eight at night, with an hour off for dinner and half-an-hour for tea. It would not be a very inspiring job, but it would keep him occupied until his father's financial position improved, and even though the money was not very much, it compared favourably with what the other boys got, and it would at least do something to help the family. Besides, James said, he would give Charles some lessons each day during the lunch hour.

The worried parents accepted the offer with gratitude. Six shillings a week was a good enough wage for an artisan's child of Charles's age, and the hours quite usual. They agreed that it was a pity that he could not go back to school, as he wanted to; but, then, most boys had no more schooling than he had had, and many started work much younger.[11] It was not as though the boy showed any exceptional promise, except in the comic singing line. He was bright enough, that was clear, and Mr Giles had praised him. But, after all, they argued, there were the other children to think of, and there *were* all these debts to be paid.

Charles, however, could not see it in this light. He was *not* an artisan's child. He did not openly complain, but he felt as though he had been sentenced to death.

How could his father and mother do this to him, he wondered in his bitterness and outraged pride. And he never ceased to wonder for the rest of his life how they could have treated him so, never ceased to pity this poor child who had been so cruelly disregarded.

It is wonderful to me, [he said], how I could have been so easily cast away at such an age. It is wonderful to me that, even after my descent into the poor little drudge I had been since we came to London, no one had compassion enough on me—a child of singular abilities, quick, eager, delicate, and soon hurt, bodily or mentally—to suggest that something might have been spared, as certainly it might have been, to place me at any common school. Our friends, I take it, were tired out. No one made any sign. My father and mother were quite satisfied. They could hardly have been more so, if I had been twenty years of age, distinguished at a grammar-school, and going to Cambridge.[12]

He was just twelve years of age—his birthday had been two days before —and he was starting work instead, on 9 February 1824, at 30 Hungerford Stairs, whose decaying floors have long since disappeared beneath the rails of Charing Cross Station.

It was a forlorn, dirty, ramshackle old building overlooking the river, 'the last house on the left-hand side of the way, at old Hungerford-Stairs', as Dickens described it. 'It's wainscotted rooms, and its rotten floors and staircase, and the old grey rats swarming down in the cellars, and the sound of their squeaking and scuffling coming up the stairs at all times, and the dirt and decay of the place, rise up visibly before me, as if I were there again.'[13]

Charles was given a place of work, separate from the other boys, in a little alcove in the counting-house, below whose grimy windows he could see the river, the disturbing, troubled river, and the coal barges working their way downstream to Limehouse and the Kentish shore.

His work, boring and repetitive, consisted of covering the pots of blacking, first with a piece of oil paper, then with a bit of blue paper, tying them round with string, clipping the paper close and neat, then sticking on the labels—WARREN'S BLACKING, 30 Hungerford Stairs, STRAND, WARREN'S BLACKING, WARREN'S BLACKING, WARREN'S BLACKING.

Although he managed, during his lifetime, to keep secret these days of his childhood, which filled him with such shame, remorse and bitterness, he could not afterwards forbear to bring the name and the advertisements which made it famous, into book after book, beginning with *Sketches by Boz* (in which the shabby-genteel man looks as though he wrote poems for Warren's), and *Pickwick Papers* (in which Tony Weller decides that 'poetry's unnatural; no man ever talked in poetry 'cept a beadle on boxin' day, or Warren's Blackin''); and ending with less obvious allusions in *Our Mutual Friend* and *Edwin Drood*.

In *Great Expectations*, the first thing Joe Gargery does when he comes up to London is to go and look at the Blacking Ware'us. But he doesn't find that it comes up to its likeness in the red bills on the shop doors; as, in the bills, so he tells Pip, 'it is drawd too architectooralooral'.* In *Barnaby Rudge*, the old house, 'mouldering to ruin', in which the secrets of the past are buried—one of many such houses in Dickens's work which are used as symbols of repression and restriction—is called The Warren. And in *The Old Curiosity Shop* Dickens introduces one of the men who called at Warren's to sell his verses to James Lamert in the character of Mr Slum,

* *Great Expectations*, ch. XXVIII.

'No words can express the secret agony of my soul'

from whose facile pen come the advertisements for Mrs Jarley's wax-works at three-and-six a time. Mr Slum, 'a tallish gentleman with a hook-nose and black hair', is dressed in once smart but now threadbare clothes which are much too small for him, and a pair of pumps 'in the winter of their existence'. He is, however, full of confidence in his talents:

'Ask the perfumers, ask the blacking-makers, ask the hatters, ask the old lottery-office-keepers—ask any man among 'em what my poetry has done for him, and mark my words he blesses the name of Slum.

If he's an honest man, he raises his eyes to heaven, and blesses the name
of Slum—mark that! You are acquainted with Westminster Abbey,
Mrs Jarley?'

'Yes, surely.'

'Then upon my soul and honour ma'am, you'll find in a certain
angle of the dreary pile, called Poet's Corner, a few smaller names than
Slum,' retorted that gentleman, tapping himself expressly on the
forehead, to imply that there was some slight quantity of brains behind
it. 'I've got a little trifle here now,' said Mr Slum, taking off his hat,
which was full of scraps of paper, 'a little trifle here, thrown off in the
heat of the moment, which I should say was just the sort of thing you
wanted to set this place on fire with. It's an acrostic—the name at this
moment is Warren, but the idea's a convertible one, and a positive
inspiration for Jarley.'* (14)

In his memoirs, Dickens's sixth son, Henry Fielding, describes how his
father, without ever telling his children anything about this period of his
childhood, could not resist making mysterious references to it.

One night, Henry remembered, the family were playing a memory
game.

It was quite a simple game but required a rare 'staying power'. The
players sitting in a circle, one of them starts by giving some name or
object such as Beefsteak, the next person has to repeat Beefsteak and
add something such as Caligula, and so on, each person having to
repeat all the names in the order in which they were given.

It was on Christmas night, the Christmas before his death. My
father had been ailing and had been troubled with his leg, which had
been giving him considerable pain, and he was lying on a sofa when we
started this Memory Game. The game had been proceeding for some
time and the volume of words had grown to a fairly staggering length
when it came once more to my father's turn: and this is where the
interest of my story comes in. After successfully repeating the string of
words the time came for him to add his own contribution. There was a
pause for a while, and then, with a strange twinkle in his eye and a
curious modulation in his voice, he gave it as *'Warren's Blacking,
30 Strand'*. The way in which he said this at once attracted my attention;
why, I could hardly tell.15

5

After a few days' work in the warehouse, when Charles had learned how
to do the work of wrapping and pasting without getting either his hands

* *The Old Curiosity Shop*, ch. XXVIII.

or the pots in a mess of glue and bits of string and paper, it was suggested that it was too inconvenient having him working in the counting-house and he was brought downstairs into the general workroom.

For Charles this enforced contact with working-class boys, illiterate and uncouth, was even more degrading than the drudgery of his work. He seemed now for ever cut off from the world of the Stroughills and the boys he had known at Chatham.

His father claimed relationship with the Dickenses of Staffordshire and he himself, although the College of Heralds did not recognise his claim, later assumed the right to use their crest: 'my father's crest; a lion couchant, bearing in his dexter paw a Maltese cross'.[16]

As behoved a man who claimed title to this crest, John Dickens had taken care to cultivate an acceptable accent, and he had expected his son to do the same.[17] There was, as a Chatham acquaintance said of them, 'more than a ghost of gentility hovering in their company'.

And now Charles was to be thrown into the company of boys such as Paul Green whose father was a fireman at Drury Lane Theatre and who had a little sister—Charles believed it was a sister—who did imps in the pantomime; and he was to be put to work with boys like Bob Fagin who wore a paper cap and lived with his brother-in-law, a waterman. They called Charles the 'young gentleman', and he, 'though perfectly familiar with them', was for ever conscious of what he called 'the space between us' placed there by his 'conduct and manners'.

Later on, when he got used to working with the men in the warehouse, two of them (the foreman who had been a soldier and the carman who wore a red jacket) called him 'Charles', but this, as he commented, was when they were 'very confidential, and when I had made some effort to entertain them with the result of some of the old readings which were fast perishing out of my mind'.

At other times he was always the 'young gentleman'. Paul Green, an egalitarian, protested against the older men referring to Dickens in this way, not recognising perhaps the sardonic tone of the description, but Bob Fagin, a kind-hearted, considerate and conservative boy despite the rough Cockney talk, the common paper hat and the tattered apron, showed himself strongly in favour of observing the convention. The two boys had an angry quarrel about it, and this made Charles all the more forcibly aware of what he felt to be his social degradation.

'No words can express the secret agony of my soul as I sunk into this companionship', Dickens wrote in a fragment of autobiography he could not bring himself to publish, but which later appeared almost word for word as a description of David Copperfield's distress at being put at the age of ten to work in Murdstone and Grinby's warehouse in Blackfriars,

> as I compared these every day associates with those of my happier childhood; and felt my early hopes of growing up to be a learned and distinguished man, crushed in my breast. The deep remembrance of the sense I had of being utterly neglected and hopeless; of the shame I felt in my position; of the misery it was to my young heart to believe that, day by day, what I had learned and thought, and delighted in, and raised my fancy and my emulation up by, was passing away from me, never to be brought back any more; cannot be written. My whole nature was so penetrated with the grief and humilation of such considerations, that even now . . . I often forget in my dreams . . . even that I am a man; and wander desolately back to that time of my life.[18]

His misery once again aggravated his ill-health; and one day as he sat at his bench he suffered a violently painful seizure which made him roll on the floor in his agony. Bob Fagin made him a bed of straw in his old alcove in the counting-house and filled empty blacking bottles with hot water and held them against his side and back where the spasmodic contractions were causing him such excruciating pain. Gradually he began to feel better, and Bob Fagin said he would take him home.

Charles let Fagin go with him part of the way, but then he tried to get rid of him. Fagin, though, insisted on accompanying him all the way, so, as Dickens said, 'I shook hands with him on the steps of a house near Southwark Bridge on the Surrey side, making believe that I lived there. As a finishing piece of reality in case of his looking back, I knocked at the door, I recollect, and asked, when the woman opened it, if that was Mr Robert Fagin's house.'

It was not that Charles was unwilling to let his family see what sort of companions he had been forced among, but that he was too proud to let Fagin know where he was going to. For he was going to visit his father. And his father, within a fortnight of Charles's beginning work at Hungerford Stairs, had at last been arrested for debt and taken to the Marshalsea prison.

6

John Dickens had spent the first three nights of his detention in a sponging house (a detention house for debtors), where Charles had visited him and discovered him crying. Charles had cried, too, and for the whole of that weekend, as he ran about London carrying messages and trying to raise the £40 which would have secured his father's release, he found difficulty in keeping the tears out of his eyes. On the Monday, no one offering to lend him the money, Charles went with his father to the Marshalsea,

an oblong pile of barrack building, partitioned into squalid houses standing back to back, so that there were no back rooms; environed by a narrow paved yard, hemmed in by high walls duly spiked at the top. Itself a close and confined prison for debtors, it contained within it a much closer and more confined jail for smugglers. Offenders against the revenue laws, and defaulters to excise or customs, who had incurred fines which they were unable to pay, were supposed to be incarcerated behind an iron-plated door, closing up a second prison, consisting of a strong cell or two, and a blind alley some yard and a half wide, which formed the mysterious termination of the very limited skittle-ground in which the Marshalsea debtors bowled down their troubles.*

At the prison gates John Dickens, in a characteristic comment of extravagant self-pity, said that the sun had now set on him for ever; and Charles believing that it might be true, thought that his own heart was really broken.

Feeling more lonely than ever now, he worked on at Warren's in utter misery. In the evenings after work he went to visit his father, who met him in the lodge and took him up the stone steps to his little room on the top floor but one. They sat down together and his father wept as he told his son to take warning from his sad and bitter fate. Charles stared at the fireplace through his tears, and the two bricks placed in the rusty grate to prevent it burning too much coal remained fixed in his memory for ever.

One evening he was sent upstairs to borrow a knife and fork from a Captain Porter who lived in the attic, and he remembered thinking as he stood nervously in the doorway that he would not like to borrow Captain Porter's comb. There were four people in the room, the shabby Captain with his uncut beard, and his 'old, old brown great-coat, with no other coat below it', two washed-out looking girls with rumpled hair, and a very dirty woman whom Charles knew instinctively 'was not married to Captain P.'

This glimpse of Captain Porter's room with its dishevelled inmates and a bed rolled up in the corner, and a row of plates and pots on a shelf, was not only used as a scene in *David Copperfield* but seems like a tableau

* *Little Dorrit*, Bk I, ch. VI.

in which the characters will soon move and talk to play their parts in a prison scene from *Pickwick Papers* or *Little Dorrit*.

Indeed, the man downstairs, crying by the rusty grate, seems already himself designed to form the model for William Dorrit, the 'father of the Marshalsea' and for twenty-three years a prisoner there. The resemblance between the two men is unmistakable. William Dorrit's social pretensions, his ornately verbose style, his nervous habit of fluttering his fingers in front of his lips when he first enters the prison, and the way in which, during the later years of his incarceration, he sits down in his chair with a 'wonderful air of benignity and patronage', are all drawn closely from life.

For John Dickens, once recovered from his early despair and recurrent outbursts of weeping, became once more the talkative, gregarious fellow he had been before, resuming his former pompous manner, taking comfort from the fact that the Navy Pay Office had not yet stopped his salary. Elected chairman of the committee which organised the debtors' lives and which saw to their needs and meagre comforts, he was soon well known and respected in the prison; and as the King's birthday approached, it fell to him—as it fell to Mr Micawber in the King's Bench—to draw up the petition in which the prisoners begged for a royal bounty to enable them to drink His Majesty's health.

Charles asked to be present on the day appointed for them to sign the petition. The document was placed on an ironing board, and the prisoners were formed up in a queue outside the door and allowed in one at a time to sign it.

Whatever was comical in this scene, and whatever was pathetic, I sincerely believe I perceived in my corner, as well as I should perceive it now [Dickens wrote in later life]. I made out my own little character and story for every man who put his name to the sheet of paper. I might be able to do that now, more truly: not more earnestly, or with a closer interest. Their different peculiarities of dress, of face, of gait, of manner, were written indelibly upon my memory. I would rather have seen it than the best play ever played; and I thought about it afterwards, over the pots of paste-blacking, often and often. When I looked, with my mind's eye, into the Fleet-prison during Mr Pickwick's incarceration, I wonder whether half-a-dozen men were wanting from the Marshalsea crowd.[19]

Those prisoners who experienced any difficulty in reading the petition, or showed the least doubt as to the purport or importance of its contents were required to wait while Captain Porter, in a cleaner and better brushed state than usual, read it out to them in a resonant, imposing voice, lingering over the more mellifluous phrases, while John Dickens sat 'listening with a little of an author's vanity, and contemplating (not severely) the spikes on the opposite wall'.

While Dickens based William Dorrit, like Mr Micawber, on some of the superficial mannerisms and idiosyncrasies of his father, the fundamental humiliation of Dorrit, his shame and fears, helplessness and concealments are really Charles's own. It was he who felt imprisoned, just as all the leading characters in *Little Dorrit*, and not only William Dorrit himself, feel imprisoned or are shown in conditions or institutions, or states of mind, which are as imprisoning as the spiked walls of the Marshalsea.

All his life from now on Dickens was to be obsessed with prisons, prisoners and imprisonment. There is scarcely a book in which they do not play a part. They are repeatedly used as symbols of suffering, inescapably linked with childhood memories, and binding him, however reluctantly and with whatever subsequent reservations, to the fears and hopes of the oppressed. To Edmund Wilson it seems that even in Dickens's first and most cheerful novel the hero was destined for the Fleet from the beginning.[20] And it is certainly there in the Fleet that the earlier shadows cast by the gloomy, interpolated stories come together to darken the spirit of the *Pickwick Papers*.

There is no squalor in Pickwick's Fleet to compare with that of the real prison; the only vermin in the room in which he is put is a dingy-looking fly which crawls over his pantaloons; the atmosphere, which in reality was poisonous, strikes him merely as 'intolerably close', except in the coffee-room gallery where the smell of tobacco smoke is 'perfectly suffocating'. But it is here that Pickwick for the first time sees men who have 'lost friends, fortune, home and happiness'; it is here for the first time that he feels 'a depression of spirit and sinking of heart' as he thinks of being left alone in such a 'coarse vulgar crowd'; it is here for the first time that he turns away from a fellow human being, unable to stand the sight of 'a woman with a child in her arms, who seemed scarcely able to crawl, from emaciation and misery'. The woman was

> walking up and down with her husband, who had no other place to see her in. As they passed Mr Pickwick, he could hear the female sob bitterly; and once she burst into such a passion of grief, that she was compelled to lean against the wall for support, while the man took the child in his arms and tried to soothe her.

Mr Pickwick's heart was really too full to bear it, and he went upstairs to bed.*

It is a theme to which Dickens persistently returns. Fagin in the condemned cell; Pip who is shown the gallows at Newgate and the Debtors' Door by a man in mildewed clothes 'bought cheap off the executioner', and who watches the scene at visiting time when 'a potman was going his round with beer . . . and a frowzy, ugly, disorderly, depressing scene it was';† Barnaby Rudge who can understand so little but who does, at least, know that prison is 'a dull, sad, miserable place', a place in which it is better to be mad like he is, so his fellow-prisoner, Hugh, tells Dennis the Hangman, than sane as they are;‡ Mr Micawber and William Dorrit, whose reactions to imprisonment so closely resemble those of John Dickens; Arthur Clennam who makes no friends in the Marshalsea, who is 'too depressed to associate with the herd in the yard' and 'too retiring and too unhappy' to go down to the tavern, and who feels that imprisonment is changing his whole character, so that he begins to be afraid of himself as the shadow of the wall grows dark upon him;§ Mrs Clennam and Miss Havisham who, by choosing to live a life of imprisonment, develop a prisoner's mentality—all these, amongst many others, reflect Dickens's need to probe constantly into that painful past which so very few of his readers knew had ever existed.

Nor was it only in imagination that Dickens felt this compulsion to turn over and re-examine these days of misery and social disgrace which centred round the Marshalsea. In England, in America, Italy and France he found his way to the prison in each new town he visited in the way that another man might seek out a museum or a church. In New York in the 1840s, for example, the first building he investigated was a prison. Crossing Broadway into the Bowery, so he recorded, he came to a 'dismal fronted pile of bastard Egyptian, like an enchanter's palace in a melodrama!—a famous prison called The Tombs.' 'Shall we go in?' he asks; and, of course, he does go in.¶

These inspections of prisons that Dickens was to make throughout his life had already begun. His way home from the Marshalsea to Gower Street took him past Newgate, and he would linger there staring at the great walls and the studded door, wondering about the life inside.

He would never forget, he wrote later, the mixed feelings of awe and

* *Pickwick Papers*, ch. XL. † *Great Expectations*, ch. XXXII.
‡ *Barnaby Rudge*, ch. XXVI. § *Little Dorrit*, Bk. II, ch. XXVIII.
¶ *American Notes*, ch. VI.

respect with which he used to gaze at those forbidding walls, that huge door plated with iron and mounted with spikes, the turnkeys sitting round a fire inside the white-washed lodge. He wondered how on earth the hackney coachmen could 'cut jokes in the presence of such horrors and drink pots of half-and-half so near the last drop'.*

Sometimes he would go past the Fleet and look at the iron cage in the wall, behind which 'was posted some man of hungry looks, who from time to time rattled a money-box and exclaimed in a mournful voice, "Pray, remember the poor debtors; pray remember the poor debtors." The receipts of this box, when there were any, were divided among the poor prisoners; and the men on the poor side relieved each other in this degrading office.'†

7

On getting back to Gower Street from the prison, Charles would be given supper by his mother and then sent out to the pawnshop with bits of her remaining jewellery or a boxful of kitchen utensils, which it was hoped would fetch enough money to provide food for the family next day.

All hope of their creditors agreeing to the execution of a new deed of composition had by now been abandoned, and insolvency proceedings had been initiated. Under the law the clothing and personal effects of the debtor and his dependants must not exceed £20. Charles, accordingly, had to go to the official appraiser for his clothing to be valued. When he arrived at the appraiser's house, 'somewhere beyond the obelisk', he wished he had not brought with him his grandfather's fat old silver watch which Grandmother Dickens had given him and which was now ticking loudly in his pocket.

But the appraiser came into the office from his dining-room where he was evidently in the middle of a meal (for his mouth was full and he smelled strongly of beer), and, having made a cursory inspection of the boy's white hat, small jacket and corduroy trousers, said good-naturedly that 'that would do', and dismissed him. Charles bowed and returned, profoundly relieved, to Gower Street.

One night when he got home he found, as David Copperfield does on returning to Mrs Micawber from a visit to her husband in the King's

* *Sketches*, 'Criminal Courts'. † *Pickwick Papers*, ch. XLI.

George Cruikshank

'Charles would be given supper by his mother and then sent out to the pawnshop with bits of her remaining jewellery or a boxful of kitchen utensils'

Bench, that most of the furniture had gone, and all that remained in the house were a few chairs and beds and the kitchen table. Mrs Dickens and the children then moved into the two front rooms and they all lived there with the orphan maid night and day.

On the next rent day, when there was scarcely any more money left in the house, and little of any value that could be sold, they moved out and went to live with John Dickens in his room in the Marshalsea. It was hardly big enough for himself, let alone for his family, but at least they could be together there; and, since the Navy Pay Office had still not stopped his salary, they would not go hungry. Nor would they be confined to the prison; for although the debtors were not allowed outside the walls, their families could move freely in and out of the gateway until it was shut and locked at night. The few pieces of extra furniture they needed could be hired from the turnkeys, while food could either be cooked in the prison kitchen or brought in from a cook-shop.

There was, however, no room for the little maid, who was found a cheap room nearby and came into the prison each morning. And there was no room either for Charles, who was sent out to live on his own in Little College Street, Camden Town, with a Mrs Roylance, a 'reduced old lady' who 'took children in to board'. She had earned her living for a number of years in this way in Brighton, and (like the dame-school owner in Chatham) 'with a few alterations and embellishments', so her young lodger later admitted, 'she unconsciously began to sit for Mrs Pipchin in *Dombey* when she took me in'. There were three other children living in the house, a brother and a sister, 'somebody's natural children, who were very irregularly paid for, and a widow's little son'. Charles and the two boys all slept in the same room.

His father paid for Charles's lodging here. But out of his six shillings a week Charles had to provide for all his other wants, including his own food.

Uusually for breakfast he had 'a penny cottage loaf and a pennyworth of milk'; though sometimes on his way to work in the morning he could not resist the pieces of pastry put out in trays at confectioners' doors in Tottenham Court Road. Being stale they were sold cheap, yet even so, when he had bought a slice, he found that he could only afford a saveloy sausage and a penny loaf for his dinner, or perhaps bread and cheese and a glass of beer in 'the miserable old public house over the way: the Swan, if I remember right or the Swan and something else that I have forgotten'.

Sometimes he contented himself with a bread roll and a slice of pudding.

This pudding was of two sorts: the best, with fresh hot currants, could be bought in a pudding-shop in a small court behind St Martin's-in-the-Fields; but more often Charles had to content himself with the heavier, stodgier sort which had raisins struck in very far apart and was sold in a cheap and smelly shop in the Strand, 'near where the Lowther-arcade is now'.[21]

When he had resisted the stale pastry on his way down Tottenham Court Road, or someone had given him an extra shilling, he would go out for a special dinner. There were so many pudding-shops and coffee-rooms and eating-houses in the courts around St Martin's-in-the-Fields that it was known as 'Porridge Island'. And here, or in the Strand or in Drury Lane or in the Adelphi, the little boy would eat in the place of his choice. In Clare Court there were two of the best known alamode beef-shops in London. 'The beef and liquors at either house are equally good', the *Epicure's Almanack* reported, 'and the attention of all who pass is attracted by the display of fine sallads in the windows—red beetroot conspicuous'.

Charles's attention was certainly attracted, and one day he went by himself to one of these beef-houses, the 'New Thirteen Cantons', more familiarly known as Johnson's, after its proprietor. Tucked under his arm was his own bread wrapped up in a piece of paper so as to look like a book. He went into the best dining-room and ordered a plateful of larded beef. 'What the waiter thought of such a strange little apparition, coming in all alone, I don't know,' he wrote; 'but I can see him now, staring at me as I ate my dinner, and bringing up the other waiter to look. I gave him a halfpenny, and I wish, now, that he hadn't taken it.'[22]

Having a single customer who was only twelve years old was curious enough, but Charles looked even younger than that and was still very small for his age. And this childlike appearance, though combined with an air of assumed self-confidence, induced the landlords of the public-houses he sometimes entered for a glass of beer to hesitate before serving him.

Once, so he said, having got a little extra money to spend, Charles went into the bar of a public-house, the Red Lion in Parliament Street at the corner of the short street leading into Cannon Row, and said to the landlord,

'What is your very best—the VERY *best*—ale, a glass?' For the occasion was a festive one, for some reason: I forget why. 'Twopence,' says he. 'Then,' says I, 'just draw me a glass of that if you please, with a good head to it.' The landlord looked at me, in return, over the bar, from head to foot, with a strange smile on his face; and instead of drawing the beer, looked round the screen and said something to his wife, who came out from behind it, with her work in her hand and joined in surveying me. . . . They asked me a good many questions, as to what my name was, how old I was, where I lived, how I was employed, etc., etc. To all of which, that I might commit nobody, I invented appropriate answers. They served me with the ale, though I suspect it was not the strongest on the premises; and the landlord's wife, opening the little half-door and bending down, gave me a kiss that was half-admiring and half-compassionate, but all womanly and good, I am sure.[23]

If he had any money left at tea-time, Charles went out, during the half-hour break he was allowed, for half-a-pint of coffee and a slice of bread and butter in a coffee-shop. But he did not always have enough money left, and then he was reduced to staring unhappily and longingly through the windows, and thinking of the loaf and cheese which were waiting for him 'on a particular shelf of a particular cupboard' at Mrs Roylance's.

There was one particular coffee-shop in St Martin's Lane, he recalled, with an oval glass-plate in the door 'with COFFEE-ROOM painted on it, addressed towards the street. If ever I find myself in a very different kind of coffee-room now, but when there is such an inscription on glass, and read it backward on the wrong side MOOR-EEFFOC (as I often used to do then, in a dismal reverie) a shock goes through my blood.'[24]

When he could not bear the sight of the COFFEE-ROOM inscription any longer he would wander off into Covent Garden to stare at the pineapples and melons and the bundles of asparagus piled up outside the shops 'like fortifications'. Looking down the side avenues he saw rows and rows of old women sitting on upturned baskets, shelling peas; and passing the doors of the herbalists he snuffed up the smell which was like that of 'veal stuffing yet uncooked, dreamily mixed up with capsicums, brown paper and seeds'.

In the poultry markets, 'ducks and fowls, with necks unnaturally long, lay stretched out in pairs, ready for cooking', speckled eggs lay in mossy baskets, and on every side there were country sausages, 'new cheeses to any wild extent; live birds in coops and cages, looking much too big to be natural, in consequence of those receptacles being much too little; rabbits, alive and dead, innumerable'; and huge, red lobsters on 'cool, refreshing, silvery fish-stalls'.*

* *Martin Chuzzlewit*, ch. XL.

'What is your very best—the VERY *best*—ale, a glass?'

Sometimes he would walk down to the back streets of the Adelphi and explore the Adelphi arches, or go down to 'the toy-shop in Fleet Street to see the giants of Saint Dunstan's strike upon the bells', or to the tea-tray shop on the corner of Bedford Street and King Street and stare at one particular tray on which was painted a touching scene of two boys leaving for school at breakfast-time, 'one boy used to it; the other not'. Or he would sit on a bench outside the waterside tavern, the Fox-under-the-Hill, to watch the halfpenny steam-boats chugging along in the river between Salisbury Stairs and London Bridge.

Little steamboats dashed up and down the stream incessantly. Tiers upon tiers of vessels, scores of masts, labyrinths of tackle, idle sails, splashing oars, gliding row-boats, lumbering barges, sunken piles with ugly lodging for the water-rat within their mud-discoloured nooks; church steeples, warehouses, house roofs, arches, bridges, men and women, children, casks, cranes, boxes, horses, coaches, idlers and hard labourers—there they were all jumbled up together.*

Often Charles went down to Scotland Yard, then a haphazard collection of buildings, shops and eating-houses between the gardens of Northumberland House and the river, where the coal-heavers repaired each morning to fill their wagons with coal from the barges moored at the wharf. The district was more or less given over to the needs of the coal-heavers—a tailor's shop displayed, as an advertisement, a pair of little leather gaiters, a diminutive apron and, on each door post, the model of a coal sack; the eating-houses 'exhibited joints of a magnitude and puddings of a solidity which coal-heavers alone could appreciate'; the public-houses were full of men with blackened faces and coalies' hats drinking Barclay's best and smoking their long-stemmed pipes.

Charles used to listen to their portentous discussions and to their songs in which the last few words were dwelt upon with a 'length of emphasis which made the very roof tremble above them', and once he found them dancing in the open space before the inn. He sat down on the bench to watch them and, like David Copperfield, he wondered what they thought of him. Occasionally he played with Paul Green and Bob Fagin on the coal barges, but usually he was alone and miserably unhappy.

'No advice, no counsel, no encouragement, no consolation, no support, from any-one that I can call to mind', Dickens wrote in the autobiographical fragment that he could not bear to publish in his lifetime,

* *Ibid.*

discussing with acute self-pity the plight of his young self almost as though this sad little boy were quite a different person altogether.

I know I do not exaggerate, unconsciously and unintentionally, the scantiness of my resources and the difficulties of my life. I know that if a shilling or so were given me by anyone, I spent it on a dinner or a tea. I know that I worked, from morning to night, with common men and boys, a shabby child. I know that I tried, but ineffectually, not to anticipate my money, and to make it last the week through; by putting it away in a drawer I had in the counting house, wrapped up in six little parcels, each parcel containing the same amount, and labelled with a different day. I know that I lounged about the streets, insufficiently and unsatisfactorily fed. I know that, but for the mercy of God, I might easily have been, for any care that was taken of me, a little robber or a little vagabond.[25]

One evening on his visit to the family in the Marshalsea, Charles broke down and cried bitterly. He was all the more upset for he had, up till then, confided his loneliness and misery to no one. He had 'never said, to man or boy' how he came to be working in the blacking warehouse; he 'never gave the least indication' that he was sorry to be there. That he suffered 'in secret', and that he suffered 'exquisitely', no one had known but he.

But now he could not control his tears, and his father, immediately touched by the unhappiness he had succeeded till then in hiding from himself, made arrangements for him to move from Mrs Roylance's to a little back attic in Lant Street, Southwark, in the house of an Insolvent Court agent, which was then occupied by a good-hearted fat old man with a gentle wife, and a 'very innocent grown-up son', lame like his father. The room looked out over a timber-yard, and the family—later to become the plump and placid Garland family of *The Old Curiosity Shop*— were kind and understanding, all three of them sitting up one whole night by his bedside when he had an attack of his recurrent illness. Charles, after moving there from Camden Town, thought it all 'quite a paradise'.

Lant Street [he wrote later] was colonised by a few clear-starchers, a sprinkling of journeymen bookbinders, one or two prison agents for the Insolvent Court, several small housekeepers who are employed in the Docks, a handful of mantua makers, and a seasoning of jobbing tailors. The majority of the inhabitants either direct their energies to the letting of furnished apartments, or devote themselves to the healthful and invigorating pursuit of mangling. The chief features in the still life of the streets, are green shutters, lodging-bills, brass door-plates, and bell-handles; the principal specimens of animated nature, the pot-boy, the muffin youth, and the baked-potato man. The population is migratory, usually disappearing on the verge of quarter-day, and generally by night. His Majesty's revenues are seldom collected in this happy valley, the rents are dubious, and the water communication is very frequently cut off.*

Now that he was living in Lant Street, Charles did not have nearly so far to walk home after his evening visits, and was able to go to the prison for breakfast and supper. And after supper on Saturdays, as he made his way home 'over Blackfriar's Bridge and down that turning in the Blackfriar's Road which has Rowland Hill's chapel on one side, and the likeness of a golden dog licking a golden pot over a shop door on the other', his money burned a hole in his pocket. Occasionally he was forced to spend his money on something essential like bootlaces. But more than once, as he confessed, 'I have been seduced by a show-van at a corner; and have gone in, with a very motley assemblage, to see the Fat Pig, the Wild Indian, and the Little Lady. There were two or three hat-manufactories there, then (I think they are there still); and among the things which, encountered anywhere, or under any circumstances, will instantly recall that time, is the smell of hat-making.'[26]

After seeing the show in the travelling circus van, he might call at a shop selling Hunt's roasted corn, which had become a popular substitute for coffee, and which he enjoyed making for his Sunday breakfast, or he might spend twopence on the latest issue of *The Portfolio of Entertaining and Instructive Varieties in History, Science, Literature and Fine Arts*, (a magazine which specialised in burlesque and parody), or he would linger perhaps at a street corner to watch a Punch and Judy show.[27] And he remembered once going into a theatre 'of the lowest description' and seeing a performance which included two dramas, a comic song sung from a donkey's back, and a display of fireworks.

On Sunday he spent all day in the prison, going first to fetch Fanny from the Academy of Music so that he could walk with her from Tenterden Street to the Borough. One day he went to the Academy to see his sister presented with a prize, and felt overwhelmed by the contrast between her acclaimed success and his own neglect and hopelessness. 'I could not bear to think of myself—beyond the reach of all such honourable emulation and success', he wrote. 'The tears ran down my face. I prayed, when I went to bed that night, to be lifted out of the humiliation and neglect in which I was. I had never suffered so much before.'

* *Pickwick Papers*, ch. XXXI.

8

And then, in April 1824, John Dickens came into his inheritance from his mother, and the debts could be paid at last. The family moved out of the prison, first to stay with Mrs Roylance, then to Hampstead, before finding a more permanent home in a seedy house in Johnson Street between Camden Town and Somers Town. [28] While he was in prison John Dickens had applied for a retirement pension, in the hope that he would be granted one before the disgrace of his insolvency rendered him ineligible to receive it. He had had no reply to his application, however, and he went back to work trusting that the Office would over-look his lapse from respectability now that the debts had been paid.

With his father back at work, Charles felt sure that he would be allowed to go back to school. He waited for something to be said. But nothing was said. And Charles continued with his hated work. He was not so poor now, for his mother provided him with his dinner which he carried to the warehouse in a basin tied up in a handkerchief; yet he was, in his own words, 'just as solitary and self-dependent as before'.

The only real changes were that Warren's, having prospered, had moved to larger, lighter and less tumbledown premises on the corner of Chandos Street and Bedford Street, [29] and that Charles had become so adept at his work that he and Bob Fagin were set to work together in the light of one of the ground-floor windows overlooking Bedford Street, where they were the subject of great interest to the passers-by who collected on the pavement outside to watch them.

Charles, no doubt, rather enjoyed being watched at his work, as most boys do when they are performing a task skilfully and at speed; and he had always liked showing off, was always to enjoy playing a part, even in his private relationships. But his father, it seems, was deeply distressed by this public display of his son's manual dexterity and of his own vicarious disgrace. He quarrelled with James Lamert who told Charles that he could not possibly keep him on.

Instead of being pleased by this longed-for dismissal, however, Charles, as he admitted, 'cried very much, partly because it was so sudden, and partly, because in his anger [James Lamert] was violent about my father, though gentle to me. Thomas [the foreman] comforted me, and said he was sure it was for the best. With a relief so strange it was like oppression, I went home.'

At home his mother was not at all pleased by what had happened. More realistic in such matters than her husband, she realised how foolish it was to quarrel with one of the few people who had done something to help the family in the time of their distress. Besides, who could tell how long her husband would be kept on at the Navy Pay Office, having been in prison for mismanaging his own financial affairs? And, in the meantime, Charles's weekly wage (recently increased to seven shillings a week) was very useful.

She went to see James Lamert, settled the differences between him and her husband, and persuaded him to take Charles back. This seemed to her son an unforgivable betrayal. 'I know how these things have worked together to make me what I am,' he confessed. 'But I never afterwards forgot, I never shall forget, I never can forget that my mother was warm for my being sent back.'[30]

His father, however, shocked by what he had seen in Warren's Bedford Street window, and determined that his family should be seen to have regained their former gentility, decided that Charles should not be sent back, but should go instead to school again, whether he could afford it or not.[31]

So the blacking warehouse episode was over. His parents never again referred to it; and in later life his wife, like his children, knew nothing of it until after he was dead. Perhaps even then they would not have done so had not Charles Wentworth Dilke[(32)] mentioned to John Forster that he had once seen Dickens as a child working in a warehouse near the Strand. Forster told Dickens this, how Dilke had gone into the place with his father, given Charles half-a-crown and received in acknowledgment a low bow. Dickens listened in silence while Forster repeated the story and remained silent 'for several minutes'. Forster felt that he had 'unintentionally touched a painful place in his memory', and after the long silence was broken, they spoke of other things. Some time later, however, Dickens told his friend the full story of the imprisonment in the Marshalsea and of his time at Warren's, and gave him a written account of it.

In this written account Dickens said, 'I have no idea how long it lasted; whether for a year or much more or less'. In fact it lasted for less than six months. But since while he was there, overwhelmed by a sense of deprivation, degradation, loneliness and despair, he had no idea when, if ever, he would be released from his bondage, it seemed to the child interminable. And although released in fact, he was never to be released in spirit.

It is not merely that superficial references to boot-blacking, to Warren's, to debtors and to prisons occur repeatedly throughout his work; it is not only that, as most noticeably in *Little Dorrit*, modern society is seen as a prison like the Marshalsea, and in terms of imprisonment like his life at Warren's; it is not only that his books are filled with ill-treated victims of society who, though adult, seem like children, nor only that they do not contain a single example of a completely happy, self-fulfilled child; it is that the very spirit of his imagined world reflects the atmosphere and the experience of these days.[33]

Most of Dickens's heroes begin their lives cut off from other people, insecure, obliged to make their way in a strange, discordant, threatening world, endeavouring to become accepted by it and a part of it, trying to understand themselves, and, in the meantime, sharing the sense of deprivation which makes Paul Dombey live with 'an aching void in his young heart, and all outside so cold, and bare, and strange'.[34]

Even Samuel Pickwick feels compelled to conclude 'we are all the victims of circumstances, and I the greatest'. For though his adventures are comic, the world in which they take place is essentially a menacing, savage world where only the fittest will survive and the unprotected, the simple and the good will be treated with indifference if not with cruelty. It is a world in which men live secret lives, in which, as Sairey Gamp says, 'we never know wot's hidden in each other's hearts; and if we had glass winders there, we'd need keep the shutters up, some on us, I do assure you!'* Most men, in fact, 'live in a world of their own'.†

The disquieting sense of being watched in this world, of being spied upon and caught out by gleaming eyes, eager eyes, spying eyes, eyes that stare, inquisitive eyes, which constantly and disturbingly appear; and of being choked or suffocated in a stifling room, or lost in a labyrinth of streets, as in *Oliver Twist*; the images of crumbling riverside houses that totter suddenly into ruin as the houses of Tom-All-Alone's do in *Bleak House* and the Clennams' house does in *Little Dorrit*; the desire to escape from the imprisoning city back to the countryside of innocent childhood, as shown in *The Old Curiosity Shop*; the comfort of pretence that soothes the fears of the characters in *Martin Chuzzlewit*; the fascination with dirty, muddled, crowded, fungus-laden interiors; the concern with money; the plots which time and again revolve round a family mystery and the dread of its revelation; and, of course, the difficulties of the relationships between parents and their children which are investigated in novel after

* *Martin Chuzzlewit*, ch. xxix.   † *Nicholas Nickleby*, ch. xxviii.

novel—all these ideas and symbols and themes, that repeatedly occur in Dickens's writing, can be interpreted in the light of the traumatic experiences and sufferings of these few months of his thirteenth, pre-pubescent year.

The problems faced by children who have inadequate or neglectful parents, or who do not have any parents at all and are searching for compensatory substitutes, are—to take but one example of these themes—discussed over and over again as Dickens diffuses and recreates his own childhood, torn between the desire for reconciliation and the urge to condemn.

The novels are far more crowded with orphaned children, and with characters suffering from the effects of orphanage, than the usefulness of having such malleable and pathetic agents in a work of fiction would seem to demand. In *David Copperfield*, for example, Emily, Traddles, the Orfling, Mrs Copperfield, Martha Endell and Rosa Dartle are all orphans; Agnes and Dora have no mother; Steerforth, Heep, Ham and Annie Strong, as well as David himself, have no father. In *The Old Curiosity Shop*, in which Little Nell is an orphan and in which Kit Nubbles, her admirer, has no father, Dick Swiveller, the *jeune premier*, cries out in self-pity, 'Left an infant by my parents, at an early age . . . cast upon the world in my tenderest period. . . . Here's a miserable orphan for you.' And Dickens himself, after reading Browning's poetic drama, 'A Blot on the Scutcheon', said passionately, 'I know nothing that is so affecting, nothing in any book I have ever read, as Mildred's recurrence to that "I was so young—I had no mother".'[35]

Miserable as orphans are, though, there is a worse state. For 'not an orphan in the wide world can be so deserted as the child who is an outcast from a living parent's love'.* In *Dombey and Son* there are three parents, including Dombey himself, who so desert their children. In *Barnaby Rudge* there are five whose relationships with their children are unsatisfactory, and remain so. Lionel Trilling has drawn attention to the 'remarkable number of false and inadequate parents in *Little Dorrit*. To what pains Dickens goes to represent a delinquent parenthood, with what an elaboration of irony he sets it forth'.[36] In *Nicholas Nickleby*, Dotheboys Hall itself, as Bernard Bergonzi says, is 'one huge indictment of the failure of parental responsibility'.[37] In *Great Expectations*, it is the criminal Magwitch whom the orphaned Pip, ill-treated by his surrogate mother, comes to accept and to love as a true father.[38] In *David Copperfield* every adult who assumes

* *Dombey and Son.* ch. XXIV.

some sort of parental responsibility for the orphaned child—the Murd-
stones, the Micawbers, Betsey Trotwood, and even Mr Dick—reflect
some aspect of Dickens's resentment towards his mother and of his
ambivalent attitude towards his father.

Of course, he loves Mr Micawber; but when he allows David to warn
Traddles not to lend Micawber any money and to say, in reply to
Traddles's protest that he hasn't got any money, 'You've got a name, you
know', Dickens quietly reminds the reader of the unsavoury methods that
the old sponger employs to obtain a needed loan.

Only in *Pickwick*, which was written at a time when John Dickens's
improvidence had not yet begun to make heavy demands on his own
stretched finances, can he bring himself to idealise the relationship between
himself and his father and to view such a parent as Tony Weller with
good-humoured tolerance. And even here, in the interpolated stories,
there are wicked fathers enough.[39]

9

This continued habit of drawing on his own past is, though, of more
than psychological interest, since it is also, as Humphry House said, 'of
the greatest importance to anybody who wants to treat Dickens's books
as historical documents, or to see them in relation to their age; for it
meant that he tended to push his stories back in time so that the imaginary
date was a good deal earlier than the date of writing'.[40]

This did not mean that he wanted to make them into accurate 'period'
pieces: he had little historic sense, and no fear of anachronisms. But it did
enable him to colour his narrative from his own past experiences, so
closely observed and vividly remembered. He had no sentimental
affection for the historical past, as the titles he chose for the mock books
in his study and the vehement judgments in his *Child's History of England*
show. But he did have an abiding affection for the immediate past, that
'better world' of his early childhood.

Barnaby Rudge and *A Tale of Two Cities* had, of course, to be set in
periods of which he had no personal knowledge. But in most of the other
novels the period against which the action is set is a period in the immediate past, the time of his boyhood and youth. The adventures of Pickwick, so the author tells us in his first chapter, begin in 1827 (nine years
before they were written down) and, although even in 1836 the coach had
not yet been displaced by the railway carriage, the spirit of the book

seems to belong to a much earlier time. In *Little Dorrit*, which first appeared in 1855, the author again immediately makes it clear that the action is to be set in the 1820s, reminding the reader as the book progresses that he is recounting a story of the past. John Chivery, as he mournfully composes the inscription for his tombstone in St George's Churchyard, for instance, thinks that he will die of a broken heart 'about the end of the year one thousand eight hundred and twenty-six'. And when Clennam follows Tattycoram down the Adelphi towards the Terrace which overhangs the river, Dickens pauses to comment,

> there is always, to this day, a sudden pause in that place to the roar of the great thoroughfare. The many sounds become so deadened that the change is like putting cotton in the ears, or having the head thickly muffled. At that time the contrast was far greater; there being no small steam-boats on the river, no landing-place but slippery wooden stairs and foot cause-ways, no railroad on the opposite bank, no hanging bridge or fish market near at hand, no traffic on the nearest bridge of stone, nothing moving on the stream but watermen's wherries and coal-lighters. Long and broad black tiers of the latter, moored fast in the mud as if they were never to move again, made the shore funereal and silent after dark; and kept what little water-movement there was, far out towards midstream.*

The railroad on the opposite bank was not there until 1848; the stone bridge is Waterloo Bridge, opened in 1817; and the fish market was part of Hungerford Market rebuilt in 1831–33. Dickens is remembering the river front as he knew it when he was working at Hungerford Stairs.

In the novels where no specific date is given, the atmosphere is still of the recent past. This is so in *The Old Curiosity Shop* and *Nicholas Nickleby* as well as *Martin Chuzzlewit*. In *Martin Chuzzlewit*, though the book was written in 1843–44 and the characters in it are constantly on the move, the only indication we are given that England is in the ferment and excitement of the Railway Age, is when Mrs Gamp suddenly breaks out in wrath against it, as she looks down upon the Antwerp packet:

> 'Oh, drat you!' said Mrs Gamp, shaking her umbrella at it, 'you're a nice, sputtering, nisy monster for a delicate young creature to go and be a passinger by, ain't you? *You* never do no harm in that way do you, with your hammering, and roaring, and hissing, and lamp-iling, you brute! Them Confugion steamers,' said Mrs Gamp, shaking her umbrella again, 'has done more to throw us out of our reg'lar work, and bring events on at times when nobody counted on 'em (especially

* *Little Dorrit*, Bk. II, ch. IX.

them screeching railroad ones), than all the other frights that ever was took.'*

In *David Copperfield* and *Great Expectations*—as, indeed, in other books —Dickens is obliged to set the early action back in time before the Railway Age, because the narrative covers so long a span. And here again we are constantly aware of Dickens's feeling for the background of the past, so different from his feeling for the present scene. We are aware, too, of a voice taking pains to remind us that we are to imagine an 1820s setting: 'I derived from this last, that Joe's education, like Steam, was yet in its infancy'—'this happened in the days of the extinct red-waistcoated police'—'At that time jails were much neglected.'†

In other books the setting is less firmly established; and Dickens draws on his early memories in an erratic way which makes it difficult to fix the action in any particular period. In *Bleak House*, for example, though the events appear to be taking place about ten years before the book was written, that is to say in the early to mid-1840s, Esther Summerson, speaking of the journey between Bleak House and Deal, says that 'it was a night's journey in those coach times'. And there are references in the book to the Spanish refugees, 'walking about in cloaks, smoking little paper cigars', who lived in Somers Town at the time Dickens was there in the late 1820s.[41] Certainly the whole atmosphere of the legal parts of the book and numbers of small details 'are drawn out of the inexhaustible store of memories from Dickens's early days'.[42]

10

Apart from David Copperfield, who is made to go through the same experiences, the most obvious parallel to Charles Dickens the boy worker is Oliver Twist, the son of a gentleman who becomes the workhouse orphan, 'a poor houseless, wandering boy, without a friend to help him, or a roof to shelter his head'.

Charles was instructed in his warehouse duties by the young, kind Bob Fagin whose name is borrowed for the old shrivelled Jewish villain. And this choice of name is significant. It may well be, as John Bayley has suggested, that Charles felt about Bob Fagin's benevolent and protective interferences on his behalf as Oliver feels about the other Fagin whose

* *Martin Chuzzlewit*, ch. XL.   † *Great Expectations*, chs. VII, XVI, XXXII.

affection he wants and needs and yet dreads as the greatest threat to his moral existence.

No wonder Fagin the criminal is such an ambivalent figure when the real Fagin's kindness had, so to speak, threatened to inure Dickens to the hopeless routine of the wage-slave. So passionate was the young Dickens's desire for the station in life to which he felt entitled and so terrifying his sense that it was being denied him, that he must have hated the real Fagin for the virtue which he could not bear to accept or recognise in that nightmare world, because it might help to subdue him into it. The real Fagin's kindness becomes the criminal Fagin's villainy. [43]

While writing *Oliver Twist*, Dickens became so absorbed in his work that it was as though he were actually experiencing the events he was describing; he began to suffer a recurrence of the feverish spasms of his boyhood illness. Twice he fell ill during the writing of *David Copperfield*, the first time when he was about to begin his description of David in the warehouse. Throughout his life, indeed, he was subject, in times of stress, to these agonising spasms of renal or intestinal colic, that 'unspeakable pain in the side'.

As he himself knew, the weeks of misery in the blacking warehouse had helped to make him what he was; but, at the same time, he dreaded the thought of having to have any further physical contact with the place of his degradation. For years he could never bring himself to go near Hungerford Stairs, and rather than pass the warehouse in Chandos Street he would make a wide detour. Walking back from Southwark across Blackfriars Bridge to Camden Town, by way of the streets he passed along when returning to his room after a visit to his father in the Marshalsea, made him cry even after his eldest child could speak; and to avoid the smell of the cement which was used on the blacking corks, he would cross to the other side of the Strand whenever he drew near to Robert Warren's factory.

Indeed, the whole of the London scene as presented in his novels, particularly in the later novels, is a gloomy, decaying, vaguely menacing one, criss-crossed by 'cold, wet, shelterless, midnight streets'. London seemed to him, when he first came to know it, as it seemed at first sight to David Copperfield, 'an amazing place . . . fuller of wonders and wickedness than all the cities of the earth'. But the London he describes—and describes with so much more imagination and emotion than the scenes of the countryside where he had been happy—is far less full of wonders than of wickedness and corruption. The real London, smoky, dirty, and ill-lit, is marvellously, romantically transformed. Yet Dickens's London, at once strange and familiar, seems pervaded by an underlying despondency.

Its streets are shown as being like that faded, tumble-down street near Golden Square, with its 'two irregular rows of tall meagre houses, which seem to have stared each other out of countenance years ago. The very chimneys appear to have grown dismal and melancholy, from having had nothing better to look at than the chimneys over the way. Their tops are battered and broken, and blackened with smoke; and here and there some taller stack than the rest, inclining heavily to one side, and toppling over the roof, seems to meditate taking revenge for half a century's neglect, by crushing the inhabitants of the garrets beneath.'*

Or they are like the street where Mr Dombey lives, between Portland Place and Bryanston Square, in a dismal house with 'great wide areas containing cellars frowned upon by barred windows', leered at by crooked-eyed doors leading to dustbins, and overlooked by two gaunt trees with blackened trunks and branches whose leaves were so smoke-dried they rattled rather than rustled.

The sun was never on the street but in the morning about breakfast-time, when it came with the water-carts and the old clothes-men, and the people with geraniums, and the umbrella-maker, and the man who trilled the little bell of the Dutch clock as he went along. It was soon gone again to return no more that day; and the bands of music and the straggling Punch's shows going after it left it a prey to the most dismal of organs, . . . until the butlers whose families were dining out began to stand at the house-doors in the twilight, and the lamplighter made his nightly failure to brighten up the streets with gas.†

The squares and courts off Holborn are miserable, muddy, mean and poor, with the most dismal trees, 'and the most dismal sparrows, and the most dismal cats, and the most dismal houses . . . dilapidated . . . crippled . . . cracked . . . dusty . . . miserable makeshift', decayed by 'dry rot and wet rot and all the silent rots that rot in neglected roof and cellar'.‡

The impression that such descriptions inevitably make is that Dickens came to agree with Mortimer Lightwood and Eugene Wrayburn that London—although he could not work for long away from its stimulation —was in fact, as well as symbolically in his work, 'such a black shrill city,

* *Nicholas Nickleby*, ch. xiv.   † *Dombey and Son*, ch. iii.
‡ *Little Dorrit*, Bk. i, chs. ix, xii, xxvii; *Great Expectations*, ch. xxi.

combining the qualities of a smoky house and a scolding wife; such a gritty city; such a hopeless city, with no rent in the leaden canopy of its sky'.*

In the opening sentences of *Bleak House* the streets of London are shown to us as cold and muddy; there is a black drizzle of soot lowering down from the chimney-pots, and the fog that is everywhere in this 'great (and dirty) city' is as pervasive as it is inescapable. There is a certain re-deeming, if ill-tempered, vitality in the people who jostle their way through the gloom. But in *Little Dorrit* even this has gone.

Mews Street, Grosvenor Square, is a hideous, smelly 'little street of dead wall, stables, and dunghills'. Covent Garden has become a desolate place full of arches where miserable children in rags, 'like young rats, slunk and hid, fed on offal, huddled together for warmth, and were hunted about'. Even in the area of Park Lane in summertime, streets that try to be stately, succeed only in being more melancholy. And, of course, down by the river the crooked and descending streets are all mouldy, dingy, sad and smoke-blackened.†

Everywhere on a Sunday evening,

> melancholy streets in a penitential garb of soot, steeped the souls of the people who were condemned to look at them out of windows, in dire despondency. In every thoroughfare, up almost every alley, and down almost every turning, some doleful bell was throbbing, jerking, tolling, as if the Plague were in the city and the dead-carts were going round.... Nothing to see but streets, streets, streets. Nothing to breathe but streets, streets, streets. Nothing to change the brooding mind, or raise it up.‡

* *Our Mutual Friend*, ch. xii.   † *Little Dorritt*, chs. x, xiv, xxxii.
‡ *Ibid.*, ch. iii.

3

WELLINGTON HOUSE ACADEMY
1824-1827
aet. 12-15

GRANBY STREET HAMPSTEAD ROAD LONDON

What would they say, who made so light of money, if they could know how I have scraped my halfpence together, for the purchase of my daily saveloy and beer, or my slices of pudding? How would it affect them, who were so innocent of London life and London streets, to discover how knowing I was (and was ashamed to be) in some of the meanest phases of both?

David Copperfield

3

1

When his father told him that he was to go back to school again, Charles's eyes filled with tears of gratitude, and he went to ask for a card of terms at a nearby school in a state of high excitement.

The school, Wellington House Academy, on the corner of Granby Street and Mornington Place in Hampstead Road,[1] was kept by a Welshman, William Jones, who took both boarders and day pupils. When Charles arrived there to ask for the prospectus, it was dinner-time and Mr Jones was carving the joint. He came out wearing a pair of holland sleeves and gave Charles what he wanted. He seemed at first sight an agreeable man; it looked like a good school, and Charles hoped that he would soon become a pupil there.

A few days later, at seven o'clock of a June morning in 1824, his name was entered on the books of the school and he was taken into the class-room in a wooden building in the bare and dusty playground.

'I gazed upon the schoolroom, the most forlorn and desolate place I had ever seen,' says David Copperfield—and his description of the deserted schoolroom at Salem House was, as one of Charles's fellow pupils afterwards testified, an accurate enough description of the school-room at Wellington House:

I see it now. A long room, with three long rows of desks, and six of forms, and bristling all round with pegs for hats and slates. Scraps of old copy-books and exercises litter the dirty floor. Some silkworms' houses, made of the same materials, are scattered over the desks. Two miserable little white mice, left behind by their owner, are running up and down in a fusty castle made of pasteboard and wire, looking in all the corners with their red eyes for anything to eat. A bird, in a cage very little bigger than himself, makes a mournful rattle now and then in hopping on his perch, two inches high, or dropping from it; but neither sings nor chirps. There is a strange unwholesome smell upon the room, like mildewed corduroys, sweet apples wanting air, and rotten books. There could not well be more ink splashed about it, if it had been roofless from its first construction, and the skies had rained, snowed, hailed, and blown ink through the varying seasons of the year.*

★ *David Copperfield*, ch. v.

When Charles entered this schoolroom for the first time, it was in the middle of a term. The boys were sitting on each side of the three long desks that stretched almost across the entire width of the room, with the master at a raised desk in the middle of the side wall.

Charles felt like an impostor at first, afraid that the other boys would discover what he had been doing and where he had been during the last few months and despise him for it:

> My mind ran upon what they would think, if they knew of my familiar acquaintance with the Prison. Was there anything about me which would reveal my proceedings in connection with all those pawnings and sellings. . . . What would they say who made so light of money, if they could know how I have scraped my halfpence together, for the purchase of my daily saveloy and beer, or my slices of pudding? How would it affect them, who were so innocent of London life and London streets, to discover how knowing I was (and was ashamed to be) in some of the meanest phases of both?*

When he wrote about these fears of David Copperfield, Dickens was thirty-seven and had thought about them for twenty-five years. There had not been a book—there was not to be a book—in which their influence cannot be traced.

In his work as a whole, the qualities which he seems most to admire are usually to be found in such poor and ill-educated, loyal and unselfish characters as Sam Weller, Nancy, Kit Nubbles, Daniel Peggotty, the fisherman, and Joe Gargery, the smith. But the young Dickens himself, like the young Pip, wanted to be taken for a gentleman. The concealments which this entailed, the guilt and unhappiness they caused him— and the uncertain wavering between secretiveness and the relief of confession—had already become a part of his life by the time he went to school again. 'What would they think, if they knew . . .?'

2

There were five masters at the school in addition to Mr Jones—the junior master, Mr Shiers; a French master, who was short and brisk and always carried an umbrella; a fat little dancing and music master, who drove up to the school in a gig and tried to teach Charles the piano and violin without success; a Latin master, 'a colourless doubled-up nearsighted man with a crutch, who was always cold, and always putting

* *David Copperfield*, ch. XVI.

onions into his ears for deafness, and always disclosing ends of flannel under all his garments, and almost always applying a ball of pocket handkerchief to some part of his face with a screwing action round and round. He was a very good scholar, and took great pains where he saw intelligence and a desire to learn: otherwise, perhaps not.'* Lastly, there was Mr Taylor, a kind, lame man who taught English and mathematics, played a broken trombone, and made a practice of calling at the homes of boys who were away from school through illness to ask how they were getting on.

Charles liked Mr Taylor and later—using some ideas from *Roderick Random* and John Forster's *Life of Goldsmith*, as well as his own imagination —transformed him into Mr Mell, the Master at Salem House, 'a gaunt, sallow young man, with hollow cheeks. . . . He was dressed in a suit of black clothes which were rather rusty and dry, and rather short in the sleeves and legs; and he had a white neckerchief on, that was not over clean.' Charles did not suppose that 'this neckerchief was all the linen he had, but it was all he showed or gave any hint of'. He talked to himself and his boots were beyond repair.†

Charles did not, however, on closer acquaintance, take to Mr Jones, the headmaster, an ignorant, excitable, portly man with a heavy tread and a rolling gait, and an irritating habit of clearing his throat. Now that he had induced the boy's parents to hand him into his charge for the fees mentioned in his prospectus, Mr Jones saw no reason to remain as pleasant as he had seemed at first. Dickens transformed him into Mr Creakle.

Mr Creakle's face was fiery, and his eyes were small, and deep in his head; he had thick veins in his forehead, a little nose and a large chin. He was bald on the top of his head; and had some thin wet-looking hair that was just turning grey, brushed across each temple, so that the two sides interlaced on his forehead. But the circumstance about him which impressed me most, was, that he had no voice, but spoke in a whisper.‡

Mr Jones, like Mr Creakle—as many of his pupils had cause to remember —was very free both with his cane and with a 'bloated mahogany ruler' with which he was 'always ruling ciphering books, or smiting the palms of offenders'. He had 'an undoubted love of the cane' one of these pupils said. Jones and the cane seemed inseparable, and he would lash out indiscriminately with it at the boarders. Once one of them called out,

---

* *Reprinted Pieces*, 'Our School'.   † *David Copperfield*, ch. v.
‡ *David Copperfield*, ch. vi.

'Shame! Shame!' when he was being particularly savage, and another threw an inkpot at his head. They had no respect for him, of course, and the more he beat them the less amenable they became. He had a habit, according to Dickens, of 'viciously drawing a pair of pantaloons tight with one of his large hands, and caning the wearer with the other'.

> He had a delight in cuffing at the boys, which was like the satisfaction of a craving appetite. I am confident that he couldn't resist a chubby boy, especially; that there was a fascination in such a subject, which made him restless in his mind, until he had scored and marked him for the day. I was chubby myself, and ought to know. I am sure when I think of the fellow now, my blood rises against him with the disinterested indignation I should feel if I could have known about him without ever having been in his power; but it rises hotly, because I know him to have been an incapable brute, who had no more right to be possessed of the great trust he held, than to be Lord High Admiral, or Commander-in-Chief—in either of which capacities it is probable that he would have done infinitely less mischief.*

This is David Copperfield talking. But Dickens, in a speech on education given at the London Tavern in November 1857, indicated that David's experiences were his own:

> I don't like the sort of school to which I once went myself [he said], the respected proprietor of which was by far the most ignorant man I have ever had the pleasure to know, who was one of the worst-tempered men perhaps that ever lived, whose business it was to make as much out of us and to put as little into us as possible . . .
> I don't like that sort of school, because I don't see what business the master had to be at the top of it instead of the bottom, and because I never could understand the wholesomeness of the moral preached by the abject appearance and degraded condition of the teachers . . .
> I do not like that sort of school, because I have never yet lost my ancient suspicion touching that curious coincidence that the boy with four brothers to come always got the prizes. In fact, and in short, I do not like that sort of school, which is a pernicious and abominable humbug altogether.[2]

It was a type of school which Dickens brought under repeated attack. For every such place as Dr Strong's at Canterbury, and for every such schoolmaster as the 'pale, simple-looking man of a spare and meagre habit' who befriends Little Nell, there are two such monsters as the one at the Charitable Grinders (that superannuated old man of 'savage disposition, who had been appointed schoolmaster because he didn't know

---

* *David Copperfield*, ch. VI.

'No matter what a young gentleman was intended to bear Doctor
Blimber made him bear to pattern, somehow or other'

anything, and wasn't fit for anything, and for whose cruel cane all chubby little boys had a perfect fascination').*

The grotesque descriptions of Mr Squeers's methods of teaching at Dotheboys Hall are a wonderful parody of those then employed in certain establishments of a like nature:

'We go upon the practical mode of teaching, Nickleby; the regular education system. C-l-e-a-n, clean, verb active, to make bright, to scour. W-i-n, win, d-e-r, der, winder a casement. When the boy knows this out of book he goes and does it. It's the same principle as the use of globes. Where's the second boy?'

'Please, Sir, he's weeding the garden,' replied a small voice.

'To be sure,' said Squeers, by no means disconcerted. 'So he is. B-o-t, bot, t-i-n, tin, n-e-y, ney, bottinney, noun substantive, a knowledge of plants. When he has learned that bottinney means a knowledge of plants, he goes and knows them. That's our system, Nickleby. What do you think of it?

'It's a very useful one, at any rate,' answered Nicholas significantly'

'I believe you,' rejoined Squeers, not remarking the emphasis of his usher.†

Dr Blimber's school at Brighton is run on rather less haphazard lines, but its effect on the pupils is scarcely preferable:

Doctor Blimber's establishment was a great hot-house, in which there was a forcing apparatus incessantly at work. All the boys blew before their time. Mental green-peas were produced at Christmas, and intellectual asparagus all the year round. Mathematical gooseberries (very sour ones too) were common at untimely seasons. . . . Every description of Greek and Latin vegetable was got off the driest twigs of boys, under the frostiest circumstances. Nature was of no consequence at all. No matter what a young gentleman was intended to bear, Doctor Blimber made him bear to pattern, somehow or other.‡

Methods similar to Dr Blimber's are adopted also at Thomas Gradgrind's school at Coketown where the children are all crammed with Facts; and Dickens does not like this new educational method (the description was written in 1854) any better than its predecessors: 'Now, what I want is, Facts', Mr Gradgrind, founder of the school enjoins M'Choakumchild, the master.

Teach these boys and girls nothing but Facts. Facts alone are wanted in life. Plant nothing else, and root out everything else. . . . Girl number twenty . . . give me your definition of a horse'.

* *Dombey and Son*, ch. VI.   † *Nicholas Nickleby*, ch. VIII.
‡ *Dombey and Son*, ch. XI.

(Sissy Jupe thrown into the greatest alarm by this demand.)

'Girl number twenty unable to define a horse!' said Mr Gradgrind ... 'Girl number twenty possessed of no facts, in reference to one of the commonest of animals. Some boy's definition of a horse. Bitzer, yours.' ...

'Quadruped. Graminivorous. Forty teeth, namely twenty-four grinders, four eye-teeth, and twelve incisive. Sheds coat in the spring; in marshy countries, sheds hoofs, too. Hoofs hard, but requiring to be shod with iron. Age known by marks in mouth.' Thus and much more Bitzer.*

The methods of instruction at Wellington House seem to have been rather less standardised than those adopted at Dr Blimber's and Mr M'Choakumchild's, and a good deal less haphazard than those adopted by Mr Squeers. But that it fell a long way short of the ideal cannot well be doubted. For Dickens, the ideal seems to have been the public school, though he was to send only the eldest of his seven sons to one.

I believe there is not in England [he said a few years before his death], any institution so socially liberal as a public school. ... As far as I know, nowhere in this country is there so complete an absence of servility to mere rank, to mere position, to mere riches as in a public school. A boy there is always what his abilities or his personal qualities make him. We may differ about the curriculum and other matters, but of the frank, free, manly, independent spirit preserved in our public schools, I apprehend there can be no kind of question.[3]

But although Wellington House Academy seemed to Dickens a far cry from a 'frank, free, manly' public school and its headmaster unworthy of holding a post anywhere at all, he was not personally much exposed to the physical ill-treatment of which he complained. The headmaster's beatings were mostly limited to the boarders, since they had no opportunity, as day boys had, to complain to their parents at night. Nor did the threatening presence of Mr Jones make his time at Wellington House an unhappy one.

Certainly he sometimes wrote of his experiences there—exaggerating and embroidering them—with a kind of amused and amusing affection. He recalled, for instance, the sudden change in the behaviour of the school bully, 'Globson', after the receipt of a letter hinting that Charles might soon be sent some guava jelly from the West Indies:

I had mentioned these hints in confidence to a few friends, and had promised to give away, as I now see reason to believe, a handsome

* *Hard Times*, ch. II.

covey of patridges potted, and about a hundredweight of guava jelly. It was now that Globson, bully no more, sought me out in the playground. He was a big fat boy, with a big fat head and a big fat fist, and at the beginning of that Half had raised such a bump on my forehead that I couldn't get my hat of state on, to go to Church. He said that after an interval of reflection (four months) he now felt this blow to have been an error of judgment, and that he wished to apologise for the same.

Not only that but holding down his big head between his two big hands in order that I might reach it conveniently, he requested me, as an act of justice which would appease his awakened conscience, to raise a retributive bump upon it, in the presence of witnesses.

This handsome proposal I modestly declined, and he then embraced me, and we walked away conversing. We conversed respecting the West India Islands, and, in the pursuit of knowledge he asked me with much interest whether in the course of my reading I had met with any reliable description of the mode of manufacturing guava jelly; or whether I had ever happened to taste that conserve, which he had been given to understand was of rare excellence. . . .*

A profound respect for money pervaded our school, which was, of course, derived from its Chief [so Dickens wrote elsewhere]. We remember an idiotic goggle-eyed boy, with a big head and half-crowns without end, who suddenly appeared as a parlour-boarder, and was rumoured to have come by sea from some mysterious part of the earth where his parents rolled in gold. He was usually called 'Mr' by the Chief, and was said to feed in the parlour on steaks and gravy; likewise to drink currant wine. And he openly stated that if rolls and coffee were ever denied him at breakfast, he would write home to that unknown part of the globe from which he had come, and cause himself to be recalled to the regions of gold. He was put into no form or class, but learnt alone, as little as he liked—and he liked very little—and there was a belief among us that this was because he was too wealthy to be 'taken down' . . .

There was another mysterious pupil—a heavy young man, with a large double-cased silver watch, and a fat knife the handle of which was a perfect tool-box—who unaccountably appeared one day at a special desk of his own, erected close to that of the Chief, with whom he held familiar converse. He lived in the parlour, and went out for his walks, and never took the least notice of us, unless to give us a deprecatory kick, or grimly take our hat off and throw it away, when he encountered us out of doors . . . though closely observed he was never seen to do anything but make pens out of quills, write small hand in a secret folio, and punch the point of the sharpest blade in his desk.†

* *The Uncommercial Traveller,* 'Birthday Celebrations'.
† *Reprinted Pieces,* 'Our School'.

Dickens said that he himself eventually became the head boy of the school. But his fellow pupils did not remember this:

He was a handsome, curly-headed lad, full of animation and animal spirits [one of them recalled]. I do not remember that he distinguished himself in any way, or carried off any prizes. My belief is that he did not learn Greek or Latin there, and you will remember there is no allusion to the classics in any of his writings. . . . depend upon it, he was quite a self-made man, and his wonderful knowledge and command of the English language must have been acquired by long and patient study after leaving school.[4]

'My recollection of Dickens', another boy at the school afterwards wrote, 'is of a rather short, stout, jolly-looking youth, very fresh-coloured, and full of fun, and given to laugh immoderately without any apparent sufficient reason. . . . He was not particularly studious, nor did he show any special signs of ability.' He liked heavy jokes and loved singing comic songs. He delivered 'The Cat's Meat Man' with great energy and action, 'his tone displaying the full zest with which he appreciated and entered into all the vulgarity of the composition'.[5]

He was an unexceptional schoolboy, then, giving no hint to the others that he had already been out to work to earn his living in a factory, bright enough to catch up quickly with the lessons he had missed, too ashamed to admit the real reasons for his entering the school in the middle of a term.

He was always neatly and carefully dressed, almost unnaturally so for a twelve-year-old boy, wearing a smart pepper-and-salt jacket and a shirt with a turn-down collar instead of a frill so that, although he was small, he could not be mistaken for one of the little boys. He walked with a straight back, carrying his head high, 'very upright, almost more than upright, like leaning back a little': so wrote another of his schoolfellows after Forster's biography made him realise that 'Little Charley Dickens at old Jones's' was the famous author. 'He always struck me as being a sharp boy rather than a thoughtful one. He had nothing heady or dreamy about him at that time. He was very particular with his clothes . . . and I never should have thought that he had been employed at humble work. He appeared always like a gentleman's son, rather aristocratic than otherwise.'[6]

He was not in the least reserved or remote, however. Indeed, his companions found him not merely lively, but hilariously gay. Occasion-ally he was almost wildly, embarrassingly gay, suddenly breaking out into bursts of uncontrollable unreasonable laughter, as though he were trembling on the verge of hysteria. But this was the only sign of there being anything unusual about him. He joined in their games and their hobbies, made friends and seemed happy.

The main extracurricular activity at the school was the keeping of pets. All sorts of pets, 'red-polls, linnets, and even canaries, were kept in desks, drawers, hat-boxes and other strange refuges for birds; but white mice were the favourite stock. The boys trained the white mice much better than the masters trained the boys.' Charles himself kept white mice and built little boats and coaches for them, and elaborate wheels with which they could pump up water. One of them, kept between the covers of a Latin dictionary from which the pages had been cut to form a nest for him, 'ran up ladders, drew Roman chariots, shouldered muskets, turned wheels, and even made a very creditable appearance on the stage as the Dog of Montargis. He might have achieved great things, but for having the misfortune to mistake his way in a triumphal procession to the Capitol, when he fell into a deep ink-stand, and was dyed black, and drowned.'*

The Dog of Montargis was not the only play performed in the boys' toy theatre to end in unrehearsed turmoil. At the end of a performance of Pocock's *The Miller and His Men*, for instance, the destruction of the mill by firecrackers was so loud and alarming that a police constable came knocking at the door, demanding to know what was going on inside the schoolroom.

The Miller and His Men, a lurid melodrama about a gang of robbers who pass in the daytime for workers in a mill, held a particular appeal for Charles who still had a strongly developed taste for such pieces and for penny-dreadfuls. [7] His favourite amongst these penny-dreadfuls was *The Terrific*, a ghoulish magazine that came out every week at a penny and contained stories in which there was always sure to be 'a pool of blood and at least one body'.

His own compositions were considered good enough to be passed round between the other boys, and his less lurid pieces were printed in the school magazine, *Our Newspaper*, which seems to have been largely given over to facetiae. One, no doubt characteristic, example of these has survived:

'*Lost*—by a boy with a long nose, and green eyes, a very bad temper. Whoever has found the same may keep it, as the owner is better off without it.'

* *Reprinted Pieces*, 'Our School'.

On his way home from school Charles and his companions—like Mr Giles's pupils in Chatham—talked loudly that invented gibberish which children everywhere love to talk in the hope and belief that they will be taken for foreigners. A less usual and more annoying game played by the boys of Wellington House was to affect extreme poverty and various forms of painful disabilities in front of old ladies. Once Charles played this game in Drummond Street, and, going up to one passer-by after the next, he begged them for charity, then burst into that loud, uncontrollable laughter of his and ran away home.

Home at this time was still in Johnson Street, a dirty, crumbling district, which a school friend was surprised to find little better than a slum. Charles, however, did not seem to mind that his father could no longer afford the genteel way of life that they had enjoyed at Chatham. At least they were all together again, the horrors of the Marshalsea and Warren's had been put behind them, and he was at school once more with the sons of respectable middle-class families.

On Sundays he went to Chapel with one of these middle-class boys. It was not that he had temporarily overcome that strong distaste for Nonconformism which the long and boring harangues of the Baptist Minister in Chatham had instilled in him, but that attendance at the Somers Chapel in Seymour Street with his well-dressed young friend was a kind of reassurance that he had regained his lost respectability. Indeed, 'Master Dickens did not in the slightest degree attend to the service', his friend said, 'but incited me to laughter by declaring his dinner was ready, and the potatoes would be spoiled, and, in fact, behaved in such a manner that it was lucky for us we were not ejected from the Chapel'.[8]

These carefree schooldays were not, however, to be of long duration. For John Dickens had paid the Wellington House fees at the expense of his rent and rates; and soon after Lady Day 1827 his family, which now included a new (and final) baby, Augustus, were evicted from their house at 26 Johnson Street and moved, presumably as lodgers, to The Polygon, Clarendon Square, Somers Town.[(9)]

Soon after moving to The Polygon, Charles had to leave school, and Fanny had to be taken away from the Academy. Their father could not manage to pay the fees any more, and so Charles had to be found a job. It was his mother (who now appeared to one of his friends as a 'fragile woman in delicate health') who found him one. An aunt of hers, who kept a boarding-house in Berners Street, had a lodger, Edward

Blackmore, the junior partner in a firm of solicitors, Ellis and Blackmore of 5 Holborn Court, Gray's Inn. [10]

Elizabeth Dickens had met this young man on visits to her aunt; and she took it into her mind to persuade him that her son Charles, a bright, wholesome-looking lad who had attended Mr William Jones's Wellington House Academy and won the Latin prize, was just the very boy he needed in his office. He was fifteen and, though perhaps a little short for his age and young-looking, he was always smartly turned out and reliable.

Mr. Blackmore accepted the testimonial, and had a word with his senior partner. He then told Dickens that he could have a job as office-boy if he wanted it, and that he should, in that case, report for duty on the following Monday.

4

MESSRS ELLIS & BLACKMORE
1827-1828
aet. 16

6 RAYMOND BUILDINGS GRAY'S INN LONDON

I went to some theatre every night, with a very few exceptions, for at least three years: really studying the bills first, and going where there was the best acting: and always to see Mathews whenever he played.

Forster's Life of Dickens

4

1

Charles left for work at Messrs Ellis & Blackmore's wearing a smart blue jacket and a military-looking cap with a strap under the chin. The jaunty manner in which the short, plump, fresh-faced, slightly feminine-looking youth wore this cap as he was crossing over Chancery Lane, aroused the anger of 'a big blackguard fellow', who, with the words, 'Hullo! My fine soldier', walked up to him and knocked it off. Charles protested, hit the bully back, and arrived at work with a black eye.

It was not an auspicious beginning to his new career. Nor when he entered the doors of 5 Holborn Court was he encouraged by finding what one of the articled clerks remembered as 'a poor old set of chambers of three rooms, the front overlooking the Court, a room at the back, and the clerk's office which was shut off from the passage by a glass partition'.[1]

He rarely afterwards entered a solicitor's office with pleasure; and scarcely ever described one without distaste. Mr Vholes's chambers in Symond's Inn—as mouldy and smelly as those of Dodson and Fogg, as dismal as those of Mr Jaggers, and, no doubt, reminiscent of Ellis & Blackmore's—provide an example of this antipathy:

> Mr Vholes's chambers are on so small a scale, that one clerk can open the door without getting off his stool, while the other who elbows him at the same desk has equal facilities for poking the fire. A smell as of unwholesome sheep, blending with the smell of must and dust, is referable to the nightly (and often daily) consumption of mutton fat in candles, and to the fretting of parchment forms and skins in greasy drawers. The atmosphere is otherwise stale and close. The place was last painted or white-washed beyond the memory of man, and the two chimneys smoke, and there is a loose outer surface of soot everywhere, and the dull cracked windows in their heavy frames have but one piece of character in them, which is a determination to be always dirty, and always shut. . . .'*

Mr Vholes, himself, is a representative Dickensian lawyer. Reserved and serious, he never seems to enjoy himself, and 'is allowed by the greater attorneys who have made good fortunes, or are making them,

* *Bleak House*, ch. XXXIX.

'A smell as of unwholesome sheep, blending with the smell of dust and must, is referable to the nightly (and often daily) consumption of mutton fat in candles, and to the fretting parchment forms and skins in greasy drawers'

to be a most respectable man. He never misses a chance in his practice; which is a mark of respectability.'

He is but one of a long line of unpleasing attorneys whom Dickens saw as a ravenous flock of birds of prey, an avaricious tribe of extortioners making an unsavoury living out of what was, in effect, 'essentially a form of considered and organised oppression' dedicated to one great principle —'to make money for itself. There is no other principle distinctly, certainly, and consistently maintained through all its narrow turnings.'

In all his stories there is scarcely a solicitor who is not either unhappy in his profession, like Mortimer Lightwood and Mr Wickfield, or unpleasant like Uriah Heep.

Tulkinghorn is 'mechanically faithful without attachment, and very jealous of the profit, privilege and reputation of being master of the mysteries of great houses'. Jaggers, like his clerk, has 'an air of knowing something to everybody else's disadvantage', and such a bullying manner that he even seems to bully his sandwich as he eats it; Sampson Brass is 'a tall, meagre man, with a nose like a wen, a protruding forehead, retreat-eyes, and hair of a deep red . . . a cringing manner but a very harsh voice'. And Hiram Grewgious is 'an arid, sandy man, who if he had been put into a grinding mill, looked as if he would have ground immediately into high-dried snuff. He had a scanty flat crop of hair, in colour and consistency like some very mangy yellow fur tippet.'*

Amongst the partners of Messrs Dodson and Fogg, Snitchey and Craggs, Kenge and Carboy, Wickfield and Heep, Spenlow and Jorkins, there are few characters to be found who are more prepossessing than these. Barristers are treated less harshly; but they, too, are generally either as gloomily aware of the unpleasantness of their profession as Sydney Carton and Eugene Wrayburn, or as unscrupulous as Mr Stryver.

It would not be difficult, then, to deduce from all this, even if other evidence were not available, that Dickens did not take very happily to his new work at Messrs Ellis and Blackmore. He found, in fact, his own duties, as a clerk and errand boy, tedious and trivial, and the practice of the law in general, cumbersome, tortuous and distasteful. He had left Warren's with a determination to succeed, never to be poor or victimised again, but he soon decided that he had no wish to make his mark as a distinguished lawyer, even if his father had been able to afford the premium for his articles. He had neither the patience to wait for his opportunities, nor the necessary cast of mind.[2]

Much of his working day was spent in carrying documents to and from a succession of offices whose names seem more like those of departments of the Circumlocution Office than those of real public offices—the Dispensation Office and the Alienation Office, the Six-Clerks' Office and the Sixpenny Receivers' Office, the Hanaper Office, the Protonotaries' Office, and the Office of the Clerk of the Escheats. Sometimes he had to go to the law stationer's off Chancery Lane where a man such as Mr Snagsby, 'a mild, bald, timid man', dressed in a grey shop-coat and black calico sleeves, dealt in 'all sorts of blank forms of legal process; in skins and rolls of parchment; in paper—foolscap, brief, draft, brown, white, whitey-brown, and blotting; in stamps; in office-quills, pens, ink, India-rubber, pounce, pins, pencils, sealing-wax, and wafers; in red tape, and green ferret; in pocket-books, almanacks, diaries, and law lists; in string

* *Bleak House*, ch. XXXVI; *Great Expectations*, ch. XX; *Old Curiosity Shop*, ch. XI; *Edwin Drood*, ch. IX.

boxes, rulers, inkstands—glass and leaden, penknives, scissors, bodkins, and other small office-cutlery'.*

Between visits to these offices and shops Charles derived his main pleasure and profit from his new life, by observing the people around him. And the firm did at least offer him a wealth of human material on which his imagination could work. Mr Ellis, the senior partner, for instance, bore more than a passing resemblance to Mr Perker, solicitor of Gray's Inn, 'a little high-dried man, with a dark squeezed-up face, and small restless black eyes', who wore shiny black boots and had a habit of 'thrusting his wrists beneath his coat-tails, with the air of a man who was in the habit of propounding some regular posers';† while one of the oddest of the regular visitors to the firm's offices, the broken-down black sheep of a respectable family named Newman Knott, was easily recognised by those who knew him as being represented in the character of Mr Newman Noggs, 'a tall man of middle-age with two goggle eyes whereof one was a fixture, a rubicund nose, a cadaverous face, and a suit of clothes (if the term be allowable when they suited him not at all) much the worse for wear, very much too small, and placed upon such a short allowance of buttons that it was quite marvellous how he contrived to keep them on'.‡

Also, there were his fellow clerks, and Dickens never forgot the amusement one of these, a young man named Thomas Potter, caused after having too much to drink at a wedding. The fearful hangover, Potter insisted, was nothing to do with the wine; it *must* have been the salmon. It was a comment Dickens felt compelled to reproduce in an early chapter of his first novel, adding, 'Somehow or other, it never *is* the wine in these cases'.

The clerks, indeed, in Dickens's offices lead a far gayer life than their superiors can ever be supposed to have done. It is true that neither the first-floor clerk in Mr Jaggers's office who looked like 'something between a publican and a rat-catcher', nor 'the flabby terrier of a clerk with dangling hair' on the second floor shows much promise of being able to enjoy himself. Nor does 'the high-shouldered man with a face-ache tied up in dirty flannel' who sits copying notes in a back room in clothes that bear the appearance of having been waxed.§ But these are not the type of salaried-clerks most in evidence in Dickens's offices.

There are [as Dickens explains] several grades of Lawyers' Clerks. There is the Articled Clerk, who has paid a premium, and is an

* *Bleak House*, ch. x. † *Pickwick Papers*, ch. x.
‡ *Nicholas Nickleby*, ch. II. § *Great Expectations*, ch. XXIV.

attorney in perspective, who runs a tailor's bill, receives invitations to parties, knows a family in Gower Street and another in Tavistock Square, goes out of town every long vacation to see his father, who keeps live horses innumerable; and who is, in short, the very aristocrat of clerks. There is the salaried clerk who devotes the major part of his thirty-shillings a week to his personal pleasure and adornment, repairs half-price to the Adelphi at least three times a week, dissipates majestic-ally at the cider cellar afterwards, and is a dirty caricature of the fashion which expired six months ago. There is the middle-aged copying clerk, with a large family, who is always shabby, and often drunk. And there are the office lads in their first surtouts [overcoats], who feel a befitting contempt for boys at day-schools, club as they go home at night, for saveloys and porter, and think there's nothing like 'life'.*

The clerks whom Mr Pickwick finds at Messrs Dodson and Fogg's are evidently salaried clerks, cheeky young assistants preoccupied with mixing seidlitz powders and relating their adventures of the previous evening:

'It was half past four when I got to Somers Town, and then I was so precious drunk, that I couldn't find the place where the latch-key went in, and was obliged to knock up the old 'ooman. I say, I wonder what old Fogg 'ud say, if he knew it. I should get the sack, I s'pose—eh?'
At this humorous notion, all the clerks laughed in concert.†

After discussing their revelries, Dickens's clerks usually find the morning drags as heavily by as do Mr Guppy and Young Smallweed, clerks to Messrs Kenge and Carboy.

Mr Guppy, of 87 Penton Place, is paid £2 a week by his employers, but he appears to do little work in return for this remuneration. 'By the time Mr Guppy has blunted the blade of his penknife, and broken the point off, by sticking that instrument into his desk in every direction . . . he finds that nothing agrees with him so well, as to make little gyrations on one leg of his stool, and stab his desk, and gape.' After trying all the other office stools in succession and finding none of them comfortable, he puts his head into the iron safe 'with a notion of cooling it' and spends the rest of the morning lolling out of the window.

Young Smallweed, 'now under fifteen and an old limb of the law . . . a town-made article of small stature, and weazened features', is sent out twice for effervescent drinks, mixes them in the two official tumblers and stirs them up with a ruler. 'Mr Guppy propounds, for Mr Smallweed's

* *Pickwick Papers*, ch. xxx.   † *Pickwick Papers*, ch. xx.

'. . . cheeky young assistants preoccupied with mixing seidlitz powders
and relating their adventures of the previous evening'

consideration, the paradox that the more you drink the thirstier you are; and reclines his head upon the window-sill in a state of hopeless languor.'*

Thus were many summer mornings spent at 5 Holborn Court and, after the firm moved, towards the end of the year, at 6 Raymond Buildings, a fairly new block of chambers, built in 1819.(3)

Charles, like Mr Guppy, carved his name on his desk. He also dropped cherry-stones from his second-floor window on to the hats of passers-by, and entertained his fellow clerks by performing lively imitations of the speech and manners of the office charwoman who was always ready with an excuse for sweeping the dust under the carpet or forgetting to light the fire. He had a wonderful gift of mimicry, one of his friends recalled. 'He could imitate, in a manner that I never heard equalled, the low population of the streets of London in all their varieties, whether mere loafers or sellers of fruit, vegetables or anything else.' He was equally skilful in caricaturing the idiosyncrasies of the best-known actors and singers of the day.

2

Now that he could afford it, with his ten shillings a week, soon rising to thirteen and six and then to fifteen shillings, he became once more a regular visitor to the theatre and the music hall, so that he had plenty of opportunity to study his originals. He also now, so Mr Blackmore said, took to performing himself, at those private theatres where the seats were cheap and the parts were played by amateurs who paid a fee for the privilege of doing so.

The fees paid for performing the parts were a good deal higher than the cost of the seats, for everyone wanted to act, not watch. In *Richard III*, for instance, the Duke of Gloucester's role might cost as much as £2, and the Earl of Richmond's, £1, though the lines spoken by the Lord Mayor could be bought for half-a-crown. In an article contributed some years later to the *Evening Chronicle*, Dickens decried the stage-struck youths who were prepared to pay these sums for the benefit of exhibiting their 'lamentable ignorance and boobyism on the stage of a private theatre'. They were, so he said, mainly 'dirty boys, low copying-clerks in attorneys' offices, capacious headed youths from City counting houses, Jews whose business, as lenders of fancy dresses, is a sure passport to the

* *Bleak House*, ch. xx.

amateur stage, shopboys who now and then mistake their master's money for their own, and a choice miscellany of idle vagabonds'.

The men who ran these theatres were not much better than their patrons:

> The proprietor of a private theatre may be an ex-scene-painter, a low coffee-house-keeper, a disappointed eight-rate actor, a retired smuggler, or an uncertificated bankrupt. The theatre itself may be in Catherine Street, Strand, the purlieus of the City, the neighbourhood of Gray's Inn Lane, or the vicinity of Sadler's Wells: or it may, perhaps, form the chief nuisance of some shabby street, on the Surrey side of Waterloo Bridge. The lady performers pay nothing for their characters, and, it is needless to add, are usually selected from one class of society.*

Despite the rather prudishly disapproving tone of the article—written, of course, for middle-class readers who rarely if ever went to the play-house, patronised as it was by young bloods, prostitutes, drunkards and lower-class citizens generally—there can be no doubt that Dickens's acquaintance with the private theatres of London, both as a member of the audience and as a backstage participant, was not limited to that of an alert and conscientious reporter. As he was soon to show, he had an expert knowledge of the mechanics of theatrical production, and was a practised as well as a natural actor.

He was to show, too, how often his mind, in dwelling on the behaviour of his characters, would imagine them against the background of a play-house stage or auditorium. Nadgett, the enquiry agent for the Anglo-Bengalee Disinterested Loan and Life Insurance Company, for instance, always makes his appearance amongst the other characters of *Martin Chuzzlewit* as though 'he had that moment come up a trap'. And Dick Swiveller, Sampson Brass's clerk, when trying to wake the 'single gentleman' by raining a shower of blows on his door with a ruler, adopts a position, close to the wall and standing on a stool, 'after the method of those hardy individuals who open the pit and gallery doors of theatres on crowded nights'.

Also, Dickens's characters are often presented to his readers as though he were sharing with us a view of them upon a stage, allowing them to reveal themselves to us by their speech and making them speak not so much to each other but *at* each other, so that an audience can overhear them as 'they soliloquise in a world of their own'.[4]

By putting Nicholas Nickleby and Smike into the employment of

* *Sketches by Boz*, 'Private Theatres'.

Vincent Crummles, the actor-manager of a company of strolling players, Dickens revealed his knowledge of the theatre and his delight in its denizens to the full:

> Mr Crummles looked from time to time with great interest at Smike, with whom he had appeared considerably struck from the first. He had now fallen asleep, and was nodding in his chair.
>
> 'Excuse my saying so,' said the manager, leaning over to Nicholas, and sinking his voice, 'but—what a capital countenance your friend has got!'
>
> 'Poor fellow!' said Nicholas with a half smile, 'I wish it were a little more plump and less haggard.'
>
> 'Plump!' exclaimed the manager, quite horrified. 'You'd spoil it for ever.'
>
> 'Do you think so?'
>
> 'Think so, sir! Why, as he is now,' said the manager, striking his knee emphatically, 'without a pad upon his body, and hardly a touch of paint upon his face, he'd make such an actor for the starved business as was never seen in this country. Only let him be tolerably well up in the Apothecary in *Romeo and Juliet* with the slightest possible dab of red on the tip of his nose, and he'd be certain of three rounds, the moment he put his head out of the practicable door in the front grooves O.P.'
>
> 'You view him with a professional eye,' said Nicholas laughing.
>
> 'And well I may,' rejoined the manager. 'I never saw a young fellow so regularly cut out for that line since I've been in the profession, and I played the heavy children when I was eighteen months old.'*

The world of Mr Crummles and Mr Crummles himself, in fact, that splendid creation whose huge face is quite proportionate to the size of his body, whose voice is hoarse from so much shouting, and whose hair is shaved off nearly to the crown of his head 'to admit of his wearing character wigs of any shape or pattern', seem of much more interest to Dickens than the plot and theme of Nicholas Nickleby to which they bear the most tenuous relevance. And it is with quite evident reluctance that Dickens takes Nicholas back to London, makes him say good-bye to Mr Crummles (who inflicts upon him 'a rapid succession of stage embraces, which, as everybody knows, are performed by the embracer's laying his or her chin on the shoulder of the object of affection, and looking over it'), and thus leaves the so congenial world of Mr Crummles's touring company.(5)

As well as the private theatres of Catherine Street and Gray's Inn Lane

---

* *Nicholas Nickleby*, ch. XXII.

there were the 'major' theatres of Drury Lane, Covent Garden, and the Haymarket, which, until the passing of the 1843 Theatres Act, held a monopoly in 'legitimate' drama (that was to say five-act tragedy or comedy without music). There were also an uncertain number of 'minor' theatres which did, in fact, also present spoken drama, but interspersed their productions with songs and called them 'burlettas'. 'Even *Hamlet* with a song or two for Ophelia and a lugubrious ditty for the melancholy Prince, could pass unchallenged as a "burletta".'[6] And, in the outlying suburbs, there were many theatres, subject to different regulations which presented everything from circuses to cabarets, from melodramas about Jack Sheppard to operettas about Ancient Rome.

Astley's, indeed, a theatre in Westminster Bridge Road, of which Dickens was particularly fond, presented an extraordinarily diverse fare, including circus clowns, acrobats, sword fights, performing horses, as well as exotic melodramas with an eastern setting, in which, as Mr George discovered one night, the Emperor of Tartary was quite likely to get up into the cast and 'condescend to bless the united lovers, by hovering over them with the Union-Jack'.*

It is to Astley's that Kit Nubbles takes his family and Barbara. And

dear, dear, what a place it looked, that Astley's! With all the paint, gilding and looking-glass, the vague smell of horses suggestive of coming wonders, the clean white sawdust down in the circus, the company coming in and taking their places, the fiddlers looking carelessly up at them while they tuned their instruments, as if they didn't want the play to begin, and knew it all beforehand! What a glow was that which burst upon them all, when that long, clear, brilliant row of lights came slowly up; and what the feverish excitement when the little bell rang and the music began in full earnest. . . . Then the play itself! The horses, the firing . . . the forlorn lady . . . the tyrant . . . the man who sung the song with the lady's maid and danced the chorus . . . the pony who reared up on his hind legs when he saw the murderer . . . the clown who ventured on such familiarities with the military man in boots . . . the lady who jumped over the nine and twenty ribbons and came down safe upon the horse's back—everything was delightful, splendid and surprising.†

Although few theatres offered the wonderful variety of Astley's, even Covent Garden—as David Copperfield had occasion to observe before being pushed out dazed into the streets at twelve o'clock at night, feeling that he had been leading a romantic life for ages and was now 'a stranger

---

* *Bleak House*, ch. XXI.   † *The Old Curiosity Shop*, ch. XXXIX.

'Dear dear, what a place it looked that Astley's!'

upon earth'—even Covent Garden sometimes presented a double bill of
Julius Caesar and the new pantomime.

In the smaller cheaper theatres, the plot of the melodramas presented
was often incomprehensible, for no one cared much about plots, or even
about the words spoken. What the audience came to see and hear was
passionate, full-blooded acting. The plot of the piece in which Nicholas
Nickleby watched Miss Snevellici performing with some others of Mr
Crummles's company may be taken as typical:

> The plot was most interesting. It belonged to no particular age, people,
> or country, and was perhaps the more delightful on that account, as
> nobody's previous information could afford the remotest glimmering
> of what would ever come of it. An outlaw who had been very success-
> ful in doing something somewhere, and came home in triumph, to the
> sound of shouts and fiddles, to greet his wife—a lady of masculine mind,
> who talked a good deal about her father's bones, which it seemed were
> unburied, though whether from a peculiar taste on the part of the old
> gentleman himself, or the reprehensible neglect of his relations, did not
> appear. This outlaw's wife was somehow or other mixed up with a
> patriarch, living in a castle a long way off, and this patriarch was the

father of several of the characters, but he didn't exactly know which, and was uncertain whether he had brought up the right ones in his castle, or the wrong ones, but rather inclined to the latter opinion, and, being uneasy, relieved his mind with a banquet, during which solemnity somebody in a cloak said 'Beware', which somebody was known by nobody (except the audience) to be the outlaw himself, who had come there for reasons unexplained, but possibly with an eye to the spoons. . . .

A last it came out that the patriarch was the man who had treated the bones of the outlaw's father-in-law with so much disrespect, for which cause and reason the outlaw's wife repaired to his castle to kill him, and so got into a dark room, where, after a great deal of groping in the dark, everybody got hold of everybody else, and took them for somebody besides, which occasioned a vast quantity of confusion, with some pistolling, loss of life, and torchlight; after which the patriarch came forward, and observing, with a knowing look, that he knew all about his children now, and would tell them when he got inside, said that there could not be a more appropriate occasion for marrying the young people than that, and therefore he joined their hands, with the full consent of the indefatigable page who (being the only other person surviving) pointed with his cap into the clouds, and his right hand to the ground, thereby invoking a blessing and giving the cue for the curtain to come down, which it did, amidst general applause.*

The players at these cheaper theatres, where such plays were performed, were obliged to put up with a great deal of heckling, abuse and ribald comments from the audience. And a production of *Hamlet*, as Pip and Herbert Pocket discover when they go to see Wopsle perform the part, was likely to entail a constant barrage of shouts from the spectators, as well as of nutshells, orange-peel and the unwanted remains of ham-sandwiches and pigs' trotters which were offered for sale throughout the performance.

Whenever that undecided Prince had to ask a question or state a doubt, the public helped him out with it. As for example; on the question whether 'twas nobler in the mind to suffer, some roared yes, and some no, and some inclining to both opinions said 'toss up for it'; and quite a Debating Society arose. When he asked what should such fellows as he do crawling between earth and heaven, he was encouraged with loud cries of 'Hear, hear!' When he appeared with his stocking disordered (its disorder expressed according to usage, by one very neat fold in the top, which I suppose to be always got up with a flat iron), a conversation took place in the gallery respecting the paleness of his leg, and whether it was occasioned by the turn the ghost had given

* *Nicholas Nickleby*, ch. XXIV.

him. On his taking the recorders—very like a little black flute that had just been played in the orchestra and handed out at the door—he was called upon unanimously for Rule Britannia.*

That Dickens was deeply influenced as a writer by these regular visits to the theatre, and based many of his comic characters on memories of parts performed on the stage, is undeniable. And even if we agree with Dr K. J. Fielding that this influence has sometimes been exaggerated by Dickens's critics, it is still true that his manner is often more that of a dramatist or of a theatrical performer than a novelist. He chose to work, in Ruskin's words, 'in a circle of stage fire'.(7)

His settings are those of the theatre; most of his famous characters are performing a part rather than developing an idea; many of his villains behave as though they are designed to provoke the repugnance of a theatre audience, and most of his heroes and heroines as though they have been created to enlist its sympathy; his plots contain all the conventional theatricalities of the early nineteenth-century stage—long lost heirs and suddenly inherited fortunes, strange disguises and improbable coincidences, exciting discoveries and mysterious secrets; his heroes and heroines are allowed to talk in the traditional voice of melodrama:

'My curse, my bitter deadly curse, upon you, boy!' [cries Ralph Nickleby when his plans are foiled].
'Whence will curses come at your command? Or what avails a curse or blessing from a man like you? I warn you, that misfortune and discovery are thickening about your head; that the structures you have raised through all your ill-spent life are crumbling into dust; that your path is beset with spies; that this very day, ten thousand pounds of your hoarded wealth have gone in one great crash!'
' 'Tis false!' cried Ralph, shrinking back.
' 'Tis true, and you shall find it so. I have no more words to waste. Stand from the door. Kate, do you go first. Lay not a hand on her, or on that woman or on me, or so much as brush their garments as they pass you by!'†

Walter Bray's sitting-room, 'not many hundred paces distant from the obelisk in Saint George's Fields', where this scene takes place, is very close in spirit to the Theatre Royal, Star Hill, Rochester, to Astley's, to the Westminster Subscription Theatre, and to the Drury Lane and Covent Garden of the 1820's.

'I think I have told you sometimes', Dickens wrote, soon after he had

---

* *Great Expectations*, ch. XXXI.   † *Nicholas Nickleby*, ch. LIV.

finished *David Copperfield*, to his 'much-loved friend', the famous traged-
ian William Charles Macready, 'how, when I was a mere boy, I was one
of your faithful and devoted adherents in the pit; I believe I was as true a
member of that true host of followers as it has ever boasted. As I improved
myself and was improved by favouring circumstances in mind and
fortune, I only became more earnest (if it were possible) in my study of
you.'[8]

His study resulted not only in a style of acting which sometimes rose to
heights that almost rivalled Macready's, but in the creation of written
scenes in which one can hear echoes of Macready's voice.[9]

As strong an influence as Macready on Dickens's work was the brilliant
and versatile Charles Mathews, a comic actor whose wonderful gifts
ranged from mimicry to singing, from ventriloquism to conjuring. His
most famous act, however, was to perform a short play in which, using
different voices and dialects, he would take all the parts. To make it
easier for the audience to recognise the different characters, and to
heighten their comic effects, he would assign to each of them a tag-line
or catch-phrase. His hesitant Mr Waglinton, for example, was always
commenting doubtfully, 'It might be so—and then again it might not';
and his preposterous Major Longbow constantly protests that his outlandish stories are real adventures: ' 'Pon my soul it's true: what'll you
lay it's a lie?'

Mr Grimwig who repeatedly asserts in *Oliver Twist*, 'I'll be content
to eat my head', and Mrs Micawber with her recurrent promise, 'But I
will never desert Mr Micawber', are but two examples of many of
Dickens's characters who follow in this tradition.[10]

One of Mathews's most famous characters was Commodore Cos-
mogory whose jerky, staccato style of speech was delighting London
audiences at the time Dickens was at Ellis & Blackmore's.

Here is the Commodore describing his improbable adventures in Egypt:

'Seen the River Nile, if you mean that—something like a river—
thousand miles long—swam down it many a time—ate part of a
crocodile there, that wanted to eat me—saw him cry with vexation
as I kill'd him—tears big as marrowfat peas—bottled one of them, for
the curiosity of the thing. True tale—pos—I'm not joking.'[11]

When Jingle addresses the members of the Pickwick Club, this is his
manner of speaking, too:

'Heads, heads take care of your heads' cried the loquacious stranger, as they came out under the low archway, which in those days formed the entrance to the coach-yard. 'Terrible place—dangerous work—other day—five children—mother—tall lady, eating sandwiches—forgot the arch—crash—knock—children look round—mother's head off—sandwich in her hand—no mouth to put it in—head of a family off—shocking, shocking. Looking at Whitehall, Sir,—fine place—little window—somebody else's head off there, eh, Sir?'*

Long after *Pickwick* was written, Dickens confessed his profound admiration for Mathews's techniques and told Forster that when he was working as a youth in London he went 'always to see Mathews whenever he played'.

He soon developed a facility for imitating him to the delight of his fellow clerks; and, in later life, would imitate his own characters in the very process of creating them. He could even hear them talking he said, and he talked back to them. He told George Henry Lewes, 'that every word said by his characters was distinctly *heard* by him'.[12]

On one occasion his elder daughter Mamey caught him thus excited by his work. He was writing 'busily and rapidly at his desk, when he suddenly jumped from his chair and rushed to a mirror which hung near and in which I could see the reflection of some extraordinary facial contortions which he was making. He returned rapidly to his desk, wrote furiously for a few moments, and then went again to the mirror. The facial pantomime was resumed, and then turning toward, but evidently not seeing me, he began talking in a low voice.'[13]

3

Charles's usual companion on his visits to the theatre was Thomas Potter, his fellow-clerk at Ellis and Blackmore's. A seat in the gallery cost a shilling, but at nine o'clock the price was reduced to sixpence, and since by then the main item of the evening's entertainment had not yet been performed, the two boys usually waited till nine before buying their tickets, as Tommy Traddles does, thinking the very smell is cheap at the money.

In the earlier part of the evening they might go together to a cheap restaurant for a chop and a pint or two of porter, or to an oyster shop where the natives, laid out in circular marble basins in the windows, were eightpence a dozen. And afterwards they would cut a dash by ordering a brandy and water and smoking a halfpenny cigar.

* *Pickwick Papers*, ch. II.

'In the earlier part of the evening they might go together to a cheap
restaurant for a chop and a pint or two of porter'

Charles by now was always dressed in a most fastidiously dapper,
even dandified way.

David Copperfield wears a gold watch and chain, a ring upon his little
finger, a long-tailed coat, straw-coloured kid gloves, shoes too small for
him, and a great deal of pomade on his hair. It sometimes takes him
two hours to dress, and in his buttonhole he occasionally sports a flower—
'pink camellia japonica, price half a crown'. His tastes are those of his
creator, who loved to parade the streets in 'crimson velvet waistcoats,
multi-coloured neckties with two breast pins joined by a little gold chain,
and yellow kid gloves'.[14]

Dickens always took a deep delight in describing his characters'
clothes, and never more so than in his earlier work. In one of his first
short stories he introduces, for instance, 'a single lady' whose clothes are
described with characteristic flair. She has 'a pelisse the colour of the
interior of a damson pie; a bonnet of the same, with a regular conservatory

of artificial flowers; a white veil, and a green parasol, with a cobweb border'.

A young man is as exactly presented to us in 'a black coat, and exceedingly short, thin trousers; with a very large white waistcoat, white stockings and cravat, and Blucher boots'.★

In his early stories, in fact, Dickens is more interested in describing what his characters wear than what they look like. Although Mr Pickwick's features are well enough known to us, this is due to the illustrator rather than the novelist who contents himself with merely telling his readers that his hero has a bald head and twinkling eyes behind circular spectacles. When Mr Jingle makes his appearance in the second chapter we are told all about his green swallow-tail coat, his stock, his black trousers, his white stockings, his mended shoes, his pinched-up hat, his gloves, and the cuffs of his coat sleeves. That his face is 'thin and haggard' is added almost as an afterthought.

There is scarcely a character in the entire book whose clothes are not described in some detail when he is first introduced into the narrative. Sam Weller is presented as being 'habited in a coarse-striped waistcoat, with black calico sleeves, and blue glass buttons: drab breeches and leggings. A bright red handkerchief was wound in a very loose and unstudied style round his neck, and an old white hat was carelesssly thrown on one side of his head'. We are left to imagine the rest of him from his behaviour and conversation.

In Dickens's later works the clothes his characters wear are more clearly seen as integral parts of their personalities: they even assume a symbolic significance. Miss Havisham's long white veil and white shoes; Mark Tapley's loose red neckcloth whose long ends stream out both in the front and at the back; Mr Tulkinghorn's black stockings which, be they silk or worsted, never shine; Sir Leicester Dedlock's blue coat with bright buttons always buttoned, all these are outward tokens of their wearers' inner lives.

But Dickens was never to lose his taste for cataloguing the entire wardrobe that a man carried on his back, from the top of his hat to the bottom of his boot leather, in a welter of minutely observed detail.

4

In these days at Ellis & Blackmore's, Charles sometimes used to go with Thomas Potter to watch other elegantly dressed young men and their

★ *Sketches by Boz*, 'The Boarding House'.

young ladies promenading at the tea gardens. The young men walked up and down, three abreast, proud of their coloured waistcoats and steel watch guards. And the girls chased each other on the grass, hoping that the young men would take notice of them and buy them a pot of shrimps or a bag of periwinkles.

On Easter Monday it was a holiday and the two friends might, if they could afford the high fare, take a horse-drawn omnibus to Greenwich Fair. Omnibuses had first appeared in the streets of London in 1829, and Charles was fascinated by the brash behaviour of the cheeky conductors (known as 'cads') whose great boast was that they could 'chuck an old gen'lm'n into the buss, shut him in, and rattle off, afore he knows where it's a-going to'. The cad

had opponents, of course; what man in public life has not? But even his worst enemies cannot deny that he has taken more old ladies and gentlemen to Paddington who wanted to go to the Bank, and more old ladies to the Bank who wanted to go to Paddington, than any six men on the road; and however much malevolent spirits may pretend to doubt the accuracy of the statement, they well know it to be an established fact, that he has forcibly conveyed a variety of ancient persons of either sex, to both places, who had not the slightest or most distant intention of going anywhere at all.*

The cad was in his element on the road to Greenwich where, amidst the hackney coaches, and the gigs, the donkey-chaises and the sociables,

the dust flies in clouds, ginger-beer corks go off in volleys, the balcony of every public house is crammed with people, smoking and drinking, half the private houses are turned into tea shops, fiddles are in great request, every little fruit-shop displays its stall of gilt ginger-bread and penny toys; turnpike men are in despair; horses won't go on, wheels will come off; ladies in 'caravans' scream with fright at every fresh occasion, and their admirers find it necessary to sit remarkably close to them, by way of encouragement; servants-of-all-work, who are not allowed to have followers, and have got a holiday for the day, make the most of their time with the faithful admirer who waits for a stolen interview at the corner of the street every night when they go to fetch the beer, apprentices grow sentimental, and straw-bonnet makers kind.†

The Fair itself was a wonderfully exciting place. At the entrance, were the old gypsies telling fortunes; the Jack-in-the-Box booth with three

* *Sketches*, 'Omnibuses' and 'The Last Cab-Driver and the First Omnibus Cad'.
† *Sketches*, 'Greenwich Fair'.

'The young men walked up and down, three abreast, proud of their coloured waistcoats and steel watch guards'

shies offered for a penny; the old pensioners selling glimpses through their telescopes of the mast house, and the river, the place where the pirates used to hang in chains, and the pretty girls runnning down the hill from the Observatory or playing Kiss in the Ring, and Threading My Grandmother's Needle on the grass. And here, at the entrance too, was the man with three thimbles and 'vun little pea' whose patter came rolling off his tongue in an uninterrupted stream:

'Here's the sort o'game to make you laugh seven years arter you're dead, and turn ev'ry 'air on your 'ed grey with delight. Three thimbles and vun little pea—with a vun, two, three, and a two, three, vun, catch him who can, look on, keep your eyes open, and niver say die! Niver mind the change and the expense: all fair and above board: them as don't play can't vin; all luck attend the royal sportsman! Bet any gen'lm'n any sum of money, from harf-a-crown up to a suverin, as he doesn't name the thimble as covers the pea.'*

Inside the entrance the gingerbread men and the toy-sellers; and the girls without bonnets trying to sell their spice nuts, and grabbing their customers by the coat with a 'Do, dear, come on, there's a love, don't be cross, now'; and the tables with their white saucers of pickled salmon (a penny each, fennel included) and the oysters with shells as large as cheese-plates. The noise was deafening—the screaming of women, the shouts of boys, the clanging of gongs, the firing of pistols, the ringing of bells, the bellowings of speaking-trumpets, the squeaking of penny whistles, and the din of a dozen bands, with three drums in each, all playing different tunes at the same time.

Outside the wild beast show was a military band all dressed up in beef-eaters' costumes with leopard-skin caps; a collection of posters depicting tigers tearing men's heads open, and lions being burned with red-hot irons to induce them to drop their terrified victims; and the lion-tamer in his scarlet coat telling the passers-by that his most ferocious lion kills on average three keepers a year ever since he arrived at maturity. 'No extra charge on this account recollect. The price of admission is only sixpence!'

Then there were giantesses and living skeletons, Wild Indians, dwarfs who lived in a box, and a 'young lady of singular beauty, with perfectly white hair and pink eyes'. And at the very centre of the fair was Richardson's theatre which offered a Melodrama '(with three murders and a ghost), a pantomime, a comic song, an overture, and some incidental

* *Sketches*, 'Greenwich Fair'.

music, all done in five-and-twenty minutes'. While for those who could bear the noise and the dust and the heat, there was the dancing booth, where boisterous young men with cigars in their mouths, bulbous cardboard noses and false spectacles danced with excited girls who kept their bonnets on and banged away on childrens' drums.

5

Exciting and stimulating as Dickens found his outings with Potter, however, his evenings were not all given over to pleasure. Determined not to spend the rest of his life in a solicitor's office, he had already begun to think of journalism as a career more suited to his talents and personality, and had taken his first steps towards entering it.

He was encouraged in this by the example of his father who had now been required to retire from the Navy Pay Office on an income of £145 16s 8d a year, and who, despite the difficulties of learning new skills at the age of forty-one, had mastered the intricacies of shorthand and found himself an appointment with the *British Press*.[15]

Charles, while still at school, had sometimes taken in short reports of fires, accidents and crimes, to the *British Press* and had been rewarded at the standard rate of a penny a printed line. But if he were to become a full-time journalist, like his father, he would have to learn shorthand as well. And so, spending almost a whole's week's salary on the purchase, he bought himself a copy of Gurney's *Brachygraphy, or An Easy and Compendious System of Shorthand*, and applied himself with sustained determination to learn its secrets.

Like David Copperfield he 'plunged into a sea of perplexity' that brought him 'in a few weeks to the confines of distraction':

> The changes that were wrung upon dots, which in such a position meant such a thing, and in such another position something else, entirely different; the wonderful vagaries that were played by circles; the unaccountable consequences that resulted from marks like flies' legs; the tremendous effect of a curve in the wrong place; not only troubled my waking hours, but reappeared before me in my sleep. When I had groped my way, blindly, through these difficulties, and had mastered the alphabet, which was an Egyptian Temple in itself, then there appeared a procession of new horrors, called arbitrary characters; the most despotic characters I have ever known; who insisted, for instance, that a thing like the beginning of cobweb, meant expectation, and that a pen-and-ink sky-rocket stood for disadvantageous. When I had fixed these wretches in my mind, I found that

George Cruikshank.

'The dancing booth where boisterous young men with cigars in their
mouths, bulbous cardboard noses and false spectacles danced with
excited girls'

they had driven everything else out of it; then, beginning again, I forgot them; while I was picking them up, I dropped the other fragments of the system; in short, it was almost heart-breaking.* (16)

But, encouraged by the knowledge that a reporter could earn twenty times as much as he was earning now, intrigued by the contrast between the bustling offices of the *British Press* compared with the quiet dullness of Ellis and Blackmore's, and driven on by a fixed and enduring determination to achieve that brighter, more secure future of which the blacking factory had threatened to deprive him, Charles persevered.

'I feel it is not for me to record how hard I worked at that tremendous shorthand', he later wrote with pride in the character of David Copperfield.

I will only add, to what I have already written of my perseverance at this time of life, and of a patient and continuous energy which then began to be matured within me, and which I now know to be the strong part of my character, if it have any strength at all, that there, on looking back, I find the source of my success. . . . I never could have done what I have done, without the habits of punctuality, order and diligence, without the determination to concentrate myself on one object at a time, no matter how quickly its successor should come upon its heels, which I then formed. . . . Whatever I have tried to do in life, I have tried with all my heart to do well; whatever I have devoted myself to, I have devoted myself to completely; that in great aims and in small, I have always been thoroughly in earnest. † (17)

Exaggeratedly self-laudatory as the passage seems, it is quite true of Dickens himself. By the beginning of 1829, some time after he had left Ellis and Blackmore's to work for another solicitor, Charles Molloy, in New Square, Lincoln's Inn, he had learned enough shorthand to make the change which he had been planning. He was too young yet to be given a job as a parliamentary reporter, but, encouraged by a small legacy he received at this time, he felt sure he could make a living as a free-lance reporter in one of the courts. His mother's aunt, the boarding-house keeper in Berners Street, knew of a young man in her husband's family who was a reporter in Doctors' Commons. He had rented a little cubicle there from which he offered his services to any of the proctors who wanted a shorthand reporter to take down a case. He kindly agreed that Charles could share this cubicle with him.

* *David Copperfield*, ch. xxxviii † *David Copperfield*, ch. xlii.

5

MISS MARIA BEADNELL
1829-1833
aet. 17-21

2 LOMBARD STREET LONDON

*In his youth he had ardently loved this woman,
and had heaped upon her all the locked-up wealth
of his affection and imagination. . . . Ever since
that memorable time he had kept the old fancy
of the Past unchanged, in its old sacred place.*

Little Dorrit

5

Charles enjoyed his new career little better than his former one; his unfavourable opinion of the law, and those who made a living out of practising it, was forcibly confirmed. At first he spent most of his days waiting for a proctor to give him a job, and he had many opportunities of exploring the different courts and watching their officers at work. He soon developed a deep disdain for them.

As well as dealing with ecclesiastical and nautical cases, Doctors' Commons (which were later taken over by the Probate Divorce and Admiralty Division of the High Court)[1] concerned themselves with the registration of wills and the granting of marriage-licences to 'love-sick couples, and divorces to unfaithful ones'.

And it is to obtain a marriage licence that the gentleman in room No. 5 at the White Hart (Mr Jingle) has to go there. He asks the way of Sam Weller:

'Do you know—what's a-name—Doctors' Commons?'

'Paul's Church-yard, sir; low archway on the carriage side, book-seller's at one corner, hot—el on the other, and two porters in the middle as touts for licences.'

'Touts for licences!'

'Touts for licences,' replied Sam. 'Two coves in white aprons—touches their hats ven you walk in—"Licence, Sir, Licence!" Queer sort, them, and their mas'rs too, Sir—Old Bailey Proctors—and no mistake.'

'What do they do?'

'Do! *You*, Sir!'*

Sam Weller's sour view of Doctors' Commons is shared by David Copperfield's friend Steerforth. David's aunt wants him to become a proctor and he asks Steerforth what this means. Steerforth, in his reply, gives Dickens's opinion:

'Why he is a sort of monkish attorney,' replied Steerforth. 'He is, to some faded courts held in Doctors' Commons—a lazy old nook near St Paul's Churchyard—what solicitors are to the courts of law and

* *Pickwick Papers*, ch. x.

'It's a place that has an ancient monopoly in suits about people's wills
and people's marriages'

equity. He is a functionary whose existence—in the natural course of
things, would have terminated about two hundred years ago. I can
tell you best what he is, by telling you what Doctors' Commons is.
It's a little out-of-the-way place where they administer what is called
ecclesiastical law, and play all kinds of tricks with obsolete old monsters
of Acts of Parliament, which three-fourths of the world know nothing
about, and the other fourth supposes to have been dug up, in a fossil
state, in the days of the Edwards. It's a place that has an ancient monopoly in suits about people's wills and people's marriages, and disputes
among ships and boats. . . . You shall go there one day, and find them
blundering through half the nautical terms in Young's Dictionary,
apropos of the "Nancy" having run down the "Sarah Jane" . . . and
you shall go there another day, and find them deep in the evidence,
pro and con., respecting a clergyman who has misbehaved himself;
and you shall find the judge in the nautical case, the advocate in the
clergyman's case, or contrariwise. They are like actors, now a man's a

judge, and now he is not a judge; now he's one thing, now he's another; now he's something else, change and change about; but it's always a very pleasant, profitable affair of private theatricals, presented to an uncommonly select audience.*

The absurdities of these 'private theatricals' Dickens was soon to present to a much wider audience; and having transcribed the judgments in some cases arising out of various petty squabbles in the vestry room of the Church of St Bartholomew-the-Great, Smithfield, he was to make use of this experience in his account of the Bumple *v.* Sludberry case, and of the type of lawyer that took part in it, a Doctor of Civil Law, whose face bespeaks nothing 'but conceit and silliness' and whose knowledge was so well concealed—'perhaps with a merciful view of not astonishing ordinary people too much—that you would suppose him to be one of the stupidest boys alive'. When this lawyer is presented in the black-wainscoted court with about ten colleagues all wearing wigs and red gowns, he has 'gathered up his robe behind, in much the same manner as a slovenly woman would her petticoats on a very dirty day, in order that he might feel the full warmth of the fire. His wig was put on all awry, with the tail straggling about his neck; his scanty grey trousers and short black gaiters, made in the worst possible style, imparted an additional inelegant appearance to his uncouth person; and his limp, badly starched shirt-collar almost obscured his eyes.'†

The description, quite without the good-tempered indulgence that marks the other character sketches written at this time, reflects the anger and frustration that the recollection of these months he spent in Doctors' Commons caused him. [2] It was not only that his work was tedious and monotonous, it was irregular and ill-paid. And he had recently discovered a very important and urgent reason for making more money quickly.

He had fallen desperately in love. The girl was very pretty, small and lively with bright eyes and dark ringlets. Her name was Maria Beadnell. She was a year older than himself and she lived with her parents and her two elder sisters next door to Messrs Smith, Payne and Smith's bank at 2 Lombard Street. [3] Her father worked in this bank and ultimately became its manager. [4]

Maria was a flirtatious, capricious, rather silly girl with an approach to young men which was at once provocative and dissuasive, and a habit—which Charles found entrancing—of drawing her eyebrows together in a simulated frown. He had been introduced to her, no doubt, by Henry

* *David Copperfield*, ch. XXIII.   † *Sketches by Boz*, 'Doctors' Commons'.

Kolle, a friend of his sister Fanny and of Maria's sister Anne. Kolle knew the Beadnells well, and perhaps recommended him to the family at Lombard Street as a young man capable not merely of enjoying but of contributing something, such as a comic song, to a musical evening. Anne Beadnell played the lute, Margaret sang, Maria played the harp. And as Charles watched Maria's soft, pale fingers plucking at the strings he felt overwhelmed by love and desire.

As the weeks passed the infatuation developed into a raging passion. He could think of little else. When she smiled at him tenderly, or touched his hand, or glanced at him invitingly out of the corner of her eye, or shook her ringlets back as she laughed at his jokes, he was overcome with happiness. When she referred to him slightingly or sulkily with a *moue* of those exquisite, torturing lips, or put out her hand to touch some other young man, or turned away from him with a petulant movement of her captivating body so tightly clothed in that raspberry-coloured dress of hers with its rows of little black velvet points on the breast, he was cast down in misery and despair.

His days were spent in longing expectation of seeing her in the evenings at Lombard Street. He became a frequent visitor there, and left in transports of delight, or in utter dejection. Mr and Mrs Beadnell took little notice of him. So many other young people came to see the girls, there seemed no reason to take particular notice of this one. He was a good-looking boy to be sure, talkative and entertaining—perhaps on occasions, a little too talkative, a trifle over-spirited, rather too ready to laugh uproariously at a joke. And perhaps he did sometimes appear rather *too* well dressed in his almost aggressively fashionable suits and immensely high black stocks, rather too proud of his own appearance, rather too emphatic in expressing opinions which were a shade unusual, even unconventional. But then, he was very young. Mr Beadnell was kind and friendly to him; so was Mrs Beadnell, though she would insist on referring to him as 'Mr Dickin'.

In imagination he had long conversations with Mrs Beadnell, on the subject of his becoming her son-in-law, and wrote letter after unsent letter to her protesting that he loved her 'adorable daughter, deeply, devotedly'. He did, in fact, send a letter to Anne, asking her to tell him what his chances with her sister were. 'My dear Charles,' Anne replied unhelpfully, 'I really cannot understand Maria, or venture to take the responsibility of saying what the state of her affection is.'

Every small detail of those agonising days of unrequited love remained fixed in his memory for ever—how disturbed he felt when Maria's little dog, Daphne, which would eat mutton chops if you cut off the fat, was accorded the exquisite privilege of being clasped to her mistress's bosom; how exhilarated he felt when he was given the task of matching a pair of Maria's blue gloves; how humbled he was one day when he caught sight of Mrs Beadnell and her three daughters (all wearing green merino cloaks) making their way down Cornhill. He had walked with them all the way to a dressmaker's shop in St Mary Axe, and on the doorstep Mrs Beadnell had turned to him and, with an unmistakable emphasis, had said, 'And now, Mr Dickin, we'll wish *you* good morning'.[5]

It was clear that a mere shorthand writer had little chance of ingratiating himself with Mrs Beadnell, and that unless he improved his prospects and financial position he was unlikely to win the love of her daughter.

On his eighteenth birthday, as soon as it was possible for him to do so, he applied for a ticket of admission to the Reading Room of the British Museum. His application slips show that he took out Addison and Goldsmith, Berges's *Short Account of the Roman Senate*, and Symonds's *Life of Shakespeare*, as well as the plays. But, although these hours of study were later seen by him as being the most useful he had ever spent in his life, they were not immediately profitable, and certainly not likely to advance his prospects with Maria Beadnell. If only, he thought, he could get a job as a reporter; but the opportunity did not present itself. And then one day he had another idea: he would become an actor.

It was a profession which was hardly likely to make the required impression on the future manager of Messrs Smith, Payne and Smith. But Charles, having made up his mind, did not hesitate. He began training himself for this new career with all the assiduity he had brought to mastering Burney's *Brachygraphy*. He began practising walking in and out of his room and sitting down in his chair with the right mixture of authority and grace; he learned a succession of parts and declaimed them to himself on solitary walks; he paid even closer attention than he had done formerly to the art of Charles Mathews, and practised his imitations of the comedian's manner and his voice; he enrolled for a series of lessons with the actor Robert Keeley. And when, at last, he considered that he had made himself good enough for an audition, he wrote to the stage manager of the theatre where Mathews played, and introduced himself as a young amateur with 'a strong perception of character and oddity', and a 'natural power' of mimicry.

He had a reply immediately. The theatre staff and actors were busy at the moment, 'getting up the Hunchback', but the stage manager would write again in a fortnight. And so he did, asking the ambitious young man to go round to the theatre 'to do anything of Mathews's' he chose in front of the great man himself and his colleague, Charles Kemble. Charles, much excited, asked Fanny to go with him as an accompanist. But, as he said himself, 'I was laid up when the day came, with a terrible bad cold and an inflammation of the face. . . . I wrote to say so, and added that I would resume my application next season.'[6]

He never did resume his application, though. For, a few weeks later, his uncle, John Henry Barrow, a versatile journalist who had written for *The Times* and had started a periodical, the *Mirror of Parliament* (composed of verbatim parliamentary reports) offered him a job. His father had already come over to the *Mirror of Parliament* from the *British Press*, and Charles immediately decided to accept his uncle's offer and join him. He also accepted an offer from a new evening paper, the *True Sun*, to join its reporting staff.

2

Given his opportunity at last, Dickens soon showed himself to be a brilliant reporter, both perfectly accurate and remarkably quick. He said himself that he 'made a great splash', and the self-congratulatory verdict was justified. 'There never *was* such a reporter', said one of his older and more experienced colleagues.[7]

The conditions in which he and the eighty-odd other reporters in the Gallery had to work in the old cramped House were peculiarly difficult. No special accommodation was made available to reporters then—this was before the rebuilding that followed the fire of 1834—and they were obliged to squeeze into the back of the Strangers' Gallery as best they could, scribble away on their knees, and then transcribe their notes standing up in 'a preposterous pen in the old House of Lords'.

Charles complained about the conditions, and he complained even more bitterly about the quality of the speeches and the debates. As he listened impatiently to the long, rancorous, inconclusive arguments over the Reform Bill, he decided that he disliked Parliament and its members as much as he disliked the Law. Instinctively on the side of reform, he recorded with contempt the blindly reactionary opinions of those who, in the face of the seething discontent in the country, the threats of revolution, the unemployment and the hunger, complacently shut their minds against change of any sort. But even when the Reform Bill became law, and a new, hard-working, conscientious Parliament passed a succession of social measures which had long been overdue, Charles's disdainful opinion of its Members and the antiquated methods by which they chose to work did not undergo any appreciable change. He had detested the opponents of the Bill, but he did not think much more highly of Lord Grey, the Prime Minister, who had done so much to carry it through. He spoke of his 'fishy coldness, his uncongenial and unsympathetic politeness', while the very shape of his head was 'a misery' to him.[8]

Never afterwards did he draw a member of parliament with sympathy. Like Cornelius Brook Dingwall, the typical member has 'a great idea of his own abilities, which must have been a great comfort to him as no one else had'. Like the Hon. Samuel Slumkey of Slumkey Hall, and Horatio Fizkin, Esq., of Fizkin Lodge, he conducts his campaign without regard either to honesty or dignity. Like Mr Merdle he is rich but hardly seems to enjoy himself much and does not shine in company; there is a 'particular kind of dull red colour in his cheeks which is rather stale than fresh, and a somewhat uneasy expression about his coat-cuffs as if they [are] in his confidence, and [have] reason for being anxious to hide his hands; he is 'tenacious of the utmost deference being shown by every one, in all things, to Society'. Like Mr Gregsbury, the typical Member also has 'a pompous manner, a tolerable command of sentences with no meaning in them . . . a senatorial gravity, and a statesmanlike habit of keeping his feelings under control'.★

Charles was not always able to keep *his* feelings under control in the House. And once when the Irish leader, Daniel O'Connell, was talking of the suffering of the peasants during an anti-tithe riot in Ireland, he could not go on with his report, but hid his head in his arms and wept. In later life he could be driven to tears by far less heartrending stories than O'Connell's, but even now he was extremely susceptible. He was, in any event, in a highly-wrought emotional state.

3

In the winter of 1831–32 his existence, as he put it himself, had been 'entirely uprooted', and his 'whole being blighted'. Maria Beadnell had been taken away from him. She had been sent by her father to Paris 'to

★ *Sketches by Boz*; *Pickwick Papers*, ch. XIII; *Little Dorrit*, ch. XXI; *Nicholas Nickleby*, ch. XVI.

finish her education' at a school for young ladies kept by Madame Martinez in the rue du Berry.

Until hit by this sudden blow, Charles had been more often made happy by Maria's smiles and flattering displays of affection, than by her coquettish sulks. It was possible even to believe that she really did love him, as in her middle-age she confessed she had done. She had answered his letters, sent him little presents accompanied by tender notes, whispered messages in his ear that filled him with a kind of ecstasy. At a dinner party at the house in Lombard Street he had perhaps gone too far, though.

He had written, specially for the occasion, a parody of Goldsmith's 'Retaliation' which he called 'The Bill of Fare'. He was rather proud of it and, with what might well have been considered rather unbecoming immodesty, read it out after dinner. The guests and some of their friends were mentioned in it in the guise of the food they had just enjoyed. It was an intermittently brash, occasionally sharp, but more often embarrassingly facetious production, and Mr Beadnell, though referred to in it as 'a good fine sirloin of beef', and his wife as 'an excellent *Rib* of the same', cannot be expected to have admired it, or to have approved of the reference to its author ('a young Summer Cabbage') having lost his heart ('not that he's heartless') to 'a sweet pair of eyes', whose death would leave him without the desire to go on living himself.

Maria's departure left him desolate. He was earning a great deal of money now, sometimes as much as twenty-five guineas a week, but he could not enjoy it. He had made friends with only one of his colleagues in the Gallery, Thomas Beard of the *Morning Herald*; to the rest he seemed a polite enough young fellow, but distant and reserved. His duties frequently kept him working late in the House, and he could not get to the theatre nearly as often as he would have liked. Occasionally on Saturdays he would meet Beard and a few other friends, including Henry Kolle, for a sing-song over a bowl of punch and a box of cigars; but his mind seemed far away.

For a time he tried living on his own. While working at Doctors' Commons he was still with his parents who had gone back to live in Norfolk Street in rooms over a grocer's shop.[9] Soon after getting his job on the *Mirror of Parliament*, however, he had moved to lodgings in Cecil Street, Strand, so as to be nearer the House. But he did not like it there. 'The people at Cecil Street', he told Kolle, 'put too much water in the hashes, lost the nutmeg grater, attended on me most miserably, dirtied the Table Cloths, etc., etc—and so (detesting petty miseries)', he gave them notice. He moved his things back to his parents' who (enforcedly peripatetic) had had to leave Norfolk Street and go round the corner to another house.

But although he was not living on his own any more, he still spent much of his time by himself, roaming the streets at all hours of the day and night, watching the people, thinking, groping his way through those lanes and by-ways, and courtyards, and passages that sprawled around Doctors' Commons, entering dingy churchyards, 'all overgrown with such straggling vegetation as springs up spontaneously from damp, and graves, and rubbish', looking into queer old taverns where old men, wheezy and asthmatical, 'expressed themselves opposed to steam and all new-fangled ways, and held ballooning to be sinful', passing through fruit-brokers' markets where the first impression was 'of oranges—of damaged oranges, with blue and green bruises on them, festering in boxes, or mouldering away in cellars. All day long a stream of porters from the wharves beside the river, each bearing on his back a bursting chest of oranges, poured slowly through the narrow passages.'*

After transcribing his notes in the House of Lords or in an upper room in an inn in Old Palace Yard, where the reporters congregated to compare their versions of passages in speeches which they had not been able to hear very well, Charles would go home, on occasions when it was nearly dawn, to spend the rest of the morning in bed.

In the cold darkness of the early morning when the stillness of death was over the streets, he would pass deserted coach-stands, costermongers sleeping under their carts, shuttered shops, bedroom windows where rushlights flickered in the glass. Sometimes in the hour before daybreak he would watch the streets come slowly back to life, the market carts and the women with fruit baskets on their heads making their way to Covent Garden, the serving-maids putting up the tables for breakfast outside the public houses, the street breakfast trolleys with the jugs of coffee boiling on charcoal fires, and the thick slices of bread and butter piled up on big white plates.

He would pass a bricklayer's labourer, perhaps, going to work with his dinner tied up in a handkerchief, a sweep's climbing boy knocking on a kitchen door and then sitting down on the doorstep until the servants came down to let him in, apprentices sweeping out shops and watering pavements in front of them, and, later, clerks coming into the City from Somers Town and Islington and Pentonville, the middle-aged men

* *Martin Chuzzlewit*, ch. IX.

'In the cold darkness of the early morning when the stillness of death was over the streets'

knowing almost everyone but speaking to no one, the office-boys in their tall hats and with ink on their trousers, looking under the bonnets of all the milliners' and staymakers' apprentice girls they passed on the way.

On some mornings Charles would feel drawn to go amongst the crowds in the Market, to listen to the piemen bawling their wares among the decayed cabbage-leaves and broken haybands, the chatter of the basket-women, the braying of the donkeys and the screech of cartwheels on the cobbles. Or he would go to a coach office to see the coaches going out, 'surrounded by the usual crowd of Jews and nondescripts, who seem to consider, Heaven knows why, that it is quite impossible any man can mount a coach without requiring at least six-pennyworth of oranges, a penknife, a pocket-book, a last year's annual, a pencil-case, a piece of sponge, and a small series of caricatures'.

Inside the coaching office, 'a mouldy-looking room ornamented with large posting-bills', he wondered

> what on earth the booking-office clerks can have been before they were booking-office clerks; one of them with his pen behind his ear is standing in front of the fire like a full length portrait of Napoleon; the other with his hat half off his head, enters the passengers' names in the books with a cockiness which is inexpressibly provoking; and the villain whistles—actually whistles—while a man asks what the fare is outside all the way to Holyhead!—in frosty weather too! They are an isolated race, evidently possessing no sympathies or feelings in common with the rest of mankind.*

Occasionally of an evening, Charles went to Seven Dials through St Giles's, where labourers in their working clothes, covered in brick dust and whitewash, argued with each other round the street posts; where half-naked children played in the open drains and Englishwomen fought Irishwomen to the shouts of encouragement from excited pot-boys: 'Hurray! Put the kye-bock on her, Mary!'; where in higgledy-piggledy confusion in a maze of streets and alleys, there were chandlers' shops and secondhand clothes shops, pawnbrokers' shops, rag-and-bone shops, shops full of birds and rabbits and old iron and kitchen stuff and mangles and advertisements for penny theatres; and where, in the crumbling houses, every room had a separate tenant and every tenant a family. In one small, wretched house with broken windows patched with rags and paper there might be a sweetmeat manufacturer in the cellar, a barber and a red-herring vendor in the front parlour and a cobbler in the back,

* *Sketches*, 'Early Coaches'.

'He wondered "what on earth the booking-office clerks can have been before they were booking-office clerks"'

a bird fancier on the first floor, three families on the second, starvation in the attics, Irishmen in the passage, a 'musician' in the front kitchen, and a charwoman and five hungry children in the back one—filth everywhere—a gutter before the houses and a drain behind—clothes drying and slops emptying from the windows; girls of fourteen or fifteen with matted hair walking about barefoot, and in white great-coats, almost their only covering; boys of all ages, in coats of all sizes and no coats at all; men and women, in every variety of scanty and dirty apparel, lounging, scolding, drinking, smoking, squabbling, fighting and swearing.*

The district appalled him yet held a continual fascination for him with its 'dirty men, filthy women, squalid children, fluttering shuttlecocks, noisy battledores, reeking pipes, bad fruit, more than doubtful oysters, attenuated cats, depressed dogs'. And amidst all the filth and smell and squalor, there were the bright, glittering, splendidly vulgar gin-shops with immense chandeliers hanging from their ceilings in cascades of brass and crystal, and huge green and gold barrels of gin stacked behind brass rails all round the walls, enticingly or intimidatingly labelled—'The Cream of the Valley', 'The Out and Out', 'The No Mistake', 'The Real Knock Me Down', 'The Good for Mixing', 'The Regular Flare Up', 'Old Tom', 'Young Tom', 'Samson'.

There was one particular gin-shop he knew, a magnificent building with a fantastically ornamented parapet, an illuminated clock, plate-glass windows surrounded by stucco rosettes, and a profusion of gas lights in richly gilt burners. Inside, a bar of French-polished mahogany, elegantly carved, extended the whole length of the saloon.

Behind the bar 'are two showily-dressed damsels with large necklaces, dispensing the spirits. They are assisted by the ostensible proprietor of the concern, a stout coarse fellow in a fur cap, put on very much at one side to give him a knowing air, and to display his sandy whiskers to the best advantage.'

It is growing late, and the throng of men, women and children, who have

been constantly going in and out, dwindles down to two or three occasional stragglers—cold, wretched-looking creatures, in the last stages of emaciation and disease. The knot of Irish labourers at the lower end of the place, who have been alternately shaking hands with, and threatening the life of each other, for the last hour, become furious in their disputes, and finding it impossible to silence one man, who is particularly anxious to adjust the difference, they resort to the expedient

* *Sketches*, 'Seven Dials', 'Gin Shops'.

of knocking him down and jumping on him afterwards. The man in
the fur cap and the pot boy rush out; a scene of riot and confusion
ensues; half the Irishmen get shut out, and the other half get shut in;
the pot boy is knocked among the tubs in no time; the landlord hits
everybody, and everybody hits the landlord; the barmaids scream, the
police come in; the rest is a confused mixture of arms, legs, staves, torn
coats, shouting and struggling. Some of the party are borne off to the
station-house, and the remainder slink home to beat their wives for
complaining, and kick the children for daring to be hungry.*

These lonely walks across London, into St Giles's and Seven Dials,
through Covent Garden and Drury Lane, down by the river from
Bermondsey to Fulham, Dickens was to continue for the rest of his life.
In later years, when his work had excited him too much to sleep, he would
walk the whole night through.

He came to rely on walking through the streets as the only means of
relieving the tensions within him, as the true source of his inspiration.
When trying to begin *The Chimes* in Genoa in 1844 he felt that he had
plucked himself out of his proper soil by leaving London, and would
not be able to write anything until he had walked again through its
streets. 'Put me down on Waterloo Bridge at eight o'clock in the evening
with leave to roam about as long as I like,' he wrote home to Forster,
'and I would come home, as you know, panting to go on. I am sadly
strange as it is, and can't settle.'[10]

Two years later in Switzerland, when working on another Christmas
book, he complained of the 'prodigious difficulty' of going at what he
called a rapid pace, and he blamed 'the absence of streets'. He was able
to work all right for a short time without them, he said. He could get on
fast with his work for a week or so even in a quiet place like Broadstairs.
But then he always felt he must get back to walking the streets. He felt
'dumbfounded' without them. 'The toil and labour of writing, day after
day, without that magic lantern is IMMENSE!!'[11] Even now, after a day's
exhausting, concentrated work, he would walk for hours on end, sometimes going as far as Hampstead and back, at others all the way to Lombard Street, merely to look up at the room where Maria lay asleep.

4

She had come back from Paris at last. But the longed-for return gave him
none of the happiness he had hoped it would. She was prettier and more

* *Sketches*, 'Gin Shops'.

'. . . two showily-dressed damsels with large necklaces, dispensing the spirits . . . assisted by the ostensible proprietor of the concern, a stout coarse fellow in a fur cap, put on very much at one side to give him a knowing air, and to display his sandy whiskers to the best advantage'

desirable than ever, yet far more capricious and petulant. He never knew from one day to the next how she would treat him; though it was more often coldly than not. He went to Lombard Street time and again, in fact and in imagination, hoping to get her on her own, but there was always someone else there, usually her father, who seemed much less friendly than before.

In an agony of distress and uncertainty, Charles took to writing Maria appealing messages which he entrusted to one of the Beadnells' maids or to Kolle who was often at Lombard Street to see Anne. But Maria's replies were unsatisfactory, shallow, inconclusive. And then, on his twenty-first birthday, came the bitterest blow of all.

His parents had promised to give a party for him in their house at 18 Bentinck Street, Manchester Square, to which their improving finances and their son's success had allowed them to move. Charles made arrangements to have his evening work done by another reporter so that he could be home by eight.

'It was a beautiful party,' he said years later, when he could bring himself to write about it. 'Everything was hired and the mercenaries in attendance were profound strangers to me.' There was music and dancing, and more than enough to drink, and 'in the crumby part of the night, when wine glasses were to be found in unexpected spots', he took Maria away from the others behind a door, so she said, and spoke to her earnestly of his love. She listened to him patiently—even, so he liked to think, with 'angelic gentleness'—but when he had finished, she called him 'a boy' and soon afterwards went home. Charles spent the rest of the evening drinking and woke up with a fearful headache.★

For the next few weeks he was utterly miserable; and he made himself more so by displaying a wounded, self-pitying heart which, of course, aroused her irritation rather than her sympathy. Unable to understand why Maria was treating him so cruelly, and anxious to make her realise how much he loved her, and how unhappy she was making him, he determined to bring the sad and unfulfilled affair to a crisis.

He tied up her letters in blue ribbon and sent them back to her, together with a present she had once given him.

Our meetings of late [he wrote in a long and sadly sententious covering letter] have been little more than so many displays of heartless indiffer-ence on the one hand; while on the other they have never failed to

★ *The Uncommercial Traveller*, 'Birthday Parties'.

prove a fertile source of wretchedness and misery. . . . I have felt too long the feeling of utter desolation and wretchedness which has succeeded our former acquaintance. Thank God I can claim for myself and feel that I desire the merit of having ever throughout our inter- course, acted fairly, intelligently and honourably; under kindness and encouragement one day and total change of conduct the next. I have ever been the same. . . . Believe me that nothing will ever afford me more real delight than to hear that you, the object of my first and my last love, are happy.[12]

Maria sent the letter back to him. But she also, as he had so fervently hoped, wrote him a reply which contained what seemed to him a hint of encouragement. Immediately he wrote again, protesting that his love for her was unchanged. This also she sent back. It was wrapped only in a small piece of loose paper.

But even now he could not bear to give way, to accept the unpalatable fact that she had grown tired of him. He knew at least that he would see her again, for he had issued invitations to all the Beadnells to come to Bentinck Street on 27 April to see him, his family and some friends perform in some amateur theatricals. He himself, as well as producing all the three pieces on the programme, writing the prologue and playing three important parts, was acting as stage manager, scenic designer, lighting adviser and playing the accordion in the band. Maria and her parents could surely not but be impressed by this new evidence of versatility, already displayed by the author and reciter of 'The Bill of Fare' at Lombard Street the year before.

Determined that nothing should go wrong he took it as a personal affront when Henry Kolle, now engaged to Maria's sister Anne, forgot to come to a rehearsal. It was well known, Charles wrote huffily, that 'a little flow of prosperity is an excellent cooler of former friendships, and that when other and more pleasant engagements can be formed, visits— if not visits of convenience—become excessively irksome'. Would Kolle be good enough to let him know whether or not he intended to retain the part? Other arrangements must be made if he did not.

Kolle had already had a letter from Dickens in which he had been offered 'heartfelt congratulations' on his engagement to Anne. 'You are', Dickens had added, 'or at all events will be, what I never can, happy and contented'. And so Kolle was more ready to understand and sympathise with his friend's touchiness than to take offence at it. He was in good time for the next rehearsal.

The theatrical evening at Bentinck Street did nothing, however, to heal the breach between Charles and Maria. It was not that the plays were a failure—though Maria, it seems, gave no indication that she had enjoyed them or admired their production—but that after they were over Charles received far less attention from Maria than he did from her friend Mary Anne Leigh.

Marianne, as she chose to call herself, was a pretty, talkative girl with a more than ordinary devotion to gossip and scandal and a well-developed taste for intrigue. She had long since established herself as Maria's closest confidante; and Dickens, alternately fascinated and repelled by her, had been drawn into the ambivalence of her friendship. He knew that she was both inquisitive and unreliable, but he found her flirtatious, sexy manner disturbingly exciting, and he sometimes found himself behaving with her and saying things to her in a way which he later regretted.

On the night of the theatricals, naturally elated by his various performances, he spent a good deal of time in her company. And afterwards she told Maria that he had confided in her many intimate details of their relationship.

Charles had known for some time that she and Maria discussed him when they were alone together, though he had never been able to decide whether Marianne's subsequent accounts of these conversations were true, exaggerated or invented. But now, when he heard that his own remarks had been taken back to Maria with he knew not what distortions, he was overwrought. He was all the more so when his sister Fanny told him that Marianne had been claiming for a long time that she was in Charles's close confidence.

Furious with Fanny for not having told him this before, he wrote to Maria saying that 'no consideration on earth' would ever induce him to forgive his sister. He went on to deny all that Marianne had claimed, and to confess himself deeply hurt that Maria should have believed her. How could she have doubted him when once they had been so close, and he so full of hopes 'the loss of which has made me the miserable reckless wretch I am'?

He intended writing to Marianne also, and asked Maria if she had any objection to this. No, she replied, but she would like to see the letter before he sent it. And she added that he could scarcely have felt such aversion to her friend as he said he did, since he had had so many intimate conversations with her. Charles wrote back to say that he had borne more from Maria than he believed 'any living creature breathing ever bore from a woman before'. However, he sent her the letter he had written to

Marianne, a letter which insisted that, 'passing over any remark which may have been artfully elicited . . . in an unguarded moment', he had made a confidante of no one. At the same time he returned Marianne's autograph album which 'want of a moment's time' had quite prevented his writing in.

Charles's covering letter to Maria was short and stiff, and revealed again the scars of his wound. He did not begin it 'Dear Miss Beadnell', as he had done before, but at the end he wrote, 'I find I have proceeded to the end of my note without even inserting your name. May I ask you to excuse the omission and to believe that I would gladly have addressed you in a very very different way?'

Any hopes he entertained of being asked to address her in a different way were, however, soon dispelled. He sent one last stilted and repetitious appeal to her, and asked Henry Kolle, his go-between, to deliver it:

I will allow no feeling of pride, no haughty dislike to making a reconciliation to prevent my expressing it without reserve—I will advert
to nothing that has passed; I will not again seek to excuse any part I
have acted or to justify it by any course you have ever pursued, I will
revert to nothing that has ever passed between us; I will openly and at
once say that there is nothing that I have more at heart, nothing I more
sincerely and earnestly desire, than to be reconciled to you. . . . I have
never loved and I can never love any human creature breathing but
yourself . . . the love I now tender you is as pure and as lasting as at
any period of our former correspondence.[13]

But it was no good. Her reply was cool, even reproachful and he knew that he had lost her. He had known her and loved her for four years. For most of that time she had ruled his emotions; and by ruling them then she had marked them for ever.

He came to understand this well enough himself. That first passionate, frustrating and finally thwarted love made so deep an impression on him that he believed it to be responsible for 'a habit of suppression which now belongs to me, which I know is no part of my original nature, but which makes me chary of showing my affections, even to my children, except when they are very young'.[14]

It was responsible for more we may suppose than 'a habit of suppres-
sion'. His pride had been wounded; his self-confidence undermined; his natural responsiveness driven beyond sensitivity into touchiness; his fundamental reserve hardened and deepened. And a subsequent determination not to be rebuffed or slighted again, combined with a fear that

he might be, or a feeling that he had been, was to lead him to adopt—often when he was least sure of himself—a masking personality, emphatically assertive, even arrogant.

There was, too, the consciousness that had he been more of a worldly success, had his family not had a background of poverty and disgrace, he might have succeeded. He was more than ever now resolved to get on in the world, to make money, to have his own way.

Later he learned how to overcome the sense that one's grief is unbearable either by using it to judge and understand and finally to delineate the grief of others, or by exaggerating its symptoms so outlandishly that they become absurd and laughable.

But even then, in his middle age, although he could bring himself to write down a history of the affair, he could not bear to show it to anyone. The blacking factory and Marshalsea experiences had been painful enough to record; yet at least he had felt able to give his accounts of these to his closest friend. His account of Maria and of the anguish of his love for her he tore up and threw into the fire, and when she is made to reappear as the pretty, provocative, silly Dolly Varden and the helpless, childlike, affectedly incompetent *ingénue* who marries David Copperfield, the reality is gone from her.

5

More than twenty years after he wrote to Maria his last despairing letter, she came into his life again. She did so at a time when he was feeling violently restless and unbearably repressed by the frustrations of his own personal existence.

He had just finished *Hard Times*. Before he began it he had been to Preston to see how a northern industrial town looked when in the grip of a long and stubborn strike, and he had been depressed by the gloom of the place and the dispirited lethargy of the strikers. The book had not come easily to him, though he had written it quickly and finished it—100,000 words of it—in five months. But he had felt 'dreary' in composing it, and had sought relief in the company of lively friends such as Mark Lemon, the fat, gregarious editor of *Punch*, Wilkie Collins, the young novelist, and George Wilkes, the brother of an American woman with whom, during his visit to the United States in 1842, he had pretended to be desperately in love.

He took Wilkes on a tour of the 'low and vicious haunts of London', and invited Collins to join him in a few days of 'amiable dissipation and unbounded licence'. He wrote to Collins from Boulogne where he had rented a villa (immediately on arrival rearranging every piece of furniture in it, as he always did when he moved into a new furnished house). If Collins would meet him for breakfast at midnight 'anywhere—any day', they would not go to bed again until they arrived back at Boulogne. He would be glad to have what he burlesqued as 'so vicious an associate'.

He had never felt so pent-up, so feverishly restive. Emotionally thwarted, he felt at the same time 'used up' by the effort of *Hard Times*, and increasingly depressed by the tragic state of the world around him, by the pitiable incompetence and sloth revealed by the country's conduct of the Crimean War, by the Government's failure to provide the people with decent houses instead of 'polluted dens', a failure that had led to the deaths of 20,000 people from cholera that summer of 1854. He could relieve his outraged sense of social injustice by fulminating in his magazine, *Household Words*, against the 'Indifferents and Incapables' in the slumberous neighbourhood of Downing Street and the House of Commons; by appealing to the workers, in alliance with the middle-class, to make their voices heard in demanding 'cheap water in unlimited quantity', wholesome air, efficient drainage, and open spaces; by writing to friends of his burning desire to cut the Emperor of Russia's throat being outweighed by an even more burning indignation at the social evils at home. But he found no outlet for his frustrated desire to escape from the enclosing trammels of his own home.

He had 'dreadful thoughts of getting away somewhere altogether' by himself, he told Forster. He thought of 'all sorts of inaccessible places' —the Pyrenees, or somewhere above the snow-line in Switzerland. Forster, he knew, would say it was '*restlessness*'. But whatever it was it was always driving him, and he could not help it. If he couldn't walk fast and far, he would 'just explode and perish'.[15]

On occasions he appeared cheerful and relaxed; and when he was at home rehearsing plays with the children or showing them conjuring tricks at parties, so excited, so sparkling, so obviously enjoying himself, infecting Mark Lemon and Wilkie Collins with his high spirits and making Thackeray laugh so much he fell off his chair, it seemed then that Dickens was a happy and contented man. But almost in a moment the joy would die within him, and then there would return this 'dishevelled state of mind', this urgent desire to get away. 'Why is it,' he asked Forster, 'that, as with poor David, a sense always comes crushing upon me now, when I fall into low spirits, as of one happiness I have missed in life, and one friend and companion I have never made?'[16]

A fortnight or so after he had written this letter to Forster, he was sitting in his study reading a book, when a servant brought in his letters. He glanced at the envelopes, found nothing immediately familiar in the handwriting on any of them, and put them back on the table. But he felt disturbed, though he did not know why, and he picked up the envelopes again. And with a flash of wild excitement, he recognised the writing of Maria Beadnell. 'Three or four and twenty years,' he replied to her immediately, 'vanished like a dream, and I opened it with the touch of my young friend David Copperfield when he was in love.' He replied at length and with a mounting animation, recalling their shared past, anxious to see her again.

He had arranged to go to Paris the next day with Wilkie Collins, but he would be glad to do anything for her while he was there. Perhaps he could buy something for her two little daughters ('the existence of these dear children appeared such a prodigious phenomenon' that he was inclined to think he had gone out of his mind, he told her, 'until it occurred to me that perhaps I had nine children of my own!'). Anyway, as soon as he returned he would get his wife, Catherine, to call on her and arrange a day for her and her husband to come to dinner.[17]

Maria wrote to him in Paris, asking him to get brooches for the girls, and a velvet collar with a clasp of blue stones for herself. He was delighted that she should have asked him, and clearly excited by what seems to have been a suggestion on her part that he should write her a letter just for herself. He wrote a long and even more intimate reply, recalling once again the love of David Copperfield for Dora, how people used to say to him how fanciful that love affair was. 'But they little thought what reason' he had to 'know it was true and nothing more nor less'. He had spoken about her in Paris to Lady Olliffe he told her, and Lady Olliffe had asked him 'if it were really true' that he used 'to love Maria Beadnell so very, very, very, very much'. And he had replied that 'there was no woman in the world, and there were very few men who could ever imagine how much'.

I have never been so happy a man since, as I was when you made me wretchedly happy [he went on]; I shall never be half so good a fellow any more. . . . I have a strong belief—and there is no harm in adding hope to that—that perhaps you have once or twice laid down that book, and thought 'How dearly that boy must have loved me, and how vividly this man remembers it!' These are things that I have locked up in my breast and that I never thought to bring out any more. But when I find myself writing to you again 'all to yourself', how can I forebear to let as much light upon them as will show you that they are still there. . . . How can I receive a confidence from you, and return it, and make a feint of blotting all this out![18]

A third letter came from her after his arrival back in London, and, oh! though it was so late to read what she now told him, he read it 'with the old tenderness softened to a more sorrowful remembrance' than he could easily tell her. How it had all happened as it had, they would never know; but if she had ever told him what she told him now, he was sure that the simple truth and energy that were in his love would have overcome everything. He refused to believe that she had become 'toothless, fat, old, and ugly'. She would always be the same in his eyes. 'You ask me to treasure what you tell me, in my heart of hearts. O see what I have cherished there, through all this time and all these changes!'

He was a dangerous man to be seen with, for so many people knew him. But he agreed that a first meeting, just the two of them together, would be better than a meeting when her husband and his wife were there. Would she not, then, call at his house on Sunday, ask first for Catherine and then for himself. 'It is almost a positive certainty that there will be none here but I, between 3 and 4. . . . Remember, I accept all with my whole soul, and reciprocate all.'[19]

Surely here, he felt, was the chance to relive his past and his youth; here, perhaps, was that one happiness that he had missed in life, that one friend and companion he had never made. He longed to see her again, as, in his next novel, he was to present Arthur Clennam as longing to see Flora Casby. 'In his youth [Arthur] had ardently loved this woman, and had heaped upon her all the locked-up wealth of his affection and imagination. . . . Ever since that memorable time . . . he had kept the old fancy of the Past unchanged, in its old sacred place.' So had Dickens, and Clennam's shock, when his eyes 'fell upon the object of his old passion', is Dickens's shock. The passion shivered and broke to pieces.

Flora, always tall, had grown to be very broad too, and short of breath; but that was not much. Flora, whom he had left a lily, had become a peony; but that was not much. Flora, who had seemed enchanting in all she said and thought, was diffuse and silly. That was much. Flora, who had been spoiled and artless long ago, was determined to be spoiled and artless now. That was a fatal blow.
    This is Flora!

'I am sure,' giggled Flora, tossing her head with a caricature of her girlish manner, such as a mummer might have presented at her own funeral, if she had lived and died in classical antiquity, 'I am ashamed to see Mr Clennam, I am a mere fright. I know he'll find me fearfully changed, I am actually an old woman, it's shocking to be so found out, it's really shocking!'

He assured her that she was just what he had expected, and that time had not stood still with himself.

'Oh! But with a gentleman it's so different and really you look so amazingly well that you have no right to say anything of the kind, while, as to me you know—oh!' cried Flora with a little scream, 'I am dreadful!' . . .

'But if we talk of not having changed,' said Flora, who, whatever she said, never once came to a full stop, 'look at Papa, is not Papa precisely what he was when you went away, isn't it cruel and unnatural of Papa to be such a reproach to his own child, if we go on in this way much longer people who don't know us will begin to suppose that I am Papa's Mama!'

That must be a long time hence, Arthur considered.

'Oh Mr Clennam you insincerest of creatures,' said Flora, 'I perceive already you have not lost your old way of paying compliments, your old way when you used to pretend to be sentimentally struck you know—at least I don't mean that, I—oh I don't know what I mean!'

Here Flora tittered confusedly, and gave him one of her old glances.*

Dickens longed for Maria to leave him, almost as passionately as he had longed for her to arrive. But even when she had gone, there was still the now unavoidable ordeal of going to dinner with her and her husband. And it turned out to be just as much of an ordeal as he had feared. Henry Winter was boring; his wife remained her chattering, tiresome, grotesquely disappointing self. She also by now had a cold. Dickens caught it.

Flora, despite her incessant chatter and the 'profoundly unreasonable' way in which she endeavoured to bring to life 'their long-abandoned girl and boy relations', notices that Arthur is disappointed in her. Maria does not seem to have noticed, or at least refused to accept, that Charles (who had written to her with such ardent intimacy and such reciprocal anticipation) could have so suddenly changed his mind on discovering that she was, after all, rather fat and forty-four and not still a girl of eighteen.

She suggested that she should call to see him with one of her daughters the next Sunday. But he replied that he could not be sure that he would be there, though the family would probably be at home. She did call; and he was out.

* *Little Dorrit*, Bk. i, ch. XIII.

She called on two further occasions, and on both of these he was out. She wrote again. But, no, people did not seem to understand how an author's mind worked:

> They don't know that it is impossible to command one's self sometimes to any stipulated and set disposal of five minutes. . . . These are the penalties paid for writing books. Whoever is devoted to an Art must be content to deliver himself wholly up to it. . . . I am grieved if you suspect me of not wanting to see you, but I can't help it, I must go my way, whether or no. . . . I am going off, I don't know where or how far, to ponder about I don't know what.[20]

Still she persisted. But, again, no, he was very busy every day of every week, and would be out of London 'several Sundays in succession'. Once he called at her house with Kate, and noticed gloomily that her little dog, Daphne, was stuffed in the hall.

Her baby died. But it was better that he did not come to see her. He would, he told her, think of her instead.

He *did* think of her a great deal. 'No one can imagine in the most distant degree what pain the recollection gave me in *Copperfield*', he told Forster. 'And just as I can never open that book as I open any other book, I cannot see the face (even at four-and-forty), or hear the voice, without going wandering away over the ashes of all that youth and hope in the wildest manner.'

The experience of being made to realise that Maria Beadnell had become Mrs Henry Winter left him 'in a state of restlessness impossible to be described—impossible to be imagined—wearing and tearing to be experienced'. He got tired of himself, yet couldn't come out of himself to be pleasant to anyone else, and went on 'turning upon the same wheel round and round and over and over again' until he felt it might roll him to his end. 'I feel as if nothing would do me the least good,' he confided in Collins, 'but setting up a Balloon.'[21]

6

He had felt just the same when the youthful love affair with that other, so much younger and so far different, Maria had come to an end. At that time he could think of nothing but her, feel nothing but a hollow sense of waste and emptiness and unfulfilment. On the evening of the day he sent to Maria his last wounded note about Marianne, he attended a dinner given by Henry Kolle's brothers for their bachelor friends. Charles got very drunk on an 'extensive assortment of choice hock' and two days later his stomach, so he told Henry, still felt like a lime basket.

It was a Sunday and the next day he had to go back unwillingly to work.

6

THE *CHRONICLE* REPORTER
1833-1835
aet. 21-23

13 FURNIVAL'S INN HIGH HOLBORN LONDON

I walked down to Westminster Hall, and turned into it for half an hour, because my eyes were so dimmed with joy and pride that they could not bear the street, and were not fit to be seen there.

Forster's Life of Dickens

6

'We take it that the commencement of a session of parliament is neither more nor less than the drawing up of the curtain for a grand comic pantomime. . . . Perhaps the cast of our political pantomime never was richer than at this day. We are particularly strong in clowns. . . . Night after night they will twist and tumble about, till two, three, and four o'clock in the morning; playing the strangest antics, and giving each other the funniest slaps on the face that can possibly be imagined, without evincing the smallest tokens of fatigue. The strangest noises, the confusion, the shouting and roaring, amid which all this is done, would put to shame the most turbulent sixpenny gallery that ever yelled through a boxing-night.'*

The better Dickens got to know the Houses of Parliament and their workings the less he liked them. Self-satisfaction, long-windedness, public protestations of good intent contradicted by private manœuvre and intrigue, emasculation of worthy social measures in the interests of established privilege, seemed to him the characteristics of a legislative body which, he said, was more like Smithfield than an elected parliament.

Take one look around you, and retire! The body of the House [of Commons] and the side galleries are full of Members; some, with their legs on the back of the opposite seat; some with theirs stretched out to their utmost length on the floor; some going out, others coming in; all talking, laughing, lounging, coughing, o-ing, questioning, or groaning; presenting a conglomeration of noise and confusion, to be met with in no other place in existence, not even excepting Smithfield on a market-day, or a cockpit in its glory.†

He listened to the debates on Bills to abolish the commercial monopoly of the East India Company, to limit working hours, to improve conditions in factories, to provide for the poor, to abolish slavery in the colonies, and he was as angered by the bluff, insensitive speeches of reactionaries as by what he took to be the weak compromises of the reformers. He admired Lord John Russell, but there were few other members of either House he could tolerate.

* *Sketches*, 'A Parliamentary Sketch'.   † *Ibid.*

He recorded their speeches, though, with unabated speed and remarkable accuracy. He had resigned from the *True Sun* towards the end of July 1832; but he was now one of the *Mirror of Parliament*'s most valued employees, entrusted with duties more varied than those which normally fell to a stenographer's lot. His uncle, John Henry Barrow, realising that the young man's talents were worthy of wider recognition, made enquiries for him about employment on the staff of one of London's daily papers. A friend of his, J. P. Collier, was on the *Morning Chronicle*, and Barrow wrote to him recommending his nephew. But Collier was not too sure that he could pass the recommendation on without knowing more about him, how old he was, where he had been to school, what his qualifications were, how he had previously earned his living. Barrow answered the questions without demur, except the last, which skated over very thin ice. 'At one time', he replied evasively, 'he had assisted Warren, the blacking-man, in the conduct of his extensive business', adding an implication that his nephew was employed on the advertising side of the business and had composed one of the firm's most famous rhymes.[1]

Collier thought that he had better see the young man for himself; so Barrow asked them both to dinner at his home in Norwood with some other friends. Collier was immediately struck by how very young Dickens looked for his age, but he had to agree that he seemed clever, and—since Barrow had given all his guests plenty to drink—was certainly good company. The young man was persuaded, after more urging than usual, to sing two of his comic songs, one of them—about a milkmaid, 'Sweet Betsey Ogle', who has an affair with a barber—being his own composition.[2]

Collier, after this gay evening, agreed to put the name of his friend's nephew forward. Nothing came of the recommendation, however, and it was not until Charles's friend, Thomas Beard, was appointed to the staff and, on being asked to suggest a suitable colleague, said that Dickens was 'the fastest and most accurate man in the gallery', that Charles got the job he was hoping for.

His salary was to be the 'Fleet Street minimum', five guineas a week, which did not seem very generous compared with what he had been getting during parliamentary sessions at the *Mirror of Parliament*; but at least it was to be paid all the year round, whether the House was sitting or not.

Dickens was delighted with this new chance in life and this new security. One of his first thoughts was to buy some smart clothes, and the next time Collier saw him he was wearing 'a new hat and a very handsome blue cloak with velvet facings, the corner of which he threw over his shoulder *à l'Espagnol*'. He was in very good spirits, Collier thought, and as they walked together through Hungerford Market, Dickens stopped to buy a bag of cherries which he popped, one by one, into the mouth of a dirty little child that a coal-heaver was carrying over his shoulder.[3]

The high stamp duty imposed on newspapers made them extremely expensive at sevenpence a copy, and there were many of them competing for the readership of those who could afford to pay so high a price—nine in 1830, twenty-two by 1865. The daily circulation of the *Morning Chronicle* was only 6,000. But, even so, only *The Times* had a larger circulation, and *The Times* sold more copies than any other newspaper in Europe.[4] The *Chronicle* had an excellent reputation as an independent liberal paper with a fine standard of journalism, and Dickens felt justifiably proud to be working for it.

He was not kept in London to sit scribbling away in the Gallery, but was sent out to report political meetings and elections in the provinces. He went to Birmingham and Bristol. He followed Lord Grey to Edinburgh, and reported, with gusto, how the guests at a banquet, tired of waiting for the arrival of the guest of honour, fell upon 'the cold fowls, roast beef, lobster, and other tempting delicacies' to shouts of 'Shame!' from their fellow-guests, some of whom were munching away as hungrily as they were. He went up to Ipswich and Sudbury to report the elections of January 1835, and then into Essex, where he drove a gig at full gallop from Chelmsford to Braintree, 'tooling in and out of the banners, drums, conservative Emblems, horsemen, and go-carts, with which every little Green was filled. . . . Every time the horse heard a drum he bounced into the hedge, on the left side of the road; and every time I got him out of that, he bounded into the hedge on the right. . . .' A few weeks later he was in Devon recording Lord John Russell's speech in a pelting rainstorm in the castle yard at Exeter, and then galloping back to London with *The Times* reporters hard on his heels hoping to get their reports in first, and failing to do so.

This busy, exciting, competitive life was the very stimulant he needed to help him shake off the depressive effects of his recent gloom. Rattling across country on the top of a stage-coach; arriving at strange towns and strange inns in the middle of the night; playing bagatelle with other reporters in the bedroom of the White Hart, Kettering; making plans

'There never was anybody connected with newspapers, who, in this
same space of time, had so much express and post-chaise as I'

in the George and Pelican at Newbury to beat his rivals by the use of saddle horses and a chaise and four; writing letters in the Black Boy, Chelmsford, and reports in the Bush Inn, Bristol; eating a Christmas dinner of cod and oyster sauce, roast beef, a pair of ducks, plum pudding and mince-pies in Northamptonshire; watching the wild frenzy of the hustings, 'the bells ringing, candidates speaking, drums sounding, a band of *eight* trombones', and the voters, some of them 'drinking and guzzling and howling and roaring' and others being set upon by horsemen, '*led* by Clergymen and Magistrates'—'would you believe that I saw one of these fellows with my own eyes unbuckle one of his stirrup-leathers and cut about him in the crowd, with the iron part of it?'—compiling his vivid reports by the light of a guttering candle in the corner of a bar or in a swaying post-chaise, spending most of his time 'in such a chaotic spate of confusion, surrounded by maps, road-books, ostlers and post-boys' that he had 'not time to devote to anything but business'.[5]

There never was anybody connected with newspapers, who, in the same space of time, had so much express and post-chaise as I [he later told a friend, recalling those coaching days when a journey from London to Bristol, *via* Reading, Marlborough and Bath took thirteen hours by day and fourteen hours by night]. I have had to charge for the damage of a great coat from the drippings of a blazing wax candle, in writing through the smallest hours of the night in a swift-flying carriage and pair. I have had to charge for all sorts of breakages fifty times in a journey without question, such being the ordinary results of the pace which we went at. I have charged for broken hats, broken luggage, broken chaises, broken harness—everything but a broken head, which is the only thing they would have grumbled to pay for.[6]

Returning home from exciting political meetings in the country to the waiting Press in London [he continued, in a speech at an annual dinner of the Newspaper Press Fund], I do verily believe I have been upset in almost every description of vehicle known in this country. I have been, in my time, belated on miry by-roads, towards the small hours, forty or fifty miles from London, in a wheelless carriage, with exhausted horses and drunken post-boys and have got back in time for publication, to be received with never-forgotten compliments by the late Mr Black [editor of the *Morning Chronicle*] coming in the broadest of Scotch from the broadest of hearts I ever knew.[7]

2

It was not only the excitement and hustling competition of this new life as an active reporter, however, that was helping Dickens to get over the miseries Maria Beadnell had caused him: he was also deriving deep satisfaction from his successes in a different field.

Already, before he had been offered his job on the *Morning Chronicle*, he had written a humorous short story—using Marianne Leigh's coarse, loud-voiced father as a model for its most odious character, Octavius Budden of Poplar Walk—which, 'with fear and trembling' he had dropped one evening through the letter-box of the *Monthly Magazine*. This magazine did not pay its contributors, since it was hard put to it to meet its other costs, with a circulation of less than six hundred; and Dickens heard nothing from its proprietor as to whether or not he had accepted it.

When the new issue was on sale, Dickens walked into a bookshop in the Strand, paid his half-a-crown, and, with his heart beating wildly and his hand shaking with excitement, turned away to flip quickly over the pages. He had called the story 'A Sunday Out of Town', and there was no story of that name there. But, with its title changed to 'A Dinner at Poplar Walk', there it was, after all!

Overwhelmed with relief and pride and happiness he walked out of the shop and across the Strand and into Westminster Hall; and then for half-an-hour he walked up and down, his eyes brimming with tears.

Nor was this all, for the owner of the magazine now wrote to him and asked him for another contribution. Only too anxious to comply with so flattering a request, Dickens sent him one—this time using the scandal-mongering Mrs Leigh as a model for 'Mrs Joseph Porter Over the Way'. This, also, was accepted. And then Dickens sent two more; and then another, in two parts; and the second part, though the earlier stories had appeared without the author's name, he signed 'Boz'.

It was his youngest brother Augustus's nickname, given to him by Charles in its original form of Moses, 'in honour of the *Vicar of Wakefield*', a name which 'being facetiously pronounced through the nose, became Boses, and being shortened, became Boz'.

It was a pseudonym and the trademark of a distinctive style which soon became known to a far wider public than the readers of the *Monthly Mazagine*; for not only did other papers comment favourably upon the pieces that now regularly appeared there, not only did pirates adapt the stories for publication in similar periodicals and for the stage of the Adelphi Theatre, but the *Morning Chronicle* and then the *Evening Chronicle*, also, began printing the work of Boz, whose true identity no one troubled to conceal. On a visit to the *Morning Chronicle*'s offices, William Harrison

'He has described himself dropping this paper ['A Dinner at Poplar Walk', his first published piece] stealthily one evening at twilight, with fear and trembling, into a dark letter-box up a dark court in Fleet Street'

Ainsworth, whose novel *Rookwood*, based on an idealized version of the
Dick Turpin story, had recently been published, caught sight of his bright,
excited face, flashing eyes, and thick—but at that time still short—brown
hair, asked who he was, and was told that he was the well-known Boz.

Ainsworth, short, handsome, and dressed in a more self-consciously
elegant style than the younger Dickens could yet afford, went out of his
way to get to know this Boz. He asked him to dinner at his house,
Kensal Lodge near Willesden, where (with the help of a witty, malicious
woman who had once been married to his cousin and who now acted as
hostess in the absence of his wife from whom he was separated), Ainsworth entertained a gay circle of friends and acquaintances. These included
the young artist, Daniel Maclise (usually late), George Cruikshank
(often drunk), Benjamin Disraeli (in a gold waistcoat), Edward Bulwer
(as ornately bejewelled as his host), and, most important of all for Dickens,
John Macrone, Ainsworth's publisher.

One night as he was leaving Kensal Lodge Macrone suggested to
Dickens that they should walk back to Holborn together. On the way
Macrone complimented the young man on his sketches which he thought
were 'capital value'. Had he ever thought of collecting them together
in a book? If he wrote one or two new ones they might even fill two
volumes. Illustrated by Cruikshank, whose reputation had long since
been established, they might go very well. Dickens was elated by the
idea. He could certainly write more; he had numerous ideas which could
be worked up. Well, then, Macrone would pay him £150 for the
copyright of the first edition which he would bring out the following
year. It was agreed.[8]

For the time being, though, Dickens was finding it hard to live on his
salary. He had persuaded the *Chronicle* to give him another two guineas
a week for the articles he wrote for them in addition to his political
reporting—and seven guineas a week was a very good income indeed for
a young man of twenty-three in the 1830s—but he could only use part of
it on himself.

For his father was again in trouble. He had lost his job on the *Mirror
of Parliament*, and, although he had succeeded in getting another one on
the *Morning Herald*, he was heavily in debt, still borrowing money
which he had no expectation of being able to repay. Charles described
his behaviour to Kolle as 'the damnable shadow' over his life. But
concerned as he was by it, and conscious of the shameful methods his
father used in order to allay the apprehensions of his intended victims

and the impatience of his creditors, Charles still loved and, indeed, admired him. He was to hint at his foibles and absurdities, his pomposity, shabby gentility, wayward selfishness and financial irresponsibility in numerous character studies. But, at heart, he remained devoted to him. 'His industry has always been untiring', he wrote of him once in a commendation which his conduct could scarcely be said to justify. 'He never undertook any business, charge or trust, that he did not zealously, conscientiously, punctually, honourably discharge.'9

Charles could even find it in his heart to write with a kind of humorous tolerance of the ruses his father employed in extracting a loan from a newly discovered friend. Here is Montague Tigg borrowing, with flattering and reassuring cajolery, half a sovereign from the kind-hearted Tom Pinch:

'Sir,' [Tigg asks Pinch] 'you have been impressed by my friend Slyme?'

'Not very pleasantly, I must say,' answered Tom, after a little hesitation.

'I am grieved, but not surprised,' said Mr Tigg, detaining him by both lapels, 'to hear that you have come to that conclusion; for it is my own. But, Mr Pinch, though I am a rough and thoughtless man, I can honour Mind. I honour Mind in following my friend. To you of all men, Mr Pinch, I have a right to make appeal on Mind's behalf, when it has not the art to push its fortune in the world. And so, Sir—not for myself, who have no claim upon you, but for my crushed, my sensitive and independent friend, who has—I ask the loan of three half-crowns. I ask you for the loan of three half-crowns, distinctly, and without a blush. I ask it almost as a right. And when I add that they will be returned by post this week, I feel that you will blame me for that sordid stipulation.'

Mr Pinch took from his pocket an old-fashioned red-leather purse with a steel clasp, which had probably once belonged to his deceased grandmother. It held one half-sovereign and no more—all Tom's worldly-wealth until next quarter-day.

'Stay!' cried Mr Tigg, who had watched this proceeding keenly. 'I was just about to say that, for the convenience of posting, you had better make it gold. Thank you. A general direction I suppose to Mr Pinch, at Mr Pecksniff's—will that find you?'

'That'll find me,' said Tom. 'You had better put Esquire to Mr Pecksniff's name, if you please. Direct to me, you know, at Seth Pecksniff's, Esquire.'

'At Seth Pecksniff's, Esquire,' repeated Mr Tigg taking an exact note of it with a stump of pencil. 'We said this week I believe.'

'Yes; or Monday will do,' observed Tom.

'No, no, I beg your pardon. Monday will *not* do,' said Mr Tigg.

'If we stipulated for this week, Saturday is the latest day. Did we stipulate for this week?'

'Since you are so particular about it,' said Tom, 'I think we did.'

Mr Tigg added this condition to his memorandum; read the entry over to himself with a severe frown; and that the transaction might be the more correct and business-like, appended his initials to the whole. That done, he assured Mr Pinch, that everything was now perfectly regular; and, after squeezing his hand with great fervour, departed.*

After his father's death Dickens still wrote with amused tolerance of John Dickens's methods. He describes a begging letter addressed to Arthur Clennam from Edward Dorrit, which

set forth that Mr Clennam would, he knew, be gratified to hear that he had at length obtained permanent employment of a highly satisfactory nature, accompanied with every prospect of complete success in life; but that the temporary inability of his employer to pay his arrears of salary to that date (in which condition said employer had appealed to that generous forbearance in which he trusted he should never be wanting towards a fellow-creature), combined with the fraudulent conduct of a false friend, and the present high price of provisions, had reduced him to the verge of ruin, unless he could by a quarter before six that evening raise the sum of eight pounds. This sum, Mr Clennam would be happy to learn, he had, through the promptitude of several friends, who had a lively confidence in his probity, already raised, with the exception of a trifling balance of one pound seventeen and fourpence; the loan of which balance, for the period of one month, would be fraught with the usual beneficent consequences.†

When one of his creditors threatened to have John Dickens arrested Charles found the necessary money, borrowing what he could not raise himself, from a solicitor, Thomas Mitton, a friend he had made when they were clerks together at Charles Molloy's in Lincoln's Inn. But there were other impatient creditors, and no sooner had his father been saved from this one, than he was being pressed by another. By the end of 1834 he was again in a sponging house, having 'been arrested by Shaw and Maxwell, the quondam Wine People', of Woburn Place.

Charles had recently moved from the family house at 18 Bentinck Street to a set of third-floor rooms at 13 Furnival's Inn, High Holborn, 'a shady quiet place, occupied for the most part by unmarried lawyers, and echoing the footsteps of the stragglers who have business there, and rather monotonous and gloomy on summer evenings'.‡ [10] He had

---

* *Martin Chuzzlewit*, ch. VII.   † *Little Dorrit*, Bk. I, ch. XXII.
‡ *Martin Chuzzlewit*, ch. XLV.

had to pay £35 rent in advance; and now had nothing left to give his
father. Again he applied to Mitton, and with the loan that his friend
made him, a second loan from Thomas Beard, and what he himself
could provide by mortgaging his salary for the next fortnight, Charles
was able to save his father from prison once more.

But he knew that the improvident, generous, plausible man, who could
manage other people's business so much better than his own, and whose
wife's family had by now refused to have anything more to do with him,
would soon be in trouble again if he were allowed to go on living above
his means in Bentinck Street. So Charles found for his mother and the
younger children cheaper lodgings nearby, took his brother Frederick
to live with him in Furnival's Inn, and left his father to find a room in
Hampstead, where—from 'Mrs Davis's (laundress), North End'—he was
writing to Thomas Beard a few weeks later for a loan of two sovereigns.[11]

Having spent so much on his father, Charles could not afford to live
in much comfort in Furnival's Inn. He had no dishes, no curtains and no
carpets; one day when an American journalist, Nathaniel Parker Willis,
called with Macrone, unannounced and unexpected, he found that the
furniture in the 'bleak-looking' sitting-room comprised 'a deal table,
two or three chairs, a few books', and that was all. Dickens was wearing
a ragged office coat which he changed for a 'shabby blue'.[12]

He asked Henry Austin, a friend of his who was an architect, to share
the room with him as a means of economising, but nothing came of the
suggestion.

Charles, however, despite 'the damnable shadow' of his father's debts
and his own poverty, was far from depressed. He was making a name for
himself at last. And—as was to be expected after his days of yearning for
Maria Beadnell—he had fallen in love again.

While he was working on the *Mirror of Parliament* he had not, apparently, been able to reconcile himself to the loss of Maria. Indeed he had
not seemed even to want the company of any girls other than his sister
Fanny, and Anne Beadnell, at whose wedding to Henry Kolle he had
acted as best man. In a letter to the Kolles he had said that he had not
been to see them for a week because of the attraction of a 'very nice pair
of black eyes' which called him to his uncle's house at Norwood. But this
was more likely an excuse which he hoped would find its way to Anne's
sister, Maria, than a reference to any attachment he may have felt to
Lucina Pocock, a pretty girl who, after the separation of his aunt and
uncle five years before, had become his uncle's mistress.[13]

After this letter was written, however, Dickens had become a frequent visitor in another house where there were some young girls who did attract him very much. This was the shabby, untidy, happy-go-lucky home of George Hogarth, the Scottish editor of the *Evening Chronicle*. As Dickens proudly described him to his uncle, Mr Hogarth, though trained as a lawyer, was 'a gentleman who had recently distinguished himself by a celebrated work on music, who was the most intimate friend and companion of Sir Walter Scott, and one of the most eminent of the literati of Edinburgh'. This was a rather extravagant introduction; but Hogarth was certainly a man of some distinction, with undoubted talents as an editor and critic, who had enjoyed a close association with the intellectual society of Scotland. He had edited an anthology of writings by northern poets and authors as well as having written the *Musical History, Biography, and Criticism* which Dickens had mentioned in his letter to his uncle. He had, indeed, known Scott well; and his wife's father had been a friend of Burns.[14]

They had nine children. Catherine, the eldest daughter, was twenty. She was a good-looking plump girl with long glossy black hair, sleepy-lidded blue eyes, a small, red mouth and a slightly undershot chin. Her complexion was smooth and healthy, her breasts large and heavy, her movements sensually indolent. Her lazy grace and slow smile intrigued Dickens from the first. When he went out to see his kind and friendly editor at his house at 18 York Place, Fulham Road, he was always delighted to find her there. Soon he was in love with her and she with him. Although she was not as gay or as quick-witted or as lively as he was, she would sometimes burst into sudden laughter, as Dickens did himself; she could write a sprightly letter, and she was on occasions capable of making one of those outrageous puns that rarely failed to amuse him. Their affection for each other was increased and fortified by her family's liking for him, by their admiration of his striking looks and talent.

Her father believed him to be a young man of remarkable promise; her mother, to whom he was polite and attentive, grew fond of him; her eldest brother was taught shorthand by him; her eldest sister, Mary, who was fourteen, looked up to him in spellbound enchantment. When in the spring of 1835 Charles asked Catherine to marry him, the whole family was delighted.

7

MISS CATHERINE HOGARTH
1835-1836
aet. 23-24

II SELWOOD PLACE QUEEN'S ELM BROMPTON NEAR LONDON

If the representations I have so often made to you, about my working as a duty, and not as a pleasure, be not sufficient to keep you in the good humour, which you, of all people in the World should preserve—why then my dear, you must be out of temper, and there is no help for it.

The Letters of Charles Dickens

7

Soon after his engagement Dickens thought that he detected, slumbering beneath the apparent placidity of Catherine Hogarth's nature, a tendency to petulance and sulky irritation. This was something which he immediately made it clear to her that he was not going to tolerate. He was already a very different young man from the lovesick stenographer whose feelings had been so mauled by the offhand disrespect of Maria Beadnell; he wrote to Catherine to reprimand her for a 'sudden and uncalled for coldness . . . a sullen and inflexible obstinacy', which he had, to his regret, discovered in her attitude towards him.

With a magisterial, aloof austerity he told her: 'If a *hasty* temper produces this strange behaviour, acknowledge it when I give you the opportunity—not once or twice, but again and again. If a feeling of you know not what—a capricious restlessness of you can't tell what, and a desire to tease, you don't know why, give rise to it—overcome it; it will never make you more amiable, I more fond, or either of us more happy.' He was not writing in this tone to hurt her, or to make her resentful, but to make her realise that he could not turn away and forget a slight from her as he might do from another girl to whom he was not so deeply attached. 'If you knew the intensity of the feeling which has led me to forget all my friends and pursuits to spend my days at your side . . . you could more readily understand the extent of the pain so easily inflicted, but so difficult to be forgotten.' If she had grown tired of him already, she had but to say so. 'I shall not forget you lightly, but you will need no second warning. . . . I am *not* angry, but I *am* HURT . . .'¹

Evidently Catherine apologised. But six months later he felt obliged to write to her in the same vein. And once again, it seems that she apologised.

Charles was immediately mollified, satisfied and forgiving. Her ready apologies, he told her, displayed 'all that amiable and excellent feeling which I know you possess, and in which I believe from my heart, you are unrivalled. If you would only determine to *show* the same affection and kindness to me, when you feel disposed to be ill-tempered, I declare unaffectedly I should have no one solitary fault to find with you.

Your asking me to love you "once more" is quite unnecessary—*I have*
NEVER *ceased to love you for one moment since I knew you; nor shall I.*'²

And so they continued to be happy and affectionate. His letters were
full of lavish endearments. He called her his 'own dearest love', his 'more
than life', his 'dearest Mouse', his 'dearest darling Pig'. He signed himself,
'ever yours unchangeably'. 'I have not seen you, you know, dearest, since
seven O clock yesterday evening', he would complain. 'It seems an age.'
He sent her '99000000000000000000000000000000000000000 kisses'.

Since it was such a long way to travel after a day's hard work from
High Holborn to Brompton, and since he did not like her 'traversing the
West End of London, of all other parts, accompanied only by Fred'—
whom he sent to her with messages, asking her to come to his rooms—he
decided to take lodgings in Selwood Place, Queen's Elm, near her house
in York Place. He hoped to be able to sublet his rooms in Furnival's Inn,
which the porter assured him he would be able to do quite easily, but he
did not manage to find a subtenant and he was left with two rents to pay
until his lease expired at Christmas.

The rooms he took in Brompton were a great convenience to him,
though. Sometimes, chaperoned by her sister Mary, Kate would come
round to have breakfast with him there. But often he was so busy that he
could not spare the time to sit with her for long, and some days he had so
much to do that he could not get away from his work to see her at all.
In the early weeks of their engagement he had taken her often to the
theatre, but now he could rarely do so. And she, put out by what she
affected to believe was a preference on his part for staying away from her,
said that he was making her unhappy and 'coss'.

Less riled by this than her former 'sudden and uncalled for coldness',
which had both hurt his pride and denied his urgent need to be wanted
and loved, Charles was, nevertheless, cross in return.

> You may be disappointed:—I would rather you would—at not seeing
> me [he wrote]; but you cannot feel vexed at my doing my best with
> the stake I have to play for—you and a home for both of us. . . . I
> perceive you have not yet subdued one part of your disposition—your
> distrustful feelings and want of confidence. . . . I love you far too well
> to feel hurt by what in any one else would have annoyed me greatly. . . .
> Believe me (if you have any faith in your nature). Ever yours most
> sincerely and affectionately.³

Another evening he told her that he had not written enough to justify
his coming out, and went on: 'If the representations I have so often made

to you, about my working as a duty, and not as a pleasure, be not sufficient to keep you in the good humour, which you, of all people in the World should preserve—why then my dear, you must be out of temper, and there is no help for it.'⁴

The trouble was not so much that her being 'coss' irritated him—he, too, could use baby-talk and facetious spellings in his letters—nor that he minded that she confessed herself out of temper not to see more of him; it was that she did not seem to understand how important his work was to him, how essential it was for him to deny himself 'the least recreation and to sit chained' to his table.

When she contracted scarlet fever in the autumn of 1835 he called repeatedly to ask how she was and sent Fred to her with a jar of black-currant jam to soothe her painful throat, and some chloride of lime for 'purifying the atmosphere' of her room. But her too obvious desire for sympathy and her implied complaint that he did not do all that he might to console her, wrung from him the exasperated retort that 'it is very hard to preach consolation when one stands in no small need of it oneself. . . . Indeed, my dearest girl, your situation is almost an enviable one compared with mine.'

That was the real problem: he had undertaken far too much work. And his anxiety to get it all done, together with the worry that his father, once more in difficulties, was still causing him, had brought on a fresh recurrence of his childhood illness. Working till three o'clock in the morning, he suffered from dreadful headaches, dizziness and extreme physical inertia. One night he was prostrated by an 'exquisite torture from the spasm' in his side 'far exceeding anything' he had ever known before; and on another occasion when walking down Knightsbridge, so he told Kate, 'my head was so extremely bad, and the dizziness affected my sight so much that I could scarcely see at all, in addition to which cheerful symptoms, my tottering legs gave me the appearance of being particularly drunk'.⁵

The amount of work that he had agreed to do was truly formidable. There were not only the additional articles and stories to do to fill the two volumes of *Sketches* for Macrone, including such items as 'A visit to Newgate', which would mean a good deal of time spent collecting material; there were not only the announcements of the book to prepare for the newspapers, and the advertisements to draw up with Macrone. He had agreed to write the libretto for an operetta planned by a young composer, John Hullah, who had been at the Academy of Music with

Fanny; he had promised to write a one-act farce for the actor John Pritt Harley; he was already contributing a series of sketches to *Bell's Life in London*; and he was still writing for the *Chronicle*.(6) Then, immediately after the publication of the first volume of *Sketches by Boz* on 7 February 1836, he accepted a proposal from Messrs Chapman and Hall to write a serial to be published in twenty monthly instalments of twelve thousand words each.

2

This last offer came to him while the first exciting reviews of the *Sketches* were still running through his brain, filling him with pleasure and pride. For nearly all the critics agreed that the book marked the appearance of a new and original talent. Boz's exact observation of character and manners, of the streets and shops, inns and pleasure-gardens of London; a childlike wonder combined with an adult penetration; a sure eye for the grotesque, the pretentious and the absurd, were all widely praised. The *Satirist*, in a characteristic review, said that the *Sketches* were 'in their way inimitable', and that Boz was a 'man of unquestionable talent and of great and correct observation'. The first impression of the book was soon followed by three more.[7]

Elated by his triumph, and conscious now of his worth—the 'great success' of his book had established a name for him 'among the publishers', he told one of his uncles—Dickens would only agree to do the serial for Chapman and Hall on his own terms.

Originally the idea had been for him to write the text to accompany a series of drawings depicting the misadventures of a club of cockney sportsmen by a well-known comic artist, Robert Seymour. This was the proposition which William Hall, junior partner of Chapman and Hall, put to him at his rooms in Furnival's Inn three days after the *Sketches by Boz* had appeared. But Dickens immediately demurred. He did not know much about field sports, and he thought Seymour's idea a pretty hackneyed one anyway. Surely it would be better for him to write what he pleased, take his readers through a much wider range of scenes, and give them a far more varied selection of characters? He expected, in fact, that whatever he agreed to, he would end up going his own way in any case.

He seemed to entertain no doubt that Mr Hall would, and should, agree to his terms, no apprehension that he might be thought a little presumptuous. His self-possession was complete.

It was not the first time that he had behaved in this way, and shown this self-absorbed assurance. When the composer, John Hullah, had come to him with the idea for the operetta, it was to have a Venetian setting and be called *The Gondolier*. Dickens told Hullah that he preferred an English to an Italian setting, rustic characters to sophisticated ones, and he eventually produced the libretto for an operetta which he called *The Village Coquettes*. When Cruikshank had been rather slow in completing the plates for *Sketches by Boz*, Dickens had not troubled to disguise his impatience and had advised Macrone that the distinguished artist, twenty years his senior, 'required the spur'. And when the proprietor of the *Morning Chronicle* required his reporters to sign a new service agreement it was Dickens who, despite his youth, organised the strike against it.

So now with William Hall, Dickens waited for the publisher to give way—and he did give way. It was agreed that Dickens's text should govern Seymour's plates and not the other way round, that the author would be paid £14 for each instalment, and that these instalments would be in the publishers' hands five weeks before they were due to come out rather than the longer time which Chapman and Hall had originally stipulated.[8]

It was all fixed up within two days. And immediately, Dickens set his lively mind to work on the scheme of the book, which had so far only been mentioned in the 'vaguest terms'. Suddenly, so he said, he 'thought of Pickwick'.[9]

The work would be no joke, Dickens told Catherine, but the payment was 'too temping to resist'. Adding it to the seven guineas a week from the *Chronicle*, he was now assured of a regular income of nearly eleven pounds a week, not counting the extra money he earned from his other writings. Now at last they could make definite plans to get married.

3

In the middle of February, Charles moved to bigger and sunnier chambers in Furnival's Inn, paying a rent of £50 a year for three third-floor rooms and a kitchen in the basement; and he decided that they would begin their married life there. They were really bachelors' chambers; but his mother helped him to make them more suitable for a married couple to live in, while he himself went out to buy various things to make the place look less bleak, including 'a pair of quart Decanters, and a pair of pints, a chrystal [*sic*] Jug, and three brown dittos with plated tops,

for beer and hot water, a pair of Lustres, and two *magnificent* china
Jars'.

After all, as he wrote to remind her, Catherine had often told him that
she could be happy anywhere with him, so presumably she would not
mind living in a bachelor's apartment. He had looked at some houses in
the new streets in Pentonville, where he had gone one day in order to
persuade Cruikshank to hurry up with his plates; but the cheapest was
more than he could yet afford, taking into account all the costs of removal
and the ever-threatening danger that he might have to rescue his father
again at any moment. In any case, as he complained, he really did not have
time to go out looking for decent houses that he might get for less.

The date of the marriage was fixed for 2 April 1836, and Charles had
so much work to get through before then that he rarely left his rooms.
Confined there, writing hard and suffering from the colds which he
caught one after the other that spring, he wrote constantly to his 'ever
dearest Katie', his 'darling Tatie', his 'dearest Wig' and 'Titmouse', to
explain and apologise:

> A note and not me. I am very—very—sorry. . . . If you are unjust
> enough to be cross, I will not deprecate your anger, or ill humour. I
> have at least equal reason to be so; forced as I am to deny myself the
> least recreation, and to sit chained to my table, when a regard for my
> own health, or my own wishes, would move me away. . . . Not 'coss',
> I hope? . . . Not low this morning, I hope?—You ought not to be, dear
> Mouse, and are very ungrateful if you are.[10]

Whether or not she was low that morning, she was very happy on her
wedding-day. It was a small, quiet wedding. Dickens had first asked
Macrone to be his best man, but since 'the ladies insisted' that he '*must*
be attended to the place of execution by a single man', he had invited
Thomas Beard instead. Beard and Macrone were the only two guests who
were not members of either family, and this was the one and only thing
about the wedding that stayed in the best man's memory. While almost
all that another guest could recall was that the reception was held at the
Hogarths' house, 'then standing opposite orchards and [market] gardens
as far as the eye could reach', that the speeches were unexceptional and
short, and that everybody seemed happy, 'not the least so Dickens and his
young girlish wife'.[11]

8

THE INIMITABLE BOZ
1836-1837
aet. 24-25

15 FURNIVAL'S INN HIGH HOLBORN LONDON

If I were to live a hundred years and write three novels in each, I should never be so proud of any of them as I am of Pickwick; feeling as I do, that it has made its own way, and hoping, as I must own I do hope, that long after my hand is as withered as the pens it held, Pickwick will be found on many a dusty shelf with many a better work.

The Letters of Charles Dickens

8

1

Catherine Hogarth was only twenty at the time of her marriage. Dickens was twenty-four. He took her away, after the reception, to a little cottage in the village of Chalk near Chatham. There, for the single week of their honeymoon, they were alone together for the first and only time in their lives. He had longed for this, as he had often told her, and confessed himself 'in a fever' to be with her. It was not only that he was passionately impatient to make love to her, he had a deep and urgent need for the comfort of warm, absorbed devotion. How eagerly he had told her, did he long to be in her company. 'I wish you were a fixture here—I should like to have you by me SO much.'

'How much delight it would afford me to be able to turn around to you at our own fireside when my work is done', he wrote in another letter, 'and seek in your kind looks and gentle manner the recreation and happiness which the moping solitude of chambers can never afford.'[1] This sort of admiring, comforting, reassuring companionship his mother, he felt, had denied him, and his sister Fanny had only offered him as a child.

But now, as well as his pretty young wife, there was also her sister Mary.

Mary came to stay with them in Furnival's Inn soon after they returned from their honeymoon. She was now sixteen. A portrait of her done about this time by Hablot Knight Browne (the 'Phiz' who illustrated the later numbers of *Pickwick* and several of Dickens's other books) indicates that she did not have her sister's voluptuous good looks; but Dickens thought her beautiful, and considered Browne's portrait to be 'worthless' as 'a record of that dear face'. During his engagement, when he had felt he should arrange for a chaperone, he had included Mary in invitations to Kate almost as a matter of course, and now that he was married it evidently never occurred to him that he might see her less often. She was gay and lively and understanding, and she surrounded him with the comfort and the stimulus of heartfelt and inextinguishable admiration. 'Winning, happy and amiable', she sympathised with all his thoughts and feelings more than anyone he had ever known or ever would know. 'So perfect a creature', he thought, 'never breathed.'[1]

Kate was not in the least jealous, it seems. The two sisters had always been devoted to each other, and so they always remained. The month they all spent together at Furnival's Inn after the honeymoon was a time of real happiness.

A most delightfully happy month, [Mary called it when writing breathlessly to a cousin that spring]. I only wish you could see dearest Katherine in her own house! . . . She makes a most capital housekeeper and is as happy as the day is long—I think they are more devoted than ever since their Marriage if that be possible—I am sure you would be delighted with him he is such a nice creature and so clever he is courted and made up to by all the literary Gentleman, and has more to do in that way than he can well manage. . . . It is not exactly a house but a suite of rooms opening from one to another they were formerly a set of Chambers which Charles had for 3 years, and they thought it would be a very nice and prudent way of beginning by staying out the expiration of his time, they have furnished them most tastefully and elegantly, the drawing-room with Rose-wood, the dining-room with Mahagony furniture—I hope you are fully satisfied with *this* description.[3]

Dickens, for his part, would never be 'so happy again as in those Chambers three Stories high', he wrote in his diary after he had left them, remembering a day when he and Mary had wandered up and down Holborn looking in the secondhand furniture shops for a table for Kate's bedroom; 'never so happy again—never if I roll in wealth and fame. I would hire them to keep them empty, if I could afford it'.[4]

But it was the memory of Mary there that made him think of them with such deep and lasting affection; and Kate, though she had never shown any resentment towards her more lively, more intelligent and more entertaining sister, was forced in the end to realise this.

2

A few weeks before his marriage, he had confidently and proudly written to Chapman and Hall to tell them that *Pickwick* was begun 'in all his might and glory'. But the opening numbers had not been received with anything like the enthusiasm that had greeted *Sketches by Boz*; and the sales were equally disappointing. The first number was limited to a mere four hundred copies, and although a wholesale bookseller advised printing an additional 1,500 copies of the subsequent numbers and distributing them on a 'sale or return' basis in the provinces, all but about fifty of them came back each month. Then, in the week after his return from his honeymoon, came an even greater disaster: Robert Seymour committed suicide.

Ever since the artist's idea had been taken over and transformed by this self-confident young writer, Seymour's life had been made miserable. He had never had much self-confidence himself. An illegitimate child, he has been brought up in a working-class family and had had little education. His bad writing and worse spelling had caused him much humiliation; and though he had had a picture exhibited at the Royal Academy in 1822, his later offerings had been rejected. Determined to make a name and a good living for himself in a different line, he had been overworking for years and had already had a nervous breakdown in 1830.

When Dickens wrote to him to tell him that his drawing for the first interpolated story in *Pickwick*—the melodramatic 'Stroller's Tale'—was not quite the author's idea, it seemed to Seymour the final insult. He had not wanted to do the illustration, anyway: the subject was quite outside his normal field, and had nothing whatever to do with the agreed theme of the book. And now here was the young man writing to him: 'The alteration I want I will endeavour to explain. I think the woman should be younger—the "dismal man" certainly should, and he should be less miserable in appearance. To communicate an interest in the plate, his whole appearance should express more sympathy and solicitude: and while I represented the sick man as emaciated and dying, I would not make him too repulsive. The furniture of the room you have depicted, admirably'. (The furniture consisted of a bed, a table, a chair and a broken stool.) Seymour resignedly agreed to do another plate; and when he had done so, he went out to his summerhouse, put the muzzle of a fowling-piece in his mouth and blew his brains out. He left a note for the 'best and dearest of wives' asking her not to blame herself, or anyone else, for his death.

It was a tragedy which immediately put *Pickwick* in jeopardy. The serial could not continue without an artist; and could a suitable one be found in the short time available? Even if one were to be found, would it not be wiser to abandon the whole series which had not yet justified much hope for its success?

Dickens, at least, was determined that *Pickwick* must go on. He had married on the expectation of the money that the serial would bring him; and he could not afford to lose that money now. He told Chapman and

Hall that he would write a further 4,000 words for each instalment so that the number of plates in each issue could be reduced from four to two. For this additional text he would only charge them an extra guinea, until the sales improved, instead of the three guineas to which he would have been entitled on the basis of the original contract. Chapman and Hall agreed to this. But, whether for two plates or four, an artist still had to be found.

Cruikshank was too busy. A young artist, William Makepeace Thackeray —later to illustrate his own book, *Vanity Fair*—was suggested; but although, after an interview with Dickens, he was so sure he had been chosen that he took a fellow-artist out to a celebratory supper of sausages and mashed potatoes, his drawings were ultimately rejected by the author as unsuitable. Robert William Buss, a portrait painter who had exhibited several humorous narrative pictures for the Royal Academy, was then approached; but he, although a good wood-engraver, had no experience in etching, and, work as he would night and day for three weeks, he could not master the new technique in time. So, to his indignant fury—he had abandoned all his other work, including a painting for the Royal Academy, on the strength of what he had taken to be a definite agreement with Chapman and Hall—Buss was told his services were not required.

Instead, the shy and diffident twenty-year-old Hablot Knight Browne —the artist who had shared with Thackeray that celebratory supper of sausages and mashed potatoes—was given the contract and produced some ideal etchings which he signed 'Nemo', a name which he later changed to 'Phiz'.

So *Pickwick* could go on. But there were still no signs that he would go on successfully. And Dickens, though he did not show any symptoms of a failing confidence, threw himself into other work. He produced at furious speed a political pamphlet, *Sunday Under Three Heads*, a passionately humanitarian attack upon the canting righteousness of those evangelical clergy he had come to detest in his childhood, and upon a parliamentary Bill—defeated without difficulty in the Commons, in fact, before the pamphlet was published—which, with the support of these dissenting clergy, sought to prohibit Sunday recreations as well as Sunday labour. He worked hard to revise the operetta, *The Village Coquettes*. He rushed about collecting material for a second series of *Sketches by Boz*. He agreed in May to deliver by the end of August the manuscript of a novel to be entitled *Gabriel Varden, the Locksmith of London*, for which Macrone was to pay him £200 for the copyright of the first edition of 1,000 copies and half the shares of the net profits on any additional copies. And all the time he remained on the staff of the *Chronicle*, liable to be sent anywhere in the country as their star reporter.

But it was his work on *Pickwick* which was closest to his heart and in which his dearest hopes were centred; and in the summer these hopes were realised. After reading the fourth instalment, the editor of the influential *Literary Gazette* wrote to congratulate him on the creation of a new character who had made his appearance cleaning boots in the yard of the White Hart, Southwark. By then, indeed, the story had already begun to catch the public fancy.

Soon the sales were approaching 40,000 copies a month, and Samuel Pickwick was a household name. His unprecedented popularity struck across all barriers of class and age and intellect; workmen who could not afford to buy a shilling number shared in the cost of a library subscription so that one of them could read it out to the others; 'all the boys and girls talk his fun—the boys in the streets', Mary Russell Mitford wrote to a friend; 'and yet they who are of the highest taste like it most'. Doctors read it in their carriages between patient and patient; judges read it on the Bench. Critics compared him favourably with Smollett, Cervantes and Sir Walter Scott. There were Pickwick hats and Pickwick coats and Pickwick canes, Pickwick cigars and Pickwick furnishing fabrics, *Pickwick Comic Almanacs* and *Pickwick Jest Books*. Pickwick plays were performed in the theatre, and Pickwick plagiarisms appeared on the bookstalls. As each monthly part came out, long extracts were printed in most of the cheap periodicals.

There were those, of course, who derided all this 'Bozomania', and viewed with distaste what they took to be the undignified behaviour of the theatrically dressed young man who had brought it about. When *The Village Coquettes* was performed that winter at the St James's Theatre and a part of the audience called for the author, Dickens, dressed in the 'very height of the existing fashion' and with 'long brown hair falling in silky masses over his temples', actually appeared, to the 'utter amazement' of the *Morning Herald*. He was severely criticised for thus defying the customs of the time, for exhibiting himself in this way and for being so 'extremely ill-advised to come forward to receive the congratulations of a *packed* house'. It was felt that the house must certainly have been packed, for how otherwise account for the loud calls for the author of what was, in fact, a thoroughly bad libretto. 'When will this ridiculous nonsense end?' asked the *Literary Gazette*. 'Will they have Bulwer on the Covent Garden stage next Wednesday at the close of "La Valliere"?'(5)

'Bad as the opera is,' another paper commented, 'we feel assured that if Mr Braham [the popular and rich tenor who had built the St James's in fourteen weeks in 1831 for £26,000] will make arrangements to parade the real living "Boz" every night after the opera, he will ensure for it a certain attraction.' To others it seemed that the very form in which Boz's novel was appearing was, in itself, a vulgar method of publication. It was not a new method, for Pierce Egan's *Tom and Jerry* had been issued in instalments. But it was mostly used for popular reprints; and the usually accepted manner of producing a new novel was to issue it in three volumes at one and a half guineas for the calf-bound set.[6]

Dickens, though, cared nothing for these customary proprieties. He wanted *Pickwick* to make money, and to reach as wide a public as possible, and if it could be helped to achieve these ends by coming out as a serial and by being advertised by his personal appearance on the stage of the St James's Theatre, he was certainly not going to be conventional or modest. It might not be in the best of taste to behave in this way, but then, as George Santayana has said, Dickens had more genius than taste. Besides, he liked appearing on the stage, anyway.

Yet although he enjoyed showing himself to his public and feeling the warmth of their admiration, and although he was content that his work should appear in instalments bound between paper covers, he was anxious that *Pickwick* should not merely be a means to early fame and financial security. Well aware that Boz had suddenly become the most famous young author in London, he was aware, too, that he was writing a book whose popularity would outlive him. 'If I were to live a hundred years and write three novels in each,' he told Chapman and Hall, 'I should never be so proud of any of them as I am of Pickwick, feeling as I do, that it has made its own way, and hoping, as I must own I do hope, that long after my hand is as withered as the pens it held, Pickwick will be found on many a dusty shelf with many a better work.'[7]

With the critics now almost all agreed that *Pickwick* was the comic masterpiece he felt it to be himself, his confidence in his talents was complete. When Cruikshank suggested some changes in the text of the second series of *Sketches by Boz*, he told Macrone that he long suspected that Cruikshank was mad, and went on:

If you have any further communication with him, you will greatly oblige me by saying *from me* that I am very much amused at the notion of his altering my Manuscript, and that had it fallen into his hands, I should have preserved his emendations as 'curiosities of Literature'. Most decidedly am I of opinion that he may just go to the Devil. . . .

I think it is a great question whether it requires any illustrations at all, but if so, I think my Pickwick man had better do them, as he is already favourably known to the public, by his connection with that immortal gentleman.[8]

Confident as he was, however, he felt unable to relax or lessen his rate of work or refuse any offers of additional work that came to him. At the beginning of August he accepted a commission to write a series of short sketches for the *Carlton Chronicle*; a week later he agreed to do a children's book, *Solomon Bell, the Raree Showman*, for £100, and, although he had promised *Gabriel Vardon* by the end of November, he said that he would deliver this new children's book by Christmas.

Then, in the middle of the month, he was negotiating with a different publisher, Richard Bentley, for a novel 'to form three Volumes of 320 pages each and 25 lines in each page'. Bentley offered £400 for the copyright; but Dickens replied that his friends had advised him he ought to have £500.

I have thought the matter over deliberately [he went on], and when I take into consideration, the time, the labour, the casting about, in every direction, for materials: the anxiety I should feel to make it a work on which I might build my fame, and the great probability of its having a very large sale (we are justified in forming our judgment upon the rapid sale of *everything* I have yet touched) I think you will not object to raising your terms thus far. . . . Recollect that you are dealing with an Author not quite unknown, but who, so far as he has gone, has been most successful.[9]

Bentley gave way, consented to pay the additional £100 once the sales had exceeded 1,450 copies, and the contract was signed five days later. No date for the delivery of the manuscript was agreed upon; but Dickens said that he would not undertake any other 'literary production' until he had finished it, and bound himself to offer his next novel to Bentley on the same terms.

Despite this immense amount of commissioned work, Dickens did not yet feel able to give notice to the *Morning Chronicle*. That autumn, however, he was offered £20 a month to edit a new magazine, which Bentley was proposing to launch under the title of *Bentley's Miscellany*, and a further twenty guineas for his own contribution of sixteen pages to each month's issue. And on the strength of this regular additional salary, which would raise his assured income to £15 a week, he decided to hand his resignation in to the *Chronicle*.

By doing so he annoyed the *Chronicle*'s proprietor, who accused him of discourtesy in not having come to see him before leaving the office, and by undertaking this new work for Bentley he angered Macrone who foresaw that *Gabriel Vardon* would now be forgotten.

He and Macrone and their two families had been on the friendliest terms ever since *Sketches by Boz* had been published, and during a conversation that summer Dickens had gathered that Macrone would not hold him to the contract which they had made before *Pickwick*'s great success. But Macrone did not agree he had ever released Dickens from his undertaking and he was determined that the contract should be fulfilled. He called upon Harrison Ainsworth for his advice.

Ainsworth, who had himself refused offers from Bentley rather than leave his original publisher, told Macrone that he did not think Dickens had any right to break the contract, although he sympathised with Dickens in having to do the book for £200 when he could now command four times as much. He asked Macrone not to tell Dickens what he said, but he advised him to go to his solicitor. Eventually Macrone agreed to cancel the contract on condition that for £100 Dickens sold him the entire copyright of *Sketches by Boz*, in which he at present held the copyright of the first edition only.

But the quarrel did not end here. For now that Macrone could do what he liked with the *Sketches* he made plans to reissue them in monthly parts with green covers like the *Pickwick* covers. Dickens, fearful of the effect this would have upon the sales of *Pickwick*, strongly protested and said that if Macrone did, in fact, reissue the *Sketches* in this way, he would advertise everywhere that it was being done against his wishes and without any profit to himself.

Macrone refused to give way, arguing that Dickens had sold the copyright to get out of having to write the novel he had contracted to do; and so why should not he, as a publisher, make a perfectly legitimate profit out of his new investment?[10]

3

In his anxiety Dickens turned to a man who was to become his closest friend, a man whose advice many other writers, from Charles Lamb and Leigh Hunt to Landor, Tennyson, Browning, Bulwer Lytton and

Carlyle, all came to trust. 'Whenever anybody is in a scrape we all fly to him for refuge', Thackeray said. 'He is omniscient and works miracles.'

This man, John Forster, had been born in the same year as Dickens at Newcastle-on-Tyne, where his father was in an indifferent way of business as a cattle-dealer and butcher. He was educated, first at Newcastle Grammar School and then at University College, London, at the expense of an uncle. At the age of sixteen he became a law student at the Inner Temple, but four years later he had abandoned his prospects of a career at the bar to become dramatic critic of the *True Sun*. By 1830 his name as a highly talented journalist had been established, and he was the chief literary critic of an influential journal, *The Examiner*. When Dickens first met him, this short, thickset, pugnaciously good-looking young man was already one of the leading figures in the literary life of London.

Talkative, opinionated, bossy and assertive, Forster had nevertheless a wide circle of friends who were prepared to overlook his pompous, overbearing manner, his hypersensitive jealousy and notorious rudeness, because of his standing and perception as a critic, the fundamental warmth of his nature, and the tireless energy he devoted to promoting their interests. There was much to overlook, though. He could not bear to be contradicted, and was often heard shouting across a dinner-table, 'Monstrous!', 'Intolerable!', 'Incredible!', 'Don't tell me!', and then, when he had reduced his opponent to exasperated silence, he would repeat his own opinions in his loud mocking voice and end the discussion with a prolonged snort of derisive laughter, a 'horse-laugh' in Macready's opinion, a 'rhinoceros laugh' in Browning's.

Thackeray thought that a dinner party at which Forster did not behave in this way, at which he did not, in fact, say 'a single rude thing during the whole evening!' was worthy of special record. It was, indeed, rare enough. When Richard Bentley met Forster for the first time at a dinner party, the 'ill-mannered man broke up the pleasure of the party' by his rude remarks to several of the guests, 'so markedly rude as almost to precipitate personal violence'. With the aristocracy, for whose company he early developed a strong *penchant*, he behaved more circumspectly. And, although it was true that those who knew him best recognised the kindness and deep tenderness of his nature, his pretensions in public were undeniable.

These pretensions were easily ridiculed. People said that the way he came into a room with his hand on his heart, prefacing his opening remarks with some such phrase as, 'Believe me, I feel it sensibly . . .' or 'It is with infinite regret . . .', he reminded them of no one so much as Macready making an entrance on to a stage. And at dinner parties in his own house, at 58 Lincoln's Inn Fields, he provided those who disliked him with plenty of stories to his discredit. 'Good heavens, sir!' he was once heard shouting to his servant when he noticed that Count D'Orsay's fish was butterless, 'Good heavens, sir! Butter for the Count's flounders!'

'Mary,' he commanded on another occasion, 'Carrots!' There were no carrots, the maid told him. 'Mary,' he replied, waving her away with lordly assurance, 'Let there be carrots!'

Dickens enjoyed retelling these stories against his friend, and, in particular, describing how Forster had answered the question, 'How much do you pay for your champagne?' by turning to his butler and demanding with grave concern, 'Henry, how much do I pay for my champagne?', and how the butler had replied, quite as ponderously, ' 'Alf a guinea a bottle'.

But although he could laugh with an affectionate indulgence at Forster, although he was to become wary of his proprietorial patronage, and irritated by his wearisome, self-opinionated manner of denying a thing and thereby supposing that he had altogether put it out of existence, Dickens from the first recognised in him a 'dear and trusty friend'.

In *Our Mutual Friend* he may have intended to ridicule Forster's mannerisms in the character of Podsnap who, 'happily acquainted with his own merit and importance, settled that whatever he put behind him he put out of existence. . . . "I don't want to know about it; I don't choose to discuss it; I don't admit it!" Mr Podsnap had even acquired a peculiar flourish of his right arm in often clearing the world of its most difficult problems by sweeping them behind him (and consequently sheer away) with those words and a flushed face.'*

Yet Dickens, irritated by him as he often was, and happier as he was to be in later years in the gayer, less demanding company of the younger Wilkie Collins, never underestimated the value of Forster's friendship. For boorish as he could be at a dinner party and in a crowded room, in private he was kind, understanding and sympathetic, impulsively generous and capable of feeling as deeply for his friends in their misfortunes as for himself in his own. 'A most sterling man,' Bulwer Lytton thought him, 'with an intellect at once massive and delicate. Few indeed have his strong practical sense and sound judgment. . . . There is no safer adviser about literary work . . . no more refined critic.'[11]

* *Our Mutual Friend*, Bk. I, ch. XI.

It was this sound judgment which Dickens was repeatedly to call upon in the future. On the first occasion on which he had cause to seek his help—when Macrone announced his intention of reissuing the *Sketches* in monthly parts—Forster could not do much to help him. Macrone refused to reconsider his decision, and only gave way when Chapman and Hall advanced Dickens £2,250 to buy back the copyright he had sold for £100 a few months before. Forster thought the price 'exorbitant' and advised Dickens to 'keep quiet for a time' until Macrone realised that he had opened his mouth too wide. But it was not in Dickens's nature to keep quiet when there was something to be settled. Far too impatient to bide his time, he sought always to have problems settled there and then. And so Macrone was paid his £2,250 and Dickens got back his copyright.

Although he had been no party to the conclusion of this transaction—and was glad not to have been in view of the purchase price—from now on Forster was trusted by Dickens to act for him in all his negotiations. Indeed, Dickens valued his advice so highly and felt him to be so closely in tune with the tastes of his public, that he rarely let any of his work go to the printer until his friend had seen and commented upon it in manuscript.

4

The work that Dickens had at present on hand included not only the *Pickwick Papers*, still going strong in their monthly instalments, but also *Oliver Twist*, now appearing, also in monthly parts, in *Bentley's Miscellany*. He had thrown himself heart and soul into this new book, he told Bentley, and 'most confidently' believed he would make a success of it.

He was quite right. Although a very different kind of novel from *Pickwick*, although its background and characters were in such sharp contrast to those his readers had learned to expect from him, it helped to increase the circulation of the magazine until its publishers were 'fairly inundated with *orders*'.

Hard as he threw himself into his work, however, he threw himself with equal vigour into the pleasures of his success. He attended a series of literary dinners in the 'red room' of Bentley's offices in New Burlington Street; he joined the Garrick Club; he dined at Kensal Lodge; he danced quadrilles at the Chapmans' house; and he went to a succession of parties, from one of which he arrived home 'dead drunk', so he told Thomas Beard when inviting him to share a Christmas turkey with him at Furnival's Inn, 'and was put to bed by my loving missis'.

Kate did not often go out with him, even to private parties, for she was pregnant. The baby, a boy, was born on 6 January 1837, nine months after their wedding. He was christened Charles, after his father, Culliford, in deference to his Grandmother Dickens's family, and Boz, apparently because his Grandfather Dickens excitedly shouted out this name at the christening.[12]

Both Kate's mother and her mother-in-law stayed in the house on the night of the birth, so that there was no room for Mary, whom Charles took back to her father's house at Brompton. She came back the next morning, though, and remained at Furnival's Inn for the rest of the month.

It was—as Dickens remembered it afterwards—a wonderfully happy time. He was working by day at *Pickwick* or *Oliver Twist*, both of which were doing well, or going out to work on his editorial duties for *Bentley's Miscellany*, commissioning new contributors, writing tactful letters to would-be authors whose pieces he could not use, compiling his 'Answers to Correspondents' which he signed with unselfconscious pride, 'The Inimitable Boz', a name which his old schoolmaster, William Giles, bestowed upon him when sending him a present of a snuff-box with a letter of congratulations on his success. At the same time Dickens was writing another short farce for John Pritt Harley whose performance in Dickens's earlier piece at the St James's had been a great success.

Once again, however, as before his marriage, overwork had a deleterious effect on his health. Towards the end of the previous year he had been suffering from 'the torment of rheumatism in the face' and intermittent headaches of such violence that he was sometimes, so he told Bentley, 'wholly disabled from putting pen to paper'. Now the headaches had returned with the same violence as before and he was prescribed 'as much medicine as would confine an ordinary-sized horse to his stall for a week'.

Kate, too, was 'in a very low and alarming state', as she was often to be in the future after a confinement; she made increasing demands on his time and sympathy, refusing to eat anything unless he persuaded her to do so. He decided they must get out of London for a few weeks, and so, taking Mary with them, they went down to the cottage in Kent where they had spent their honeymoon.

9

MISS MARY HOGARTH
1837
aet. 25

48 DOUGHTY STREET LONDON

She was dead. No sleep so beautiful and calm, so free from trace of pain, so fair to look upon. She seemed a creature fresh from the hand of God. . . . So shall we know the angels in their majesty, after death.

The Old Curiosity Shop

9

While they were staying at the cottage in Chalk, Dickens went up to London to look for a house. His rooms in Furnival's Inn, not even suitable for a married couple, were far too cramped for a couple with a baby and a fourth member of the family so often staying with them. Now that *Oliver Twist* was consolidating his reputation he felt secure enough to pay for something larger.

He settled on a three-storey terrace house with twelve rooms at 48 Doughty Street, between the British Museum and Gray's Inn Road. Doughty Street was then a private street, 'a broad, airy wholesome street', a fellow-writer remembered; 'none of your common thorough-fares, to be rattled through by vulgar cabs and earth-shaking Pickford vans, but a self-included property, with a gate at each end, and a lodge with a porter in a gold-laced hat, and the Doughty arms on the buttons of his mulberry-coloured coat.'[1] The rents of houses there were not excessive and Dickens was able to take No. 48 for £80 a year, on condition that he painted the first-floor drawing-room and the blind frames round the windows.[2]

He and Kate and the baby moved into the house at the beginning of April 1837. Mary came to stay with them, as well as his brother Fred, now sixteen, for whom Charles had obtained a job in Macrone's accounts department the previous summer. His sisters Fanny, who married Henry Burnett that year, and Letitia, now engaged to Charles's friend Henry Austin, were frequent visitors there. Burnett remembered how one evening when he called with Fanny, while he and the women were sitting round the fire 'cosily enjoying a chat',

Dickens, for some purpose, came suddenly into the room. 'What you here!' he exclaimed: 'I'll bring down my work.' It was his monthly portion of 'Oliver Twist' for Bentley's. In a few minutes he returned, manuscript in hand, and while he was pleasantly discoursing he employed himself in carrying to the corner of the room a little table, at which he seated himself and recommenced his writing. We, at his bidding went on talking our 'little nothings',—he, every now and then (the feather of his pen still moving rapidly from side to side), put in a cheerful interlude. It was interesting to watch, upon the sly, the mind and the muscle working (or, if you please, playing) in company, as new thoughts were being dropped upon the paper. And to note the working brow, the set of mouth, with the tongue tightly pressed against the closed lips, as was his habit.[3]

The few weeks' break in the country had done Charles good; and although he had had to ask Bentley for an advance of £100 on the novel contract to pay for the expenses of moving into the house, he was no longer so much worried about money. For, at the end of March, on the anniversary of the publication of the first instalment of *Pickwick*, he received a present of £500 from Chapman and Hall in gratitude for the continuing success of the novel which had already made the publishers far more than they had ever expected.

A few weeks later, however, Dickens's happiness was shattered by a tragedy from which he never fully recovered.

2

One Saturday night after he and Kate and Mary had been to the St James's Theatre together, Mary said good-night to the others and went upstairs to bed 'in perfect health and her usual delightful spirits'. But scarcely had she shut the door when Charles heard her give a strangled cry. Followed by Kate he ran into the room, sent Fred for the doctor, and waited anxiously for him to arrive. But the doctor, when he did come, could not help; and, as Dickens said, Mary 'sank under the attack and died—died in such a calm and gentle sleep, that although I had held her in my arms for sometime before, when she was certainly living (for she swallowed a little brandy from my hand) I continued to support her lifeless form, long after her soul had fled to Heaven. . . . This was about 3 o'Clock on the Sunday afternoon. They think her heart was diseased. . . .'[4]

He was overwhelmed with grief.

You cannot conceive the misery in which this dreadful event has plunged us [he told her grandfather]. Since our marriage she has been the grace and life of our home—the admired of all, for her beauty and excellence—I could have better spared a much nearer relation or an older friend, for she has been to us what we can never replace, and has left a blank which no one who ever know [*sic*] her can have the faintest hope of being supplied.[5]

He took a ring from her finger and put it on his own, and it remained there for the rest of his life. He kept her clothes, and often afterwards went to look at them mouldering away 'in their secret places'. He found some bleak comfort in the thought, as he told Beard, that 'Thank God, she died in my arms, and the very last words she whispered were of me'. He paid for her funeral at Kensal Green Cemetery and promised himself that one day he would be buried beside her in that grave beneath a tombstone which bore an inscription of his own composition:

> Mary Scott Hogarth
> Died 7th May 1837
> Young, beautiful, and good,
> God in His Mercy
> Numbered her with his Angels
> At the early age of
> Seventeen.

He could not work; he could not even bear to stay in the house where she had died, and he went away with Kate to stay in a farm cottage near the village of Hampstead.

He visited her grave, and stood looking down at the ground beneath his feet, thinking how transitory were health and beauty, that those who were left on earth to remember her 'sweet face and winning smile', her 'guileless heart and affectionate nature', were 'indeed objects for sympathy and compassion'. No one loved her more than he did, no one lamented her 'more constantly and deeply in death'.

In the letters he brought himself to write—on sheets of black-edged writing-paper—he returned again and again to the same theme, to the same tributes to her grace and youth, her goodness and beauty, the same consciousness of his irreparable loss:

I have lost the dearest friend I ever had. Words cannot describe the pride I felt in her, and the devoted attachment I bore her. . . . She had not a single fault . . . I solemnly believe that so perfect a creature never breathed. I knew her inmost heart. . . She had not a fault. . . . I wish you could know how I weary now for the three rooms in Furnival's Inn, and how I miss that pleasant smile and those sweet words which, bestowed upon our evening's work, in our merry banterings round the fire, were more precious to me than the applause of the whole world could be. I can recall everything we said and did in those days, and could show you every passage and line we read together. . . . We might have known that we were too happy together. . . . She had not a single fault.[6]

For months after her death he dreamed of her constantly.

After she died I dreamed of her every night for many months [he confided to her mother several years later], sometimes as a spirit, sometimes as a living creature, never with any of the bitterness of my real sorrow, but always with a kind of quiet happiness, which became so pleasant to me that I never lay down at night without a hope of the vision coming back in one shape or other. And so it did. I went down into Yorkshire, and finding it still present to me in a strange scene and a strange bed, I could not help mentioning the circumstances in a note I wrote home to Kate. From that moment I have never dreamed of her once, though she is so much in my thoughts at all times (especially when I am successful and have prospered in anything) that the recollection of her is an essential part of my being, and is as inseparable from my being as the beating of my heart is.[7]

The year after he wrote this letter, though, he did dream of her again. He was in Genoa, staying at the beautiful Palazzo Peschiere, and trying to settle down to write. But although the Peschiere was an enchanting place, cool, imposing and restful, with a delicious garden enclosed by rose hedges and ornamented with sparkling fountains, Dickens found it difficult to work there. The 'tuneless, grating, discordant, jerking, hideous vibration' of the bells clanging so persistently in the town below, made his ideas spin round and round in his head; he was attacked again by the pain in his side and could not sleep, and when he did get to sleep he dreamed of a spirit draped in blue like a Madonna and knew that it was Mary's. He stretched out his arms towards it, called it 'Dear', and asked it for some token that it had really visited him. 'What is the true religion?' he asked it. If we tried to do good, perhaps the form of religion did not matter, or was the Roman Catholic religion the best? 'For *you*,' the spirit replied at last with a tender compassion, 'it is the best.' He woke up, so he told Forster, with the tears running down his face.[(8)]

When Mary's grandmother and young brother, George, died within a few days of each other, and he had to abandon his hope of sharing her grave since they were to occupy the plot, he wrote to tell Forster that he could not possibly express how great a trial this was for him.

> The desire to be buried next her is as strong upon me now, as it was five years ago; and I *know* (for I don't think there ever was love like that I bear her) that it will never diminish. . . . I cannot bear the thought of being excluded from her dust. . . . I ought to get the better of it, but it is very hard. I never contemplated this—and coming so suddenly, and after being ill, it disturbs me more than it ought. It seems like losing her a second time.

Did Forster think anything could be done? The cemetery people would move her to another grave if he gave the order, but ought he to take her away from her family? What did Forster think?

Forster evidently suggested buying an adjoining plot. But no, Dickens had already thought of that and there was no ground to be had. So, unwillingly, he decided that he must 'give it up'. All that he could do was to go over to Kensal Green when the grave was opened before her brother's funeral, to derive some morbid satisfaction and comfort from having one last look at her coffin.[9]

3

He could never forget her and how much she had meant to him; and in every novel he wrote after her death there is a hint of her presence, an apotheosis of her living nature.

The young, virginal, ethereal girls who make their appearance against the far more solid backgrounds of his art, all reveal the mind of a writer preoccupied with the sanctity of purity and innocence, with the fragile impermanence of youthful beauty, and with the dreaded urge to defloration. Little Nell, for instance, 'a creature fresh from the hand of God', and Little Dorrit, whose goodness shines forth from her 'pale, transparent face', are but the idealisations of a lost and longed-for love which their creator can never replace. When such creatures had to die, it was, for Dickens, as if Mary herself had died again. So that although he had originally intended Rose Maylie—whose character was clearly drawn from Mary's—to die, in *Oliver Twist*, he could not bring himself to follow this plan; and although, three years later, he knew that Little Nell would have to die, he could scarcely face the thought of describing it, even when Forster insisted that the death was artistically essential. Forster had never known him 'wind up any tale with such a sorrowful reluctance'. He suffered unspeakable anguish, he admitted himself, even in contemplating her death. To the artist whose sad duty it was to depict the girl lying on her death-bed he confided, 'I am breaking my heart over this story'.

'I am the wretchedest of the wretched', he told Forster. '[The story] casts the most terrible shadow over me, and it is as much as I can do to keep moving at all. I tremble to approach the place. . . . Nobody will miss her like I shall. It is such a very painful thing to me, that I really cannot express my sorrow. Old wounds bleed afresh when I only think of the way of doing it. . . . Dear Mary died yesterday, when I think of this sad story.' Eventually he overcame his 'sorrowful reluctance' to wind up his story and let Little Nell die. But although he felt a sad relief when he had done so and had left her 'so beautiful and calm, so free from trace of pain, so fair to look upon', it was a temporary catharsis rather than a permanent release.

'So beautiful and calm, so free from trace of pain, so fair to look upon'

The death of old William Dorrit is described in similar terms as though, for Dickens, death was a return to the innocence of childhood: 'Quietly, quietly, the ruled and cross-ruled countenance . . . became fair and blank. Quietly, quietly, the reflected marks of the prison bars and the zig-zag iron on the wall-top faded away. Quietly, quietly, the face subsided into a far younger likeness of her own than [his daughter, Little Dorrit] had ever seen under the grey hair, and sank to rest.'* And when it was time for Paul Dombey to die in the arms of his sister Floy, Dickens suffered the same kind of agony, and wrote with the same sense of

* *Little Dorrit*, Bk. II, ch. XIX.

personal anguish and intense emotional sentiment, the same declamatory pathos:

> He put his hands together, as he had been used to do at his prayers. He did not remove his arms to do it; but they saw him fold them so, behind her neck.
>
> 'Mamma is like you, Floy. I know her by the face. But tell them that the print upon the stairs at school is not divine enough. The light about the head is shining on me as I go!'
>
> The golden ripple on the wall came back again, and nothing else stirred in the room. The old, old fashion! The fashion that came in with our first garments, and will last unchanged until our race is run its course, and the wide firmament is rolled up like a scroll. The old, old fashion—Death!
>
> Oh, thank God, all who see it, for that older fashion yet, of Immortality. And look upon us, angels of young children, with regards not quite estranged, when the swift rivers bears us to the ocean!★

Even when Dora Spenlow dies, though the style is less rhetorical and the sentiment more constrained, the sense of personal commitment is no less unmistakable. Dora's marriage to David has not been a satisfying one; but as her husband comes to realise she is dying he feels a new and far more tender emotion for her:

> Sometimes, when I took her up, and felt that she was lighter in my arms, a dead black feeling came upon me, as if I were approaching to some frozen region yet unseen, that numbed my life. I avoided the recognition of this feeling by any name, or by any communing with myself; until one night, when it was very strong upon me, and my aunt had left her with a parting cry of 'Good night, Little Blossom,' I sat down at my desk alone, and cried to think, Oh what a fatal name it was, and how the blossom withered in its bloom upon the tree.†

Constantly recreating the pain of his personal tragedy, idealising the creatures of his imagination whose young lives wither and fade away, Dickens came to believe, it seems, that the kind of love that he had known with Mary—and that he had known with his sister as a child—provided a happiness and self-fulfilment that no other relationship could give, satisfying a need for sympathy and understanding and admiration that no other love could offer, carrying within it, perhaps, for him, the excitement and responses of sexual desire without the guilt and fear of its admission, or the disillusionment of its consummation.

★ *Dombey and Son*, ch. XVI.   † *David Copperfield*, ch. XLVIII.

Paul and Florence Dombey, Tom and Ruth Pinch, Nicholas and Kate Nickleby all know this sort of love.

What on earth would he do, Paul Dombey wonders, if his sister were to go away to live in India, as all the relatives of his fellow-pupil, Master Bitherstone, have done? Paul feels that *he* could not go on living if that beloved sister lived so far away. 'If you were in India, I should die, Floy,' he protests, 'I should die of being so sorry and so lonely.' 'What do you think I mean to do when I grow up?' he later asks Mrs Pipchin.

Mrs Pipchin couldn't guess.

> 'I mean,' said Paul, 'to put my money all together in one bank, never try to get any more, go away into the country with my darling Florence, have a beautiful garden, fields, and woods, and live there with her all my life!'
> 'Indeed!' cried Mrs Pipchin.
> 'Yes,' said Paul. 'That's what I mean to do, when I—' He stopped, and pondered for a moment.
> Mrs Pipchin's grey eye scanned his thoughtful face.
> 'If I grow up,' said Paul.*

Those who *do* grow up and fulfil this romantic ambition, find a deeper happiness than all but the rarest marriages can offer. Ruth Pinch keeps house for her brother Tom, and they are blissfully content:

> It was a perfect treat to Tom to see her with her brows knit, and her rosy lips pursed up, kneading away at the crust, rolling it out, cutting it up into strips, lining the basin with it, shaving it off fine round the rim, chopping up the steak into small pieces, raining down pepper and salt upon them, packing them into the basin, pouring in cold water for gravy, and never venturing to steal a look in his direction, lest her gravity should be disturbed; until, at last, the basin being quite full and only wanting the top crust, she clapped her hands, all covered with paste and flour, at Tom, and burst out heartily into such a charming little laugh of triumph, that the pudding need have no other seasoning to commend it to the taste of any reasonable man on earth. . . . As she sat opposite to Tom at supper, fingering one of Tom's pet tunes upon the tablecloth, and smiling in his face, he had never been so happy in his life.†

When this idyllic harmony is broken by Ruth's marriage to John Westlock, the idea that the brother and sister should be parted is unthinkable. ' "I am never to leave him, am I dear?" Ruth anxiously asks John. "I could never leave Tom. I am sure you know that." "Leave Tom!

---

* *Dombey and Son*, chs. VIII, XIV.
† *Martin Chuzzlewit*, chs. XXXIX, XXXVII.

That would be a strange beginning. Leave Tom, dear! . . . The loss of one person, and such a person as Tom, too, out of our small household of three is not to be endured; and so I have told him." '*

Nor can Nicholas and Kate Nickleby bear to be parted after they both get married. Nicholas assumes, as a matter of course, that Kate will keep house for him until she finds a husband, and when that husband is found and Nicholas marries Madeline Bray they all go to live 'within a stone's throw of one another' in Devon, where Kate remains the 'same fond sister'.†

At the end of *The Battle of Life* Marion Jeddler and her sister Grace settle down to live with Grace's husband, Alfred, who in the course of the story calls both the girls by 'the dear name of sister'. ' "Use the name!",' urges his future wife, when he does use it, rather hesitantly, for the first time. ' "Use it! I am glad to hear it. Call me nothing else." '‡

4

This story, *The Battle of Life*, was written while Dickens was staying at Geneva in 1846. He had gone to Switzerland with Kate, the six children they had at that time, and Mary's sister, Georgina, who was then nineteen.

Georgina Hogarth had joined the family four years before, and had soon become as integral a part of the household as her elder sister Mary had been. Charles, when he took Kate out anywhere, nearly always took Georgina, too. They were, so he said, his 'pair of petticoats'. He had always been happier with a pair than with Kate alone, and Georgina was so pretty, so cheerful, so responsive, so lively, so full of admiration for Charles ('a man of genius [who] ought not to be judged with the common herd of men').[10] Above all, she was so very much like Mary.

Indeed, he found the resemblance so strong that it was almost uncanny at times. 'When she and Kate and I are sitting together,' he told her mother, 'I seem to think that what has happened is a melancholy dream from which I am just awakening. The perfect likeness of what she was, will never be again, but so much of her spirit shines out' in Georgina 'that the old time comes back again at some seasons, and I can hardly separate it from the present.'[11]

In Geneva, Dickens experienced what was by then a familiar difficulty in settling down to work on a story which would carry within it some

* *Ibid.*, ch. LIII.   † *Nicholas Nickleby*, chs. III, LXV.
‡ *The Battle of Life*, Pt. I.

painful remembrance of his past. And once he had begun, it gave him
headaches and sleepless nights, and dreams in which the story turned into
'a series of chambers impossible to be got to rights or got out of'. But at
last in frustration, torment and anxiety, *The Battle of Life* was finished.

As a work of literature, it deserved both *The Times*'s dismissive review,
and Thackeray's verdict that it was 'a wretched affair'. But as a biographical document, it is extraordinarily revealing. It tells, in debilitatingly
sentimental language, the simple story of two sisters both of whom love
the same man, and both of whom are loved by him in return.

In it Dickens is playing what has been called 'the alphabet game', a
game which he had already just played in *Dombey and Son* (in which
Carker and Dombey have his own initials), and a game which he continued to play in *David Copperfield* (who has his initials reversed), in *Little
Dorrit* (whose two main characters are Clennam and Dorrit), and in *A
Tale of Two Cities* (whose principal protagonists are Carton and Dar-
nay).[12]

For how are we to understand the disproportionate agony Dickens
suffered in the composition of the hopelessly dismal story of *The Battle of
Life*, as Steven Marcus has suggested, unless we regard it as a veritable
battleground where Dickens's contending impulses to write about his
reawakening past and keep it secret meet and are mutually defeated?
How are we to explain his agony unless the two sisters, Marion and
Grace, elaborate some fantasy about Dickens's feelings towards Mary and
Georgina?[13]

In the story Marion and Grace are virtually interchangeable and in-
distinguishable, their only difference being the differences between Mary
and Georgina in Dickens's mind. They are both in love with Alfred
Heathfield, a young man who has been brought up in their home as a
brother by their father Dr Jeddler, a kindly cynical sixty-year-old man,
yet another version of John Dickens, who was sixty that year himself.
Dr Jeddler is as incapable of making distinctions between his daughters
as anyone else: ' "It's a world full of hearts," said the doctor, hugging his
daughter, and bending across her to hug Grace—for he couldn't separate
the sisters.'

When Alfred goes abroad to study he leaves Marion (whom, it is
understood, he will marry on his return) in the care of Grace, her elder
sister.

'I have been telling Grace, dear Marion,' he said, 'that you are her
charge; my precious trust on parting. And when I come back and

reclaim you, dearest, and the bright prospect of our married life lies stretched before us, it shall be one of our chief pleasures to consult how we can make Grace happy. . . .'

The younger sister had one hand in his; the other rested on her sister's neck. She looked into that sister's eyes, so calm, serene, and cheerful, with a gaze in which affection, admiration, sorrow, wonder, almost veneration, were blended. She looked into that sister's face, as if it were the face of some bright angel calm, serene, and cheerful, the face looked back on her and on her lover.*

On the day that Alfred returns to reclaim Marion, she disappears, pretending to elope with another man so that Grace, by this sacrifice, can have the man they both want. Here Dickens ends Part 2 of the story and begins Part 3 with the words: 'The world has grown six years older since that night of the return.' (He had originally written 'ten years'— the number of years since Mary Hogarth's death—but Forster advised him that the lapse of time seemed excessive.)

Alfred and Grace have grieved for Marion together, 'and remembered her together, like a person dead'. They have married, as Marion hoped they would.

'They were married on her birthday. . . . Alfred said, one night when they were walking in the orchard, "Grace, shall our wedding day be Marion's birthday?" And so it was.' They have had a child, and, as Dickens had called *his* first daughter Mary, so they call her Marion after *their* lost sister. At last Marion returns, and returns in a way that recalls Mary's return to Dickens in that dream he had had in Italy. But this 'was no dream, no phantom conjured up by hope and fear, but Marion, sweet Marion! So beautiful, so happy, so unalloyed by care, and trial, so elevated and exalted in her loveliness.'

So Heathfield is allowed to achieve what Dickens was denied. He has both the sisters and can settle down with both of them, 'living (as we must!) together—close together—talking often of old times'.†

5

The atmosphere in these *ménages à trois* (which Dickens loved to create, and in which children are always present or to be expected) may not immediately strike the reader—as it struck George Orwell[14]—as being incestuous. But the depth of Dickens's personal involvement in the

---

* *The Battle of Life*, Pt. I.   † *The Battle of Life*, Pt. III.

relationships he describes, in the close and sometimes almost claustro-phobic attachments between brothers and sisters (and those who like to think of themselves as being thus related), is unmistakable.

David Copperfield, a lonely child whose father dies before he is born, is always aware of his need for a sister. As a little boy he strolls on the beach at Yarmouth with Little Emily, a surrogate sister, picking up stranded starfish and putting them back into the water. He fancies that he is in love with her, and he tells her so, adding that unless she confesses she adores him he will be reduced to the necessity of killing himself with a sword.

In later life he writes that he loved that child, 'quite as truly, quite as tenderly, with greater purity and more disinterestedness, than can enter into the best love of a later time of life, high and ennobling as it is'.*

It is only, in fact, when Dora, his wife, is dead that David's life offers the prospect of real happiness with Agnes Wickfield, his 'sweet sister' as he calls her in his thoughts, his 'counsellor and friend'.

This 'adopted sister', as he refers to her on another occasion, gives him peace and happiness. He comes home to her 'like a tired traveller and finds such a blessed sense of rest'.

Oh, Agnes, sister of my boyhood [he writes in anguish, thinking of the time when he knew her before his marriage to Dora]. 'If I had known then what I knew long afterwards!—'
There was a beggar in the street, when I went down; and as I turned towards the window, thinking of her calm seraphic eyes, he made me start by muttering, as if he were an echo of the morning:
'Blind! Blind. Blind!† (15)

Even those brothers who prove themselves unworthy of a sister's devotion contrive to retain it, as Amy Dorrit remains faithful to Edward, and Miss Pross—despite the most outrageous provocation—to her brother Solomon.

'There never was, nor will be, but one man worthy of Ladybird,' said Miss Pross; 'and that was my brother Solomon, if he hadn't made a mistake in life.'
Here again: Mr Lorry's inquiries into Miss Pross's personal history had established the fact that her brother Solomon was a heartless scoundrel who had stripped her of everything she possessed, as a stake to speculate with, and had abandoned her in her poverty for evermore,

---

* *David Copperfield*, ch. III.
† *David Copperfield*, chs. XVIII, XXV, XXXV, XXXIX, LIX.

with no touch of compunction. Miss Pross's fidelity of belief in Solomon (deducting a mere trifle for this slight mistake) was quite a serious matter with Mr Lorry, and had its weight in his good opinion of her.*

As with Miss Pross, so with the undesirable Jane Murdstone and the grotesque Sally Brass who stay by their unpleasant brothers to the end; and so with Harriet Carker. Though her brother James has utterly rejected her—'I know no Harriet Carker. There is no such person. *You* may have a sister; make much of her. I have none'†—even Harriet Carker remembers James on his birthday every year and hopes that he may be happy. And Dickens, by pointing to James's cruel rejection of his sister, adds a final stroke to the portrait of one of the most accomplished and distasteful of his villains, the type of character in which Dickens puts much of his fears about himself, the sort of man he dreads to think he might have been, or might even yet become.

6

When his own sister Fanny lay dying, Dickens was overwhelmed with grief. He had seen less and less of her in the years before her last illness, since her husband's increasingly puritanical outlook on life was a barrier which Dickens found it difficult to overcome. But when he knew that he would soon lose her, all the love that he had felt for her as a child came flooding back.[16]

She had collapsed while singing at a party in Manchester, where she and her husband then lived, and the doctors had diagnosed tuberculosis, of which there was some history in the family. Dickens had had her brought down to London to see the specialist, Sir James Clark, who told him she had only a few weeks left to live.

He found lodgings for her and her husband in the village of Hornsey and here, in the summer of 1848, he was a regular, sometimes daily, visitor. The seriousness of her incurable disease had been kept from her at first, but when she knew she was going to die, she told her brother that she was not frightened, though it was 'hard to die at such a time'. She was worried of course about her children, especially one (supposedly the 'original' of Paul Dombey) who was crippled, and she 'spoke about an invention she had heard of that she would like to have tried for the deformed child's back'.

* *A Tale of Two Cities*, Bk. I, ch. VI.   † *Dombey and Son*, ch. XXII.

Dickens felt weighed down by pity. He was 'used up', he said, good
for nothing. He went down to Broadstairs for a few days to see the
children; but he could not get Fanny out of his mind. It was almost a relief
when the call came for him to return to her. By the time he reached the
house she was struggling for breath. He could find no words 'to express
the terrible aspect of suffering and suffocation—the appalling noise in her
throat—and the agonising look around'.

In the grip of his grief, he found it as impossible to work as he had done
when Mary died. That summer he did no more than a few articles, on
social problems, for the *Examiner*, discussing such subjects as ignorance
and crime, alcoholism and environment, the futility of forcing Christianity down the throats of Africans when its principles were not applied to
remedy distress at home, the evils of narrow religion on the one hand and
material ambition on the other, the kinds of themes, in fact, which were to
weave themselves into the fabric of his later work.[17]

But for the moment he could not bring himself to concentrate on such
themes in a work of imagination; he felt himself forced to delve once
more into his own past, and into the fragmentary nature of his own
personality. So, as his Christmas book for 1848, he wrote *The Haunted
Man*.

This story has many of the weaknesses of *The Battle of Life*, yet, like
that deeply personal fantasy, it caused him agonies to write. The difficulties of making a start on it made him grimly ill-tempered, and his family
were careful to keep out of his way when he walked about the house.
All morning he was shut up in his room; at night he paced the streets;
but the story would not come. He left London and went down to stay
at the Bedford Hotel, Brighton, and there he managed to get it done—
for the last three days, as he told Bradbury, crying his eyes out over it.

It tells the story of Mr Redlaw, seemingly successful, who, with his
hollow cheeks, grizzled hair, his sunken, brilliant eye, his black-attired
figure, looks like a haunted man. And so he is—haunted by unhappy
memories; by the sufferings and injustice of his youth; by an early love
that, coming to him when he was too young to marry, made him
resolutely determined to do well in the world; by the death of a beloved
sister, 'doubly dear, doubly devoted', who had lived on to see him
famous, and who 'died with no concern but for her brother'; by parents
'who cast their offspring loose, early, as birds do theirs; and, if they do
well, claim the credit; and, if ill, the pity'.

'I am he,' Redlaw says, 'neglected in my youth, and miserably poor, who strove and suffered, until I hewed out knowledge from the mine where it was buried. . . . No mother's self-denying love, no father's counsel aided me.' But while he speaks in tones of such self-pity, his sufferings, the reader is assured, have not hardened him. He remains a man reserved about his inmost thoughts and feelings, but of generous and charitable impulses. The ghost of himself offers him the chance of forgetting the wrongs and sorrows of his past, and the ability to pass on this gift of forgetfulness to everyone else he meets. He accepts the offer, only to find that to forget sorrow is to forget happiness as well. With the help of the angelically charitable Milly Swidger, he regains his memory and is able to restore its purifying influences to others.

But, pitying the little boy and lovesick youth that was himself, and justifying the faults in the middle-aged man he felt himself already to have become, Dickens could not bring himself to come to terms with his past in this easy, satisfactorily resolved sort of way.

The more he thought of it, the more disturbed by its injustices he felt, the more resentful of those who had neglected or ill-treated him, the more regretful for what might have been, the more sorry for himself in his bereavement and in his sense 'of one happiness' he had missed in life, one companion he had never found. *The Battle of Life* and *The Haunted Man* were in no sense therapeutic or even palliative; he needed to get closer to the roots of his discontent, to explore his childhood in a more directly personal way, to write not about Heathfield or Redlaw, but about himself.

It was at this time that he wrote those autobiographical fragments of his childhood memories, memories which had already been aroused by his work on *Dombey and Son,* and which now he decided to incorporate into *David Copperfield.*

10

THE NOVELIST TRIUMPHANT
1837-1839
aet. 25-27.

1 DEVONSHIRE TERRACE YORK GATE REGENT'S PARK LONDON

I was much struck with him and liked everything but the intolerable dandyism of his dress, which is such as he might, and I believe has, humorously described himself; but it will probably wear away with his youth. He does not look more than twenty-five and is undoubtedly under thirty. His countenance, I think, beautiful, because blended with its intelligence there is so much expression of goodness.

Caroline Fox

10

While he was staying at the cottage near Hampstead, the first burst of Dickens's grief at Mary Hogarth's death passed away; and at the end of May 1837 he felt able to return to London and to begin work again in Doughty Street on the last chapters of *Pickwick* and on *Oliver Twist*. He was soon working as hard as ever. But now that Mary was gone, he found it even more difficult to relax quietly at home than he had done when she was there to help him to do so; and the only way he was able to clear his mind of his agitating thoughts, the twists of his plots, and the activities of his characters, was to seek relief in violent exercise. It was nothing for him to walk eight miles at a pace so fast it was almost a run, or to ride out into the country for lunch and then gallop back again in the afternoon in time for a dinner (preferably of chops) at five o'clock.

'I intend ordering a Oss to be at this door at 11 Oclock in the morning to convey me on a fifteen mile ride out, ditto in, and a lunch on the Road,' he would write to Forster from Doughty Street. 'Can you spare time to join me? We will return here to dinner at 5.'

'I think Richmond and Twickenham through the Park, out at Knightsbridge, and over Barnes Common, would make a beautiful ride. I sent Fred down now, in the agonies of despair, to know if you were going.'

'I am not well, and want a ride. Will you join me—say at 2 o'Clock for a hard trot of three hours? Yes or No.'

'. . . Muffle yourself up, and start off with me for a good brisk walk over Hampstead Heath. I know a good 'ous [Jack Straw's Castle] where we can have a red hot chop for dinner, and a glass of good wine.'

'. . . Come, come, come, and walk in the Green Lanes. . . . *Come*. I shall expect you.'

Sometimes his requests for Forster's company sound quite vehement: 'Where shall it be—oh where—Hampstead, Greenwich, Windsor? WHERE????' or, 'Is it possible that you can't, oughtn't, shouldn't, musn't, *won't* be tempted?'

He hated being alone, and when Kate was out in the evening and work prevented him from getting out himself, he would ask Forster to come round to keep him company: 'My missis is going out today, and I want you to take some cold lamb and a bit of fish with me. . . . We can walk out both before and afterwards but I must *dine* at home on account of the Pickwick proofs.'

'My missis is going out to dinner,' he wrote on another occasion. 'Do you come and sit here, and read, or work, or do something while I write . . . which will be arter a lamb chop.'[1]

Although he usually turned to Forster for company, he had many other friends on whose time he would also call. He had lost touch with Kolle, his confidant of earlier days, but he still saw a good deal of Mitton, Beard and Austin, as well as of more recent and famous friends such as Harrison Ainsworth, the painter Daniel Maclise, the actor John Pritt Harley, the composer John Hullah, Hablot Browne, George Cruikshank, Bentley and various members of the Garrick and the Shakespeare Society (a literary and supper club which met on Saturday evenings at the Piazza Coffee House, Covent Garden). At the Shakespeare Society he came to know Thomas Talfourd, a barrister, dramatist and Member of Parliament for Reading, whose work on the Copyright Bill was given by Dickens as the reason—apart from the happiness he enjoyed from their 'private friendship'—for dedicating to him the *Pickwick Papers* when published as a book.[2] Here, at the Shakespeare Society, he also saw Douglas Jerrold, the radical author of over sixty plays, whom Dickens asked to write for *Bentley's Miscellany* and afterwards invited on various occasions to a meal.

At the Garrick, Dickens became better acquainted with Thackeray, whose work he also published in *Bentley's Miscellany*, and with Leigh Hunt, the vivacious, good-natured, talkative, and charming critic and poet whose superficial mannerisms Dickens—while taking care to disguise his appearance—later caricatured in the impecunious dilettante, Harold Skimpole: 'a little bright creature, with a rather large head; but a delicate face, and a sweet voice, and there was a perfect charm in him. All he said was so free from effort and spontaneous, and was said with such a captivating gaiety, that it was fascinating to hear him talk.'*

It was Forster who introduced him to Leigh Hunt. And it was with Forster, too, that, one day at Covent Garden, he met for the first time William Charles Macready, whose acting he had so long admired. Macready took an immediate liking to Dickens, as Dickens did to him, and—despite the nineteen years' difference in their ages—there developed a friendship which was never to be broken.

* *Bleak House*, ch. VI.

These friends, and others, as well as visiting Dickens at Doughty Street, also came to see him when he took Kate out of London to stay a few days at a rented cottage in Twickenham, at the Old Ship Hotel at Brighton, or at a little house at Broadstairs, a small seaside village in Kent to which, despite his later complaints that its growing popularity made it difficult for him to work there, he continued to return.

On this first visit he was delighted with it, although, as he told Forster, he was so 'queer' on his arrival, that 'for four-and-twenty mortal hours' he was compelled to 'abstain from porter or other malt liquor!!!' But soon he was drinking Holland's Gin at the Albion Hotel and confessing himself intrigued by a Roman Catholic cobbler who lived in the house on the opposite side of the High Street (and who gave an hour and a half to his devotions every morning behind his counter), by ladies and gentlemen who walked barefoot on the beach and bathed in the sea in the 'buff', and by his next-door neighbour who had a 'wife and something else under the same roof with the rest of the furniture—the wife deaf and blind, and the something else given to drinking'.[3]

But wherever he was, and whoever he was with, he was consumed by that burning restlessness which made it impossible for him completely to relax indoors when not at his writing table. Feeling confined he would burst out of the house for a long walk, or a ride, or, if by the sea, for a vigorous swim. Resting, he admitted, was a labour for him; and he found it difficult when he was meant to be on holiday to keep away from his work. It was often a relief to get back to it and to throw himself once more upon his characters whose intense vivacity was but a reflection of his own. He spoke of these characters, and thought of them, as if they were real people; and for him they did, in fact, momentarily become real, making him laugh and cry, and leading him to refer to his work on them in terms of physical assault. When the time came for them to die, he would talk of his intention of killing them off, murdering them, slaughtering them. When about to describe a scene in which they were released from prison, he would talk of his burning his way into Newgate to tear them out 'by the hair of their heads'. He could not, as he had long ago discovered, set upon them until he had—as he put it—got his 'steam up'. But once he had reached that necessary state of excitement he would fall upon them, as he fell upon *Oliver Twist*, 'tooth and nail'. He found great difficulty in keeping his 'hands off Fagin and the rest of them' in the evenings at Broadstairs; and when he got back to London he killed off Nancy, sent Sikes to the devil, and couldn't rest until Fagin (who was 'such an out and outer' he didn't 'know what to make of him') had at last been tried and hanged. He hypnotised the reader, as A. O. J. Cockshut says, because he hypnotised himself.[4]

The most refreshing of the breaks away from his writing table were those he spent gathering material for new work. With the journalist's regard for vivid and authentic detail he never considered that time spent in collecting such material was wasted. He would happily spend a whole morning wandering through Bevis Marks to find a house suitable to describe as the 'little habitation' where Sampson Brass had his office—a small dark house, 'so close upon the footway that the passenger who takes the wall brushes the dim glass with his coat sleeve—much to its improvement, for it is very dirty'.* And an hour or two spent in the Hatton Garden police office watching the notorious magistrate, Allen Stewart Laing, performing his duties on the Bench, provided not only the means of portraying the fearful Mr Fang, but, at the same time, gave Dickens an opportunity to take time off from his writing without becoming subject either to the guilty feeling that he was neglecting it or to the impatient desire to return to it.

He enjoyed the same sort of change when he and Hablot Browne went to Yorkshire in January 1838 to collect material about the Yorkshire schools (those gruesome academies, where unwanted children were boarded and supposedly educated, with 'no extras' and 'no vacations', for twenty guineas a year), a species of institution which he was soon to indict in his vivid picture of Dotheboys Hall in *Nicholas Nickleby*.

He and Browne broke their journey at Grantham, putting up at the George, the 'very best Inn' he had ever stayed at, and, continuing their journey in the Glasgow Mail, reached the George and New Inn at Greta Bridge in a heavy snowstorm. But although it was 'fearfully cold' he enjoyed himself as much as he had ever done since Mary had died.

The journey had been enlivened by a 'very queer old body', 'the Mistress of a Yorkshire School returning from a holiday stay in London', who showed him and Browne 'a long letter she was carrying to one of the boys from his father, containing a severe lecture (enforced and aided by many texts from Scripture) *on his refusing to eat boiled meat*. She was very communicative, drank a great deal of brandy and water, and towards evening became insensible.' Later on they had the pleasure of the company of 'a very droll male companion', and 'a most delicious lady's maid', who affected to believe that her carriage was coming to meet her, and

* *The Old Curiosity Shop*, ch. XXIII.

implored the other travellers to keep a sharp look out for it. 'It is scarcely necessary to say that the Coach did not come, and a very dirty girl did.' (5)

At the George and New Inn, Dickens was given 'a smoking supper and a bottle of mulled port' in 'a comfortable room with drawn curtains and a most blazing fire'; for breakfast the next morning he had 'toasts, cakes, a Yorkshire pie, a piece of beef the size and much the shape of my portmanteau, tea, coffee, ham and eggs'; afterwards he went to see Bowes Academy, a notorious school kept by William Shaw.

Shaw of Bowes Academy, like Wackford Squeers of Dotheboys Hall, had only one eye. He had been sued in the 1820s by the parents of two children who had been so neglected and ill-fed as to have gone blind. In court it transpired that no less than ten children had become blind while in his charge, that they were frequently beaten, forced to eat food which was crawling with maggots and to sleep five in a single bed which was infested with fleas. Between 1810 and 1834, twenty-five boys from the school, ranging in age from seven to eighteen, had been buried in the village churchyard. Shaw lost the case and was obliged to pay damages of £500, but the school was still in existence and under his direction.

Dickens pretended to be looking at the school on behalf of a widow who had a son she could not look after. But Shaw was suspicious, and did not let him see much of it, and so he and Browne went on to look at other schools at Barnard Castle and Startforth.

2

The letter which Dickens wrote to his wife describing his adventures in Yorkshire was the first he had occasion to send to her since Mary's death, and only the second since his marriage. He began it 'My dearest Kate', and continued on a note of affection:

A thousand loves and kisses to the darling boy [their baby son, Charles] whom I see in my mind's eye crawling about the floor of this York-shire Inn. Don't leave him alone too much. Bless his heart I would give two sovereigns for a kiss. Remember me too, to Frederick who I hope is attentive to you. Take care of yourself my dearest, and let me find by your letter at the York Post Office that you are in both good health and good spirits. . . . Love to all friends. Ever my dear Kate your affectionated [*sic*] husband, Charles Dickens.[6]

But although he could write to her in terms of such affection, although he did feel affectionately disposed towards her when he was away from her, he was already giving her cause to feel that he would rather be with his friends than with her. She had not minded this much so long as Mary had been there to keep her company when Charles was out dining in one or other of his clubs, and to keep him amused on those evenings when they were all together at home. Mary had been able to talk to him and this had compensated for her own inability to think of anything to say that would entertain or interest him. But now there were just the two of them, and she could never give him what Mary had given him.

It had not been so bad just after Mary's death. Their shared misery had brought them close together. The shock of the loss of an adored sister with whom she had never once quarrelled, had made Kate miscarry her second baby. She soon recovered, however, and ten day's after her sister's death, her husband 'wondered to see her', she was, by then, 'so calm and cheerful'.

Dickens could not but admire her. In writing to a friend who was a contributor to *Bentley's Miscellany*, he said, 'Mrs Dickens has had a trying task, for in the midst of her own affliction she has had to soothe the sufferings of her bereaved mother who was called here in time to see her child expire, and remained here in a state of total insensibility for a week afterwards. She has borne up through her severe trial like what she is—a fine-hearted noble-minded girl.'[7]

But now that they had both recovered from the early anguish of their grief, it became clear to her that Charles could never be so happy alone with her as he had been when Mary had been there to supply a diverting presence. Two months after Mary's death he had taken Kate for a short holiday in France and Belgium, but he had asked young Hablot Browne to go with them. At Broadstairs he felt the need of other company, too, and was thankful when Forster came down to see them, and the two men could spend a 'merry night' together at the Albion Hotel. At Doughty Street, he had to be 'called away' from his work 'to sit with Kate'.

Kate gave birth to their second child, Mary, in March 1838; and a few hours after the baby was born, Dickens was writing to Forster to ask him to join him for a ride, 'the sooner the better for a good long spell'. The day before, he had told Bentley that 'Mrs Dickens perversely and obstinately took it into her head to fall ill at 9 O'clock this morning. I have been with her all day, but as I am advised by the most experienced authorities that I may safely absent myself from home, so that I am within reasonable call, I have ordered dinner for us at the Garrick at 5 precisely'.

The next day he and Forster 'rode out fifteen miles on the great north-road', so Forster said, 'and, after dining at the Red-lion in Barnet on our way home distinguished the already memorable day by bringing in both hacks dead lame'. Three weeks later Dickens and Forster were on the road at night again. Dickens had gone away for the week-end to stay at the Star and Garter, Richmond, as he did not want to be in London when the first number of *Nicholas Nickleby* came out (for, 'having been away from town when *Pickwick's* first number was published, he made it a superstition to be absent at all future times').[8] And from Richmond he had sent what Forster described as a 'peremptory summons':

> Richmond.
> Friday morning.
>
> My dear Forster,
>   Kate is, I think, a *little* better to-day, although she complains, and did complain all night, of great pain.
>   Any way, I hope you will spend Sunday here.[9] If she is too ill to see you, we can easily dine in another room. So meet me at the Shakespeare [Society] on Saturday Evening at 8, order your horse at midnight, and ride back with me to the bed I shall order for you.
>   *Directly you receive this* write back by the twopenny post,[10] and let me know that I may engage your bed and tell them to sit up for us. Tell Fred if you see him, to stop at home on Saturday, after 5 o'Clock till I come.
>
>   In great haste,
>   Ever Yours,
>   CHARLES DICKENS.[11]

All this, Forster said, was 'done accordingly. The smallest hour was sounding from St Paul's into the night before we started [from the Shakespeare Society], and the night was none of the pleasantest; but we carried news that lightened every part of the road, for the sale of *Nickleby* had reached that day the astonishing number of nearly fifty thousand!'[12]

3

In an early number of *Nicholas Nickleby* Dickens introduced Mr Lillyvick, 'a short old gentleman, in drabs and gaiters, with a face that might have been carved out of *lignum vitae*, for anything that appeared to the contrary'. He is a water-rate collector and his manner seems so modest and so meek that 'if he had been an author, who knew his place, he couldn't have been more humble.'*

* *Nicholas Nickleby*, ch. XIV.

Dickens himself was by now well aware of how firm was the convention in society that a young and successful author should 'know his place'. At the early literary dinners Bentley had given in his offices in New Burlington Street, he had been careful to keep rather quiet, for, as he told Bentley: 'I have seen how much ill-will and jealousy there is afloat. . . . I like to assume a virtue though I have it not.'

As he had behaved with literary men in 1836, so he behaved with the leaders of society in 1838. At the first dinner he attended at Holland House he was considered by Lord Holland to be 'very unobtrusive . . . and altogether prepossessing'.

Had he not been, he would not have been invited. Lady Holland had taken the trouble to ask Bulwer Lytton if he were 'presentable'. When assured, rather huffily, by Bulwer Lytton that he was, Lady Holland told Talfourd to bring him to the great house. It was an experience from which less self-confident men shrank with nervous apprehension. For Lady Holland was the most intimidating of hostesses. Irritable, tyrannical and intolerant, as unwavering in her friendships as in her antagonisms, she ruled her dinner-table with an imperious will. As dictatorial with Lord Russell as with Melbourne and Macaulay, she would send her husband to change his waistcoat in the middle of a meal or order the servants to remove his plate in the middle of an anecdote. Her guests were ordered about like pages and few of them protested, though once when Count d'Orsay had picked up her fan several times from the floor (as those sitting next to her were expected to do whenever she dropped it), he suggested that he should spend the rest of the evening on the floor to be in the best position to fulfil his duty. And once when she commanded Sydney Smith to ring the bell, he asked her if she would like him to sweep out the room as well.[13]

The dinner party that Dickens attended, however, went off without any recorded incidents of this nature. And Lady Holland, as well as her husband, thought that the young author would do. Lord Holland's sister, Caroline Fox, reported after a subsequent visit of Dickens to Holland House: 'I was much struck with him and liked everything but the intolerable dandyism of his dress, which is such as he might, and I believe has, humorously described himself; but it will probably wear away with his youth. He does not look more than twenty-five and is undoubtedly under thirty. [He was twenty-seven.] His countenance, I think, beautiful, because blended with its intelligence there is so much expression of goodness.'[14]

A frequent guest at Holland House was Samuel Rogers, the old banker and poet whom Carlyle described as 'a most sorrowful, distressing, distracted old phenomenon, hovering over the rim of deep eternities with nothing but light babble, fatuity, vanity, and the frostiest London wit in his mouth'. Creevey also found Rogers 'a damned bore'; and Lady Holland once said to him in her most dismissive way, 'Your poetry is bad enough, so pray be sparing of your prose'. But she liked him, and so did Dickens, who became a regular guest at the breakfasts which Rogers gave in his beautifully furnished house in St James's Place for the leading literary figures of the day.

As well as being a guest at Holland House and 22 St James's Place, the good-looking young man with his lively, eager face, his flowing brown hair and excessively fashionable clothes, was also to be seen at Gore House where the exquisite Count d'Orsay lived with the Countess of Blessington, his wife's beautiful and witty stepmother, and entertained a wide variety of fashionable celebrities from Wellington and Disraeli to the morose Prince Louis Napoleon and the ebullient Walter Savage Landor.

In this society, to which his birth and background had done so little to accustom him, the young Dickens, eager, alert, yet deferential, moved with an assured and graceful self-sufficiency. Speaking little until he felt himself to have been accepted, seeming on occasions to be rather shy, revealing the limits of his intellectual curiosity, but far too sensible and unaffected to pretend to interests and knowledge he did not possess, he showed that he was determined not to be the object of any sort of patronising condescension, not to demean himself by appearing to be an author who ought permanently 'to know his place'.

He had been concerned too long in his childhood with the fears and agonies of his own and his father's social humiliation not to feel deeply gratified and reassured by his successful entry into society—his studiedly respectful letters to Lady Holland give evidence of this—but he had too much pride, too much confidence in his exceptional gifts, too deep a sensitivity to rebuff and disparagement, ever to show by his manner that he felt flattered or honoured by the attentions he received.

Kate did not go with him to these houses. There was nothing particularly unusual in this. She was, for the most time, pregnant or ill, or both; and it was, in any event, expected of a man distinguished by his talent rather than by his birth to come out alone, and leave at home a wife who might otherwise have been considered an embarrassing and tiresome encumbrance. Also, few wives ever did dine at Gore House, owing to Lady Blessington's dubious moral status; and some would not go to Holland House because of Lady Holland's divorce. Even Mrs Carlyle, a conversationalist of rare accomplishment, did not as a rule accompany her husband on his excursions from Cheyne Row.

But Jane Carlyle was occasionally invited out, whereas Kate never was, not even to breakfast by Samuel Rogers, who did invite wives and who showed more interest in Kate than did most of Dickens's new friends who came to know her.[15] For it was soon understood in society and in the literary world that, although perfectly 'presentable', Mrs Dickens had no conversation and no wit. At home she was a competent, undemanding and uninspiring hostess; and at home she was kept, and, indeed, preferred to stay.

4

By the end of October 1839 this home was at 1 Devonshire Terrace, York Gate, Regent's Park, a far more imposing house than the one in Doughty Street.[16] The portico was impressive, the rooms were large and gracious, the tall bay windows of the drawing-room and dining-room overlooked a neat walled garden.

Dickens took the house, 'a house of great promise (and great premium)', as he described it to Forster, ' "undeniable" situation and excessive splendour', at a rent of £160 a year, and paid £800 for the remaining twelve years of the lease. Though the price was high, he was soon spending a great deal more money on improvements and furniture. New lavatories were installed; the old deal doors and wooden fireplaces went out, and mahogany panels and marble shelves and jambs came in to take their place; roller blinds were specially made for the windows; new carpets were ordered, new curtains, whole suites of furniture for the reception rooms and main bedrooms; looking-glasses were fixed to the walls, and bookcases made for the library. In these bookcases was arranged a display of books far superior to the 'three volume novels and books of travels, all obviously presentation copies' that a visitor had noticed during an early visit to Doughty Street. These were now replaced by the kind of library which a novelist and journalist needed by him for his work.

At the far end of the garden was the coach-house. And here instead of the 'small chaise with a smaller pair of ponies' which he had had when

Forster first knew him, was a 'more suitable equipage'. There was also a groom. [17]

5

Dickens would never have been able to afford so expensive an establishment while still so young a man had he not recently, after a prolonged and bitter quarrel with his publisher, entered into some new and highly profitable contracts.

The quarrel with Bentley had arisen over the publisher's determination to hold the author to the contracts they had already signed. To Dickens, whose popularity had so enormously increased since their first agreement, Bentley's attitude seemed at first unreasonable, then outrageous, and finally unforgivable. To Bentley, Dickens's attitude seemed ('quite simply') dishonest, and there were others who agreed with him. Macready summed up this view of his friend's behaviour when he wrote in his diary: 'He makes a contract which he considers advantageous at the time, but subsequently finding his talents more lucrative than he had supposed, he refuses to fulfil the contract.'

Dickens, whose contract with Bentley provided for his writing two novels for £500 each, insisted that *Oliver Twist*—although it did, in fact, constitute his contribution to *Bentley's Miscellany*—must be considered as one of these two novels. Bentley refused to concede the point, and Dickens threatened to stop writing *Oliver Twist* altogether. Bentley, anxious not to lose the services of an editor who had helped to make his magazine so popular, gave way, saying he *would* regard *Oliver Twist* as one of the contracted novels and that he would pay a higher price for both of them.

But then there were quarrels over the editorship of the magazine, about whether or not Bentley had the right to make changes in any issue without consulting Dickens, whether or not Dickens could withdraw pieces that Bentley had accepted. Soon the dispute was in the hands of solicitors, with Bentley insisting that Dickens must be held to all his agreements.

Again, however, the publisher felt constrained to give way. Dickens was offered £600 and £700 for the two novels (of which *Oliver Twist* was agreed to be one, without any deduction being made for its previous appearance in the magazine), and his editor's salary was increased to forty guineas a month. With some modifications to the advantage of the

author in respect of the term for which Bentley was to hold the copyright, these proposals were accepted.

But the quarrel soon broke out afresh. Dickens now complained that
Bentley had started to make niggling deductions from the money due
to him for his contributions to the magazine when these had to be cut
down to make room for other stories, and he wrote to ask if the publisher
considered 'that such treatment (so different from any [he] had received
elsewhere)' was likely to make him wish 'for a very long continuance
of [their] business connection?'

In fact, the business connection was not long to continue. Dickens,
oppressed by the amount of work he had undertaken to do for Bentley,
insisted that the novel which he was to provide after *Oliver Twist*
(to be called *Barnaby Rudge* instead of *Gabriel Vardon* as previously
planned) should be begun in instalments in *Bentley's Miscellany* before
its publication in three volumes. This would, at least, relieve Dickens
of having to write anything else to fill up those pages of the magazine
which were his responsibility. Bentley protested, but again gave way.
Yet Dickens was still not satisfied.

Frustrated by what he took to be Bentley's continued interference in
his running of the magazine, irritated by advertisements in it which
promised the 'forthwith' appearance of *Barnaby Rudge*, when he had not
yet had time even to start the first instalment, he broke out in anger
against the man he blamed for 'winding a net' about him:

> It is no fiction to say that at present I *cannot* write this tale. The immense
> profits which *Oliver* has realized to its publisher, and is still realizing;
> the paltry, wretched, miserable sum it brought to me . . . the conscious-
> ness that I have still the slavery and drudgery of another work on the
> same journeyman-terms; the consciousness that my books are enriching
> everybody connected with them but myself, and that I, with such a
> popularity as I have acquired, am struggling in old toils, and wasting
> my energies in the very height and freshness of my fame, and the best
> part of my life, to fill the pockets of others, while for those who are
> nearest and dearest to me I can realize little more than a genteel subsis-
> tence: all this puts me out of heart and spirits: and I cannot—cannot and
> will not—under such circumstances that keep me down with an iron
> hand, distress myself by beginning this tale until I have had time to
> breathe . . . [18]

He felt inclined to refuse to write *Barnaby Rudge* altogether. 'For I do most
solemnly declare that morally, before God and man, I hold myself
released from such hard bargains as these'. Bentley agreed to a six

months' postponement of *Barnaby Rudge*, but asked in return that Dickens, who had demanded a rest, 'and some cheerful days in the country', should not do any writing except the instalments of *Nicholas Nickleby* during that period.

This request angered Dickens still further. For, despite the oppression of the work he had undertaken to do for Bentley, he had the year before agreed to write a humorous book for Chapman and Hall, and he had also taken upon himself to edit a book for the benefit of Mrs Macrone whose husband's recent sudden death had left her and her children destitute. Dickens's answer to Bentley was to give notice that he would resign the editorship of the *Miscellany* altogether.

Bentley was utterly exasperated. But still anxious not to lose Dickens, he made him yet another favourable offer: he would pay him £40 a month to remain nominal editor of the *Miscellany*, without any duties to perform, if he would agree not to edit a magazine for anyone else. But Dickens would not give in. Bentley had to accept Harrison Ainsworth as the new editor of the *Miscellany*, and to pay Dickens £2,000 for *Barnaby Rudge*, a further £1,000 if the sales exceeded 10,000 and another £1,000 if they reached 15,000. That is to say, he would receive £4,000 for the book, if it proved anything like as popular as *Nicholas Nickleby*—a book that he had originally contracted to write for £500.

Despite this financial inducement, however, Dickens could not bring himself to get on with *Barnaby Rudge*; and soon, once more, war broke out, as Dickens put it, with the 'Burlington Street Brigand'.

The trouble was that Dickens had by now conceived an almost obsessive dislike of Bentley, a 'hound' and a 'vagabond' who was less to be trusted even than the law, bad as *that* was. 'If I were a builder or a stone-mason I might fulfil my contract with him, but write for him I really cannot unless I am forced and have no outlet for escape.' No doubt it was true: he just *could* not bring himself to write for a man whom he had come so deeply to detest. Whether or not he was conscious of having answered Bentley's proposals with what Bentley insisted was downright dishonesty and what must at least be considered disingenuousness, there could be no mistaking the heat of his anger and the depth of his animosity.

A more tactful man than Bentley would never have allowed such a situation to develop between himself as a publisher and Dickens as the most promising writer of his generation. But Bentley was not a tactful man; and that cheerful, pink, immensely bewhiskered face, and that air of open-handed geniality, belied an essentially autocratic and parsimonious temperament. Dickens was far from being the only author with whom he had quarrelled.

Whereas Chapman and Hall had always been careful to give Dickens a good deal more than his contracts with them specified, Bentley gave way to Dickens's financial demands—and gave way with a pained comment as to his legal rights—only when he was faced with the prospect of losing his most valuable author altogether. Chapman and Hall—though they could certainly afford to do so, having made £14,000 out of the monthly instalments alone—presented Dickens with about £2,000 more for *Pickwick* than they were legally obliged to do. They also gave him little presents, such as a set of silver spoons with *Pickwick* characters on the handles, which were handed to him at a banquet in the Prince of Wales Tavern, Leicester Square, to celebrate the publication of the last instalment. But with Bentley, although he and Dickens had often dined together in the early days of their relationship, there were no such intimate ties. And Dickens, wilful, determined and touchy, yet easily softened by a display of affectionate regard and admiring respect and ready to respond to it, deeply missed that happy atmosphere which Chapman and Hall's sensible generosity and understanding had created.

In the end Bentley had to accept the fact that to sue Dickens for damages for breach of contract would not be worth the cost, and that he must reconcile himself to losing him. For £1,500 he sold him his interest in *Oliver Twist*; and Chapman and Hall (who lent Dickens the money to pay for it as well as £750 for the remaining copies of the book and the Cruikshank plates) took over *Barnaby Rudge*, paying £3,000 for a six-month copyright.

So Chapman and Hall, 'the best of booksellers, past, present, and to come', had proved themselves once more Dickens's 'trusty friends'. They also continued to be pliable ones; and when Dickens informed them, through Forster, that he had received 'straightforward offers from responsible men' to publish anything he wrote at a percentage of the profits without any risk to himself, but being well disposed towards them was 'unwilling to leave them' (and would not do so provided they did something handsome for him, 'even handsomer perhaps than they dreamt of doing'), they readily complied with his wishes. These wishes were that they should publish a weekly and popular threepenny magazine—eventually to be called *Master Humphrey's Clock*—with himself not only as a contributing editor at £50 a week, but also as a proprietor, sharing in the profits though not in the costs or any losses there might be. He worked out that if the magazine were to run for two years and were to sell 50,000 copies (of which he thought there was a 'good chance') he would make a profit of between £10,000 and £11,000—over twice as much as the publishers.[19]

The self-assured determination and careful financial calculations which brought this highly profitable agreement about were to be characteristic of Dickens's future undertakings. He was now fully conscious of his value as an author; and Chapman and Hall were well aware that to retain him at all they must give way to his demands. He knew exactly what he wanted and he was defiantly determined to get it.

The profitable results of the furious arguments and bitter negotiations with Bentley were a lesson he was never to forget. That unyielding individualism and wilful determination which, as John Forster suggested, was so fiercely sharpened by his reactions to the days of the blacking factory, had beaten one publisher down, and allowed him to make a highly profitable contact with another one.

Not for the first time in his life, nor yet for the last, he had revealed a stubborn determination and an unbending self-will which were at once the seed of his genius and the source of his final, personal tragedy.

He was at heart a generous and kind man—certainly it never occurred to him that he was not so—but he was not an easy-going one. He was as capable of forcing a man to grant him far better terms than he was legally entitled to expect, as he was of spending his time—even when he had none to spare—on a subscription for the widow of a man he believed had cheated him. In the words of Angus Wilson: 'Dickens the generous and Dickens the bully grow alongside each other.'[20]

II

MRS CHARLES DICKENS
1839-1845
aet. 27-33

Mr Cruncher reposed under a patchwork counter-pane, like a Harlequin at home. At first, he slept heavily, but by degrees, began to roll and surge in bed, until he rose above the surface, with his spiky hair looking as if it must tear the sheets to ribbons. At which juncture, he exclaimed, in a voice of dire exasperation: 'Bust me, if she ain't at it again!'

A Tale of Two Cities

11

1

In May 1839 Dickens rented a cottage in Petersham for the summer. But neither here, nor at Broadstairs, where he took Kate (who was pregnant again) and the two children in August, could he sit down quietly when his work was done.

At Elm Cottage, Petersham, he played games with what Forster called 'the greatest ardour', holding his own against

> even such accomplished athletes as Maclise and Mr Beard. Bar leaping, bowling, and quoits were among the games carried on . . . and in sustained energy, what is called keeping it up, Dickens certainly balanced every competitor. Even the lighter recreations of battledore and bagatelle were pursued with relentless activity; and at such amusements as the Petersham races, in those days rather celebrated, and which he visited daily while they lasted, he worked much harder himself than the running horses did.[1]

At Broadstairs, though he was working long hours to get *Nicholas Nickleby* finished, he was just as active, taking fast walks across the sands, hurling himself into the sea from the bathing-machines, and staggering down to the pier on a stormy night, 'and creeping under the lee of a large boat which was high and dry', to watch the sea breaking for nearly an hour. He came back to the house wet through, but it was 'most superb'.

Whenever he went down to Broadstairs to spend a few days in a rented house he would, immediately on his arrival, rearrange the furniture in all the rooms, set out an inviting row of bottles of wine and spirits; and then sit down at his impeccably neat writing table to dash off a letter to a friend to join him and his family there. 'There are two pretty little spare bedrooms waiting to be occupied', he would tell Beard, who was pressed to come down by the Ramsgate boat as often and for as long as he could, or he would command Maclise to 'come to the bower which is shaded for you in the one-pair front. . . . COME'; in another letter he would beseech him to 'come down for a week, come down for a fortnight, come down for three weeks, come down for a month'.[2]

It was as though he could not bear either to be still or to be left alone with his family. Up to the Midlands he went with Browne to look at the cotton mills, then over the ruins of Kenilworth, passing on to Warwick and Stratford and Birmingham, then on to Wolverhampton and Shrewsbury, and into North Wales and on to Liverpool, and, with Forster now as well, to Manchester. He went to Manchester again, a few weeks later with Ainsworth, to attend a dinner; soon he was off to Bath to visit Landor, then up to Birmingham again, and, with Forster and his brother, he made a quick excursion to Johnson's house at Lichfield. Later he was off to Scotland, to accept the freedom of the City of Edinburgh and to make a quick tour of the country. He took Kate with him this time; but he asked his friend Angus Fletcher, the sculptor, to keep them company.

In London he was as restless as ever, giving and going to parties and to the theatre, laughing, joking, cheerful, vivid, taking long country walks and longer country rides, roaming the streets by day and night—one evening rushing to a ball given by Angela Burdett Coutts, the young heiress and philantropist, to whom Dickens had been introduced by a partner in her family's bank and with whom he was to remain on friendly terms until the separation from his wife, the next day racing up to dine in the studio at Clapham Rise where George Cattermole was working on illustrations for one of his stories, and then excitedly rolling up his sleeves in Cattermole's chambers in Albany to make punch for the 'Portwiners', a group of friends including Landseer and Maclise, Macready and Mark Lemon, Forster, Thackeray and Bulwer Lytton. Early the next morning he might dash out to see a public hanging, to gratify a whim, 'just once to watch a scene like this'.

And all the while he was working hard, keeping just ahead of the printer of *Master Humphrey's Clock* in which *The Old Curiosity Shop* had now begun to appear, contributing articles to other magazines, such as the *Examiner*, and Lady Blessington's *The Keepsake*, and writing long letters to unknown writers who sent him their work tor his advice.

The pace at which he worked, and the violent energy he brought to his other activities, had the same effect on his health that they had had before his marriage. He suffered from renewed attacks of neuralgia, which sometimes made him cry out with pain when he was working on *The Old Curiosity Shop*, and from sudden violent headaches and bilious attacks.

He suffered, too, from attacks of uncontrollable irritability; and on one occasion when Forster was dining at Devonshire Terrace with Macready and Maclise he completely lost his temper.

Forster was behaving in his peculiarly exasperating way, getting on to 'one of his headlong streams of talk (which he thinks argument)', so Macready noted in his diary, when Dickens interrupted him, only to be interrupted in his turn by one of Forster's loud, dogmatic assertions. Infuriated beyond control, Dickens asked Forster to remember that this was his house and to be good enough to leave it. Kate rushed out of the dining-room in tears, and Forster stood up to go and made angrily for the door. Macready stopped him and pleaded both with him and his host not to destroy their friendship. Dickens regained control of himself, and apologised to Forster but with the proviso that he could not be held responsible for his temper under such provocation, and if Forster acted in the same way again, so would he.

Forster stood in the doorway, 'skimbling-skambling a parcel of un-meaning words', unwilling to leave, but reluctant to stay unless Dickens made a less equivocal apology. Eventually, Macready noted, he made 'a sort of speech, accepting what he had before declined. He was silent and not recovered—no wonder!—during the whole evening.'[3]

The next day Dickens felt deeply distressed about the whole affair. He could not feel truly penitent, though, for there was no getting away from the fact, so he wrote to Macready, that there was 'no man alive or dead' who tried his friends as Forster did. But soon Forster (who was so very different when he was alone and at ease with a single companion rather than trying to overpower a dinner party) and Dickens (who valued the friendship highly) were on the same amicable footing as before.

2

On occasions there seemed something almost feverish about the pace at which Dickens led his life, the burning excitable energy that was bursting to be released. Years before, he had amazed the Hogarths by leaping through their drawing-room window dressed as a sailor, whistling the tune of a hornpipe as he danced in front of them, and then jumping out again, to appear gravely at the front door a few moments later as though nothing untoward had happened.

He still delighted in practical jokes like this one, in behaving like a crazy clown.[4] And soon after *Nicholas Nickleby* was finished, some of his friends began to believe that he really had taken leave of his senses.

It was in February 1840. In that month Carlyle had been introduced to him and been immediately struck by the 'extreme *mobility* of his face', the 'very singular manner' in which he shuttled the whole of it about when he spoke, arching his eyebrows 'amazingly'.[5]

At this time Dickens was in the middle of writing a series of letters in which he protested that he had fallen madly in love with the small fresh young Queen Victoria, a girl whose features bore more than a passing resemblance to Mary Hogarth's and whose recent marriage, he protested, had given him thoughts of doing away with himself.

'What on earth?', asked Landor when he received one of these frantic messages. 'What on earth does it all mean?'

I am utterly lost in misery and can do nothing [another of Dickens's letters protested]. The presence of my wife aggravates me. I loathe my parents. I detest my house. I begin to have thoughts of the Serpentine, of the Regent's Canal, of the razor upstairs, of the chemist's down the street, of poisoning myself . . . of hanging myself upon the pear-tree in the garden, of abstaining from food and starving myself to death . . . of murdering Chapman and Hall, of turning Chartist, of leading some bloody assault upon the palace and saving Her by my single hand. . . .

And so he went on in this, and other letters, bewildering Landor by threatening to run away to an uninhabited island with a beautiful maid of honour, telling a man he had met at Lady Blessington's that he had wandered about the grounds of Windsor Castle and felt 'so heartbroken at the glowing windows of the royal bedchamber that he had cast himself down in the mud of the Long Walk, and refused all comfort'. He now wished to be 'embalmed and to be kept (if practicable) on top of the triumphal arch at Buckingham Palace when she is in town, and on the northeast turret of the Round Tower when she is at Windsor'.[6] He carried on the pretence with relentless determination, encouraging Forster and Maclise to join in his joke, amazing bystanders, so Forster said, by unflaggingly keeping up the game in public, and loudly, despairingly lamenting that he was of no further use in life and could derive no further enjoyment from it.

So, when Landseer, commenting on Dickens's extravagant devotion to a pet raven that he had acquired, made a pun to the effect that his friend was 'raven mad', the verdict was found convincing. The rumours found their way into the papers, and Dickens, as at the time of Mary's death, when he had been unable to continue with *Pickwick* and *Oliver Twist*, was widely reported as having become demented.[7] When 'Grip', the raven, died, leaving 'a considerable property (in cheese and halfpence) in different parts of the garden', and was sent away to be stuffed, everyone was relieved, for he had been a tiresome, noisy bird calling out repeatedly, 'Halloa, old girl!', frightening the children, pecking the ankles of visitors, and biting Topping, the groom, severely. But he was soon replaced by a successor, who tore pieces out of the butcher's legs every time he called. The fantasy about Dickens's distracted, unrequited love, however, which had been carried on long after his friends had ceased to find it funny, was at last allowed to be forgotten.

Some time later at Broadstairs, though, Dickens took a fancy to play the game again. This time the object of his wild devotion was not the Queen but two unmarried ladies, one middle-aged, the other much younger, who were staying in a house in Broadstairs that had been rented by Charles Smithson, the partner of Dickens's solicitor, Tom Mitton. To both these ladies Dickens professed his undying devotion, and turning from one and then to the other would address them as 'Fair enslaver!' 'Queen of my heart!' 'Beloved of my soul!'

' 'Tis my lady! 'Tis my love!' he would exclaim at sight of one or both of them, and, continuing to address them in this style would sigh, 'Oh, that I were a glove upon that hand, that I might touch that cheek!' The elder of the two recognising the quotation asked him which one he intended to be the Juliet to his Romeo. 'Whichever you choose, my little dears,' he replied, and strolled away. Returning, he asked, 'Wilt tread a measure with me, sweet ladye?' and then, without waiting for an answer, he pirouetted on tiptoe with mock stateliness.

Another day, in the middle of a discussion of Byron's *Childe Harold*, he threw his hand to his forehead, tossed back his head, and called out, 'Stand back! I am suddenly seized with the divine afflatus!' And rushing to the shutter, he wrote upon it a verse in praise of the younger of the two ladies, an artist, Eleanor Picken, the 'maiden of the amber-dropping hair' whose beauty made him drunk.

Once he flung his arms about her and carried her off along the pier and down the slope of the jetty, clinging with her to a pole just above the water, saying that he would keep her there until the waves came up to drown them. The girl struggled to get away from him as the water rose and splashed over their legs. 'Oh! my dress,' she pleaded with him, 'my *best* dress.' It was the only silk dress she had, she told him; it would be ruined. But he held on to her and the water came up to her knees. She screamed to Mrs Dickens to help her, 'Make Mr Dickens let me go!' Kate called down to him, 'Charles! How can you be so silly? You will both be carried off by the waves, and you'll spoil the poor girl's silk dress.'

'*Dress!*' Dickens called back derisively. 'Talk not to me of *dress*! . . . Am I not immolating a brand-new pair of patent-leathers still unpaid for? . . . In this hour of abandonment to the voice of destiny, shall we be held back by the puerilities of silken raiment? Shall leather or prunella (whatever that may be) stop the bolt of Fate?'

At length Miss Picken managed to struggle free and ran back, soaking wet, to the top of the pier where Mrs Smithson, believing that the young girl must have been to blame for the undignified incident, said that she was '*surprised*' at her conduct and sent her back to the house to change.

Although she found him strangely fascinating—when she had over-come her distate for his vulgar waistcoats and fancy patent-leather shoes —Eleanor Picken was frightened of him, she confessed. And so, she came to decide, were all his family. His father and mother were staying with him while she was at the Smithsons, and she had an opportunity of observing their reactions to him. The father, who—though she did not know this—had yet again got himself into debt and been rescued by his son, seemed to watch Charles's moods warily, despite the apparent self-confidence of his conversation and portly carriage. His mother, also, appeared to be nervous of him.[8]

3

There were good reasons for his parents' apprehension. In March 1839 Dickens had felt compelled to send them both out of London. For, ever since *Pickwick* had achieved its success, John Dickens—and his second son Fred—had been plaguing Chapman and Hall for small loans which seem rarely to have been repaid. The father usually protested that the failure to comply with his requests would be 'productive of fatal consequences', and excused his importunity by reminding Chapman and Hall how much their interests were 'bound up with' those of his son. He needed £15 immediately, he had once told them, and they were the only people who could get him through 'without the appearance of disgrace, and without that annoyance to Mrs Dickens and my family which would be painful indeed'.

His needs, he always insisted, were urgent, sometimes having to be met that very day by a certain time; and he had taken care to remind Chapman and Hall that it would only distress Charles if he were to be told about these little financial arrangements. The publishers had acceded to John Dickens's requests, acceded so often and so readily, indeed, that when he was arrested for yet another debt, he had sent them a note asking them—almost as a matter of course and as though it had now become an agreed obligation—to 'do the needful'.

But John Dickens was no sooner free of one debt than he incurred another. He had taken to selling his son's autograph, cut from the bottom of letters addressed to him, and to selling pages of his manuscripts which he had purloined from his study. He had not been able by these and his more usual methods to raise enough money to meet all his debts, however, and Charles had at last come to hear of them.

Ever since he had been a full-time writer he had done what he could to help both his parents. He had employed his father as an amanuensis to take down his dictated alterations and additions to a ghosted autobiography of Grimaldi which Bentley had acquired from an incompetent writer, and he had ensured that he was invited both to the *Pickwick* dinner at the Prince of Wales and to the dinner which Charles had given for Bentley after the inauguration of the *Miscellany*. He had also kept his mother busy in looking at houses for him, and had paid her when she came to help in the house during Kate's confinements.

But when he had learned of his father's new importunities, he had felt that he must, after settling all his debts, get him out of London before he incurred any more; and in the hope of finding something suitable for them he had gone down to Devon to rent a cottage to which his parents could retire.

He had found such a place at Alphington, a mile out of Exeter on the Plymouth road. It was a small but attractive white-washed cottage, 'bright as a new pin', which could be rented for £20 a year and furnished for less than £70. 'If they are not pleased with it,' he had written to Forster, 'I shall be grievously disappointed; that's all.'

But they had been pleased with it, at first. Elizabeth Dickens came down to Mile End Cottage by 'The Telegraph' on a Thursday morning; and John Dickens, their youngest son Augustus, who was to go to school in Exeter, and their dog, Dash, two days later. Their pleasure, however, had not lasted long. Within a few weeks his mother had begun to complain, and Dickens had written in exasperation to Forster: 'I do swear that I am sick at heart with both her and father too, and think this *is* too much.' Eventually, however, he had given way and had allowed them to return from their exile. So now, at Broadstairs, they were anxious to appear to be well behaved.

4

Fred Dickens, for whom Charles had recently obtained a clerkship in the Custom House, was less nervous of Charles than the other members of his family, Eleanor Picken thought. They had a good deal in common, these two brothers—the same large full-lipped mouth, the same 'thick utterance' and gift for comic improvisation which Fred heightened by 'an amusingly oily laugh'. They went sailing together and made a practice of shouting out to each other at the tops of their voices, and with suitable gravity, a catalogue of nonsensical orders such as, 'Sheepshank your mizzen!' 'Haul up your main-top-gallant-spirits-sail-boom!' or 'Brail up your capstan-bar!'

In the evenings they all played games amongst themselves and with a succession of visitors—Mitton and Maclise, the Macreadys and the Smithsons, Angus Fletcher, Henry Austin and Charles's younger sister Letitia, a rather sickly girl who was not, in Miss Picken's opinion, 'so full of fun as the others'.(9)

Dickens, unflaggingly 'full of fun', always dominated these evenings; and at his instance the rules of games were absurdly altered, cheating became general, and confusion resulted. Even when his attention seemed to wander for a moment and a closed, absent look came over those startlingly lively eyes, he would show that he had missed nothing, by returning to the conversation with an eyebrow comically cocked to 'break forth into a wittily twisted version of all their casual remarks that they thought he had not noticed'.

In the village he was widely supposed to be mad. One day he was walking along the beach, with Angus Fletcher prancing along in front of him. Fletcher, who enjoyed showing-off as much as Dickens did, roared like a wolf when the sea water was too cold for him and 'splashed about like a fleet of porpoises, roaring most horribly all the time, and dancing a maniac dance which defied description'. A passer-by, amazed by Fletcher's odd antics and mistaking the sculptor for the novelist, said to his companion, 'Ah! How sad! You see it's quite true. Poor Boz!'[10]

The evening before, while the others had been dancing in the Tivoli Gardens, Dickens had left to go for one of his brisk walks along the front. Discovering that he was being followed by one of his inquisitive admirers, he turned round and asked him, 'Pray, Sir, may I ask, are you a native of this place?'

'No—no—sir, I am not.'

'Oh! I beg your pardon, I fancied I could detect *Broad-stares* on your very face.'[11]

He was addicted to puns, and the more atrocious they were the better he liked them. He encouraged Fred and his friends to make them, and then would endeavour to make an even more outlandish one himself. The only person not allowed to join in this game was Kate, whose punning in the days of their engagement he had found endearing rather than irritating. But now when she came up to join in, 'a pretty little woman, plump and fresh coloured', as Eleanor Picken described her, he complained with that exaggerated dismay that so often attempts to conceal a real displeasure, that this would never do, that he would get worse under this bad example. And while Kate turned up her eyes in affected terror of his wrath and then made a little *moue* before offering her contribution, which was no worse, perhaps, than many others which were far more encouragingly greeted, her husband would groan and squirm and tear his hair as if in torment.[12]

It was the reaction of a man enacting in mock earnest the suppressed exasperation that had recently helped him to create one of the most memorable and revealing characters in all his fiction. ·

5

When he began *The Old Curiosity Shop*, Dickens did not know where it would end. It was a hastily improvised story, rushed out to save the circulation of *Master Humphrey's Clock*. Recent critics have condemned the exploitation of emotion in the sentimental death scenes, for which the book seems chiefly to be remembered, 'the manipulation of "poetical" language to evade insight and instigate excited reverie around the blank fact of death'.[13]

At the time of its publication, though, critics and readers alike, from Lord Jeffrey and Edgar Allan Poe to the anxiously waiting crowds on the New York pier, broke down and wept over it. Daniel O'Connell burst into tears in a railway carriage and threw the offending pages out of the window with the heartfelt cry, 'He should not have killed her!' Even Carlyle was deeply moved.

Modern commentators, however, 'shift anxiously. Nell, they know, won't do. But, they explain, children did after all die more frequently then. And maybe, the argument runs, the Victorians were tuned in to a different emotional frequency. Tears once had a sanctioned place in the male repertoire: Homer's heroes wept. But in case Nell is impossible, there is always Quilp . . .'14

Quilp, Daniel Quilp, the violently, pathologically restless Quilp, who terrifies yet fascinates his family and dependents, is a character whom the young girl clinging to the pole at the bottom of the jetty at Broadstairs must have found strangely familiar. He is bursting with a wild vitality, he delights in practical jokes, he is determined to have his own way, he has a wonderful command of vivid language, he sometimes, 'when he found himself in a by-street, vented his delight in a shrill scream, which, greatly terrifying any lonely passenger . . . increased his mirth'.

For all his dirtiness, his dwarflike body and monstrous head, his fixed diabolical grin, his scattered, discoloured teeth, and his thin grizzled black hair 'hanging in a frowzy fringe about his ears', Quilp has married and keeps 'a pretty, little mild-spoken blue-eyed woman', 'pretty Mrs Quilp', as her husband sardonically refers to her himself, 'obedient, timid, loving Mrs Quilp . . . well-trained Mrs Quilp'.

Mrs Quilp has married this monster, 'in one of those strange infatuations of which examples are by no means scarce', and she spends most of her days in her 'bower' on Tower Hill in dread of her husband's return, yet vaguely apprehensive that he will not return.

One evening he comes back unexpectedly from the wharf (where he carries on business as a money-lender and smuggler), finds his wife's mother there, and overhears her telling some other women, who have called for a cup of tea, that her son-in-law is a tyrant who frightens her daughter to death and that her daughter 'hasn't the spirit to give him a word back, no, not a single word'.

Quilp, suddenly appearing, tells his wife he will bite her if she ever listens to these beldames again.

With this laconic threat, which he accompanied with a snarl that gave him the appearance of being particularly in earnest, Mr Quilp bade her clear the tea-board away, and bring the rum. The spirit being set before him in a huge case-bottle, which had originally come out of some ship's locker, he ordered cold water and the box of cigars; and these being supplied, he settled himself in an arm-chair with his large head and face squeezed up against the back, and his little legs planted on the table.

'Now, Mrs Quilp,' he said; 'I feel in a smoking humour, and shall probably blaze away all night. But sit where you are, if you please, in case I want you.'

His wife returned no other reply than the customary, 'Yes, Quilp,' and the small Lord of the Creation took his first cigar and mixed his first glass of grog. The sun went down and the stars peeped out, the Tower turned from its own proper colours to grey and from grey to black, the room became perfectly dark and the end of the cigar a deep fiery red, but still Mr Quilp went on smoking and drinking in the same position, and staring listlessly out of the window with the dog-like smile always on his face, save when Mrs Quilp made some involuntary movement of restlessness or fatigue, and then it expanded into a grin of delight.* (15)

' "Now, Mrs Quilp," he said; "I feel in a smoking humour, and shall probably blaze away all night" '

As well as being involved with his pretty, complaisant wife, Quilp is also involved with Little Nell, the apotheosis of Mary Hogarth, the pretty, delicate, fourteen-year-old girl, 'a fine girl of her age,' Dick Swiveller thinks her, 'but small'. Nell is an angelic martyr, ambiguously precocious, idealized and unreal. Dickens saves her from Quilp's clutches

* *The Old Curiosity Shop*, ch. IV.

by letting her die, laying her 'at rest, upon her little bed'. But not before
Quilp has jumped into her bed in London and blazed away in it with his
cigar, and not before he has asked her to be his second Mrs Quilp.

When Quilp sees Nell's grandfather kiss her smooth cheek, 'Ah!' he
says, smacking his lips, 'Just upon the rosy part. What a capital kiss!'

> Nell was none the slower in going away, for this remark. Quilp looked
> after her with an admiring leer, and when she had closed the door,
> fell to complimenting the old man upon her charms.
>
> 'Such a fresh, blooming, modest little bud, neighbour,' said Quilp,
> nursing his short leg, and making his eyes twinkle very much; 'such a
> chubby, rosy, cosy, Little Nell!'
>
> The old man answered by a forced smile, and was plainly struggling
> with a feeling of the keenest and most exquisite impatience. It was not
> lost upon Quilp, who delighted in torturing him, or indeed anybody
> else when he could.
>
> 'She's so,' said Quilp, speaking very slowly, and feigning to be quite ·
> absorbed in the subject, 'so small, so compact, so beautifully modelled,
> so fair, with such blue veins and such a transparent skin, and such little
> feet, and such winning ways—but, bless me, you're nervous. . . .'* (16)

Just as Dickens shrinks back from Quilp's lust for Little Nell, so he is
driven on to describe the delight Quilp took in frightening and shocking
his mother-in-law, Mrs Jiniwin, and the satisfaction this gave him.

Dickens had lately been on far less friendly terms with his own mother-
in-law, Mrs Hogarth; and in his anonymously edited version of *The
Loving Ballad of Lord Bateman*, which Cruikshank published with a series
of comic plates, he said that a mother-in-law who 'suddenly assumes a
new tone' when her daughter is safely married, is a phenomenon which
'most married men' will 'quickly recognise'. He had also fallen out with
Kate's uncle and aunt, the Thomsons, and in describing a visit by 'Mr and
Mrs T.', all he could say, he told Forster, was 'damn the impudence of
Mr T.'

Although it seems unlikely that Thomas Wright had any firsthand
evidence for saying that the quarrels between Quilp and Mrs Jiniwin, 'or
something like them, certainly took place in real life' between Dickens and
Mrs Hogarth,[17] there is no mistaking the delight Dickens took in describing these quarrels.

Here is his wonderfully vivid description of one such encounter between
the dwarf and the mother-in-law, who, despite her inclination 'to resist
male authority' and wage perpetual war with Daniel, stands 'in no slight

* *The Old Curiosity Shop*, ch. IX.

dread of him'. The encounter clearly has a marvellously invigorating effect on Quilp's voracious appetite:

> Mr Quilp now walked up to the front of a looking-glass, and was standing there putting on his neckerchief when Mrs Jiniwin, happening to be behind him, could not resist the inclination she felt to shake her fist at her tyrant son-in-law. It was the gesture of an instant, but as she did so and accompanied the action with a menacing look, she met his eye in the glass, catching her in the very act. The same glance at the mirror conveyed to her the reflection of a horribly grotesque and distorted face with the tongue lolling out; and the next instant the dwarf, turning about with a perfectly bland and placid look, inquired in a tone of great affection,
>
> 'How are you now, my dear old darling?'
>
> Slight and ridiculous as the incident was, it made him appear such a little fiend, and withal such a keen and knowing one, that the old woman felt too much afraid of him to utter a single word, and suffered herself to be led with extraordinary politeness to the breakfast-table. Here he by no means diminished the impression he had just produced, for he ate hard eggs, shell and all, devoured gigantic prawns with the heads and tails on, chewed tobacco and water-cresses at the same time and with extraordinary greediness, drank boiling tea without winking, bit his fork and spoon till they bent again, and in short performed so many horrifying and uncommon acts that the women were nearly frightened out of their wits, and began to doubt if he were really a human creature.*

6

The married life of Daniel and Mrs Quilp (she is given no Christian name) is in strong contrast to that of Mr and Mrs Garland, both of whom are little, plump and placid. The Garlands married late in life, have a dutiful and affectionate son, and are very happy. But they are not like adult people: they behave as though they are still innocent children and so are able to enjoy what was for Dickens the best kind of relationship of all. Yet, as in the case of Nell's perfect goodness, the unalloyed happiness of the Garlands has to be taken on trust from the author, and is not demonstrated in the way that the Quilp's incompatibility is demonstrated. Indeed, happiness in marriage, in this and other novels, has nearly always to be taken on trust; it is only the disruptive marriages that excite the author's imagination and therefore our own. The happy marriage—like that of the Garlands' son, Abel, who, at the end of the book, meets 'the

* *The Old Curiosity Shop*, ch. v.

most bashful young lady that was ever seen' and settles down with her to become 'the happiest of the happy'—seems no more than a conventional fairy-tale formula.

In Dickens's first novel, Pickwick himself and the Wellers, father and son, had already hinted at what was to come—although their respective situations, of course, are also conventional formulas, in this case the staple diet of farce. Pickwick is a bachelor and is horrified by the suggestion that he had ever seriously considered being anything else. Tony Weller, Sam's father, the coachman whose face has 'expanded under the influence of good living, and a disposition remarkable for resignation', needs all the resignation he can muster in his unwilling associations with a wife who is inclined to be 'perwerse and unpleasant'. Tony is distressed when he believes that Sam is getting married, that he also will become a 'dilluded wictim', and he is profoundly relieved when his son reassures him that he 'ain't a goin' to get married, don't you fret yourself about that'.

In the end Sam decides to marry the pretty little housemaid, Mary; but only on condition that she waits for him until Mr Pickwick needs his services no longer. She waits for two years and, since the marriage takes place on the last page, the reader is left to hope that it may perhaps be successful.

Mr Wardle of Manor Farm, Dingley Dell, was happily married for his part, he says; but then when we meet *him*, Mrs Wardle is dead.

In the later novels this scheme of things becomes a familiar pattern. Supposedly happy marriages round off plots; but marriages which are actually described, and described with vitality, are scarcely ever happy. Even those that appear to be may well not be so. The Clennams may possibly have been happy, Jeremy Flintwich, misleadingly suggests: 'As happy as most other married people, I suppose. . . . I can't say. I don't know. There are secrets in all families.'*

In *Bleak House* there are the Bagnets who love and respect each other, it seems; but there are also, in the same book, the Jellybys, the Smallweeds, the Snagsbys and the Skimpoles. And it is in the depiction of *their* relationships and conflicts that Dickens's peculiar genius takes such obvious delight, and reaches such unmatched felicities of comic invention.

Whether it is the Chicks who, on the whole, 'are a well-matched, fairly balanced couple in their matrimonial bickerings'† or the Vardens or the Crunchers, who are not well matched at all, the contests between husbands and wives are always 'very animating'.

* *Little Dorrit*, ch. xxx.   † *Dombey and Son*, ch. ii.

Mr Cruncher is quite as difficult as a husband, as Mrs Varden is as a wife:

Mr Cruncher reposed under a patchwork counterpane, like a Harlequin at home. At first, he slept heavily, but by degrees, began to roll and surge in bed, until he rose above the surface, with his spiky hair looking as if it must tear the sheets to ribbons. At which juncture, he exclaimed, in a voice of dire exasperation:

'Bust me, if she ain't at it agin!'

A woman of orderly and industrious appearance rose from her knees in a corner, with sufficient haste and trepidation to show that she was the person referred to.

'What!' said Mr Cruncher, looking out of bed for a boot. 'You're at it agin, are you?'

After hailing the morn with this second salutation, he threw a boot at the woman as a third. . . .

'What,' said Mr Cruncher, varying his apostrophe after missing his mark—'What are you up to, Aggerawayter?'

'I was only saying my prayers.' . . .

Mr Cruncher's temper was not at all improved when he came to his breakfast. He resented Mrs Cruncher's saying grace with particular animosity.

'Now, Aggerawayter! What are you up to? At it again?'

His wife explained that she had merely 'asked a blessing'.

'Don't do it,' said Mr Cruncher, looking about, as if he rather expected to see the loaf disappear under the efficacy of his wife's petitions. 'I an't a going to be blest out of house and home. I won't have my wittles blest off my table. Keep still!'*

That Dickens found this scene of 'matrimonial bickering', and scores of others like it, as animating as the reader does cannot well be doubted. Of course, the quarrels of the incompatible have a natural appeal for writers of comedy: happy marriages do not lend themselves to this kind of treatment. But in anatomising unhappy ones with such inspired verve, Dickens reveals more than a hint of his own personal relish in the discomfiture of the downtrodden partner and in the exultation of the bully.

7

It was not Catherine Dickens's fault that her husband failed to find in her what he needed in a wife. He had expected too much of her. Yet he could not avoid implying that she had let him down.

* *A Tale of Two Cities*, Bk. ii, ch. i.

As well as admiration and respect, Dickens longed for sympathy, understanding and tenderness. But the love he brought to her was never unreserved, never spontaneously intimate, never free from a hint of tolerance, even of patronage. The advice he gave her when she was moody, downcast or tearfully out of temper was studiedly reasonable and patient, yet it always carried with it a reminder of that early and well-remembered warning—if she were tired of him, she had merely to say so, he would not forget her lightly, but he would leave her immediately. She *was* moody it seems; but then his moods, too, were capable of changing abruptly and disconcertingly from elation to depression. She *was* given to self-pity; but then so, after all, was he. She *did* make demands on his time and patience when she was feeling ill or out of sorts; but his demands on her, as a wife and as a woman, were far beyond what it lay in her capacity to meet. 'My father', one of his daughters said long after he was dead, 'did not understand women', and it was true.

But Kate, for her part, had not the discernment to understand what her husband needed from her, that his work, and all that it meant to him, was more important to him than she was and that she must accustom herself to its dominance. But neither could he bring himself to understand what she wanted from him, that as a woman she needed more than the verbal assurance of his affection, the excitement of his body, and the protection and distinction of his name.

Placid, slow, lethargic, kindly, unambitious and unoriginal, her nature contrasted sharply with her husband's brilliance, restlessness and burning energy. She was made all the more aware of this herself by her husband's devotion to the memory of her younger, more lively, more intelligent sister, by his taste for flirting with women who were smarter, more attractive or more amusing than herself. She had soon grown accustomed to this, to the pleasure he took in attracting young girls like the alarmed Eleanor Picken at Broadstairs, and in pretending to be distractedly in love with them, or with susceptible women older than himself.

He proclaimed his love for Miss Mary Boyle, a cousin of Mrs Richard Watson, with the wildest extravagance, sending her poems in which he laid bare his wounded heart, writing her notes which lamented that 'the call of honour' beckoned him from happiness, that a man might seem to be happy on his domestic hearth, yet, in reality, was 'confoundedly miserable—as I am—Ever Affectionately my darling'.[18]

It was hard to be coherent, 'with a bosom full of arrows', he had protested in the same strain in 1842, to Mrs David Cadwallader Colden, the forty-six-year-old wife of an American friend of Macready. 'Inclosed is a groan. I shall not miss it. I have a great many more. . . . If this should meet HIS eye, I trust you to throw dust in the same. HIS suspicions must not be aroused. . . . When I think of futile attempts to tear two hearts asunder that are so closely knit together, I laugh like a Fiend. Ha! Ha! Ha! C UPI D.'[19]

When he left America and Mrs Colden had not been to see him off—because Kate's letter giving the time of their departure had not reached her in time—he had told her, 'It is more clear to me than ever that Kate is as near being a Donkey as one of that sex whose luminary and sun you are, *can* be'.[20] The best part of his heart, he told Mrs Colden (his 'sweet Foreigner', his 'Better Angel') was left behind in Laight Street, Boston, where she lived, and he found it difficult to get on without it.

Kate accepted all this as being harmless enough. But on his return he was protesting to a much younger girl that had he not been married, he would have taken the greatest pleasure in running a rival through the body, in no poetical or tender sense, he assured her, 'but with good sharp Steel'.

This girl was Christiana Weller, and Dickens's protestations of devotion to her were certainly much more genuine than those he had expressed to Frances Colden. He had met her at a soirée of the Liverpool Mechanics' Institute when he (in a striking 'white-and-black or magpie waistcoat') had made a speech, and she ('in a pretty green dress trimmed with fur') had played the piano. His first sight of the 'angel's message in her face' smote him to the heart, he confessed; she 'started out alone from the crowd' as soon as he saw her.

He could not joke about this girl. 'Good God!' he confided to his friend T. J. Thompson, the rich brother-in-law of his solicitor's partner, who had met him for dinner in Liverpool on the night of the soirée, 'Good God! What a madman I should seem, if the incredible feeling I have conceived for that girl could be made plain to anyone.'

Thompson was deeply attracted to her, too, and although he was worried about the difference in their ages (he was over thirty and a widower with two children), he wanted to ask the young girl to marry him. When a letter arrived at Devonshire Terrace asking for his advice, Dickens glanced at the Liverpool postmark, broke the seal, and as soon as he had opened the first page, he knew what Thompson was writing about.

'I felt the blood go from my face to I don't know where, and my very lips turn white,' Dickens replied. 'I never in my life . . . had the whole current of my life so stopped for the instant, as when I felt, at a glance, what your letter said.'

His advice was unequivocal: Thompson must not hesitate. He must marry her, and must bring her to see him; for, so Dickens said, 'I could bear better her passing from my arms to heaven than I could endure the thought of coldly passing into the World again to see her no more.'

Thompson took the advice and asked Miss Weller to marry him; and although her father did not at first approve of the match, eventually he gave his consent. 'Good Heavens what a dream it appears,' Dickens wrote excitedly when he heard the news. 'It is a noble prize you have won. The father seems to have acted like a man. I had my fears of that, I confess, for the greater part of my observation of Parents and children had shown selfishness in the first almost invariably.'

It turned out, however, that it was not only the father who had had reservations, but Miss Weller herself, as there were 'other footprints in the field'.

Dickens wrote to her and told her that she ought to reconsider her decision, that it was he who, sympathising with his friend's condition, had encouraged him to press his suit, that he meant to go on hoping for Thompson, unless, he added, 'you hold my hands; and that you wont do, I believe. Whatever happens in this case, of this I am quite sure—it will all happen Wrong, and cannot happen otherwise than Wrong, the undersigned being excluded from all chance of competition.'[21]

8

Of all this Kate had known little. But when, the next year, Charles met the pretty English wife of a Swiss banker, Emile De La Rue, who lived in Genoa (where Dickens had taken his family on the grounds that they could live twice as cheaply there as in London), Kate could not manage to hide her jealousy.

Mme De La Rue told Dickens that she had repeated visions of herself on a hillside, either surrounded by crowds of people whose faces she could not see, or alone and in great pain and terror, being pelted with stones. The hillside was haunted by a most terrible evil spirit, on whom she dared not rest her eyes, the very thought of whom made her tremble.

Dickens believed he could dispel her visions and fears by hypnosis. Several years before, Dr Elliotson, a Professor of Medicine at London

University, had interested Dickens in mesmerism, and given him some remarkable demonstrations of his powers. Since then Dickens had shown that he, too, could mesmerise a willing patient. In Pittsburgh, Kate had offered herself for an experiment, and in six minutes, so he wrote home to Forster, 'I magnetised her into hysterics, and then into the magnetic sleep. I tried again next night, and she fell into the slumber in little more than two minutes.'

He was as successful with Mme De La Rue, throwing her into hypnotic states and persuading her to tell him everything about herself, her fears and repressions. Soon he was utterly preoccupied with his influence over her, and the benefit she deemed to be deriving from his treatment. He sat with her for long periods at all hours of the day and night, until Kate was deeply upset by the absorption of his interest in her.

When he and Kate left Genoa for Rome, in January 1845, to be there in time for the Carnival and Holy Week, he was silent and abstracted on the journey, worrying that Mme De La Rue might not be able to get on without him, writing to her husband twice on the way in attempts to diagnose the origins of her 'phantom', anxious for news of her progress.

The two couples met in Rome for Holy Week, however, and immediately after his arrival Charles resumed his treatment of her illness, answering her husband's urgent calls to go to her room at night to mesmerise her, sometimes finding her 'rolled into an apparently insensible ball, by tic on the brain', and returning to his own room in such an overwrought condition that he could not immediately get back into bed, but was driven to walk up and down the room by candlelight.

Kate found Charles's preoccupation with his treatment of Mme De La Rue distressing enough; but what was even more aggravating was that his patient accompanied them whenever they went sightseeing. And when the Dickenses left Rome after Easter, both Mme De La Rue and her husband decided to travel on the same day and in the same carriage. On the journey Dickens mesmerised Mme De La Rue—sometimes in the carriage, at other times by the roadside or in the inn where they stopped—with such regular and attentive assiduity, that before they arrived back at Genoa, Kate refused to talk to her.

Jealously and tearfully she accused her husband of thinking more about Mme De La Rue than of herself; and when he told her that her suspicions were utterly unfounded, she angrily replied that if his association with her really was innocent, she couldn't understand why he didn't give it up, since he could see that it made her so unhappy. But Dickens refused to

give it up, insisting that Mme De La Rue was a sick woman who had need
of him, and that no one else could help her as he could.

The argument was unresolved. Kate continued to refuse to speak either
to Mme De La Rue or to her husband. At first, Dickens intimated to the
De La Rues that his wife's conduct was the result of her own nervous instability; but at length he felt obliged to admit to them that she was jealous.

He continued to see a great deal of the De La Rues, none the less, and
when, in June, he decided to go home to London, he left the Palazzo
Peschiere to avoid the 'miseries of moving' and went to stay with them
in their villa until all the packing up was done.

Dickens had been encouraged in his decision to return to England by
the knowledge that he could now better afford to maintain his family
in respectable style at Devonshire Terrace. Bradbury and Evans had
written to him to say that the first 20,000 copies of *The Chimes*, his little
Christmas book for the year before, had made a profit of over £1,400;
and there was another £900 from Chapman and Hall due to him from
profits of the books they still controlled. With these payments in mind,
Dickens wrote to Mitton with orders to carry on with the redecoration
of Devonshire Terrace, to have the doors and garden railings painted
green, the drawing-room papered in 'blue and gold or purple and gold'
with gold moulding, the ceiling to have 'a faint pink blush in it—and a
little wreath of flowers to be painted round the lamp'; and the walls of
the hall and staircase to be green, 'not too decided, of course, to spoil
the effects of the prints'.

Mitton did not like the idea of the green hall; so Dickens asked Kate's
opinion, which he rarely did, usually relying on Georgina, and sometimes on Forster, to settle all domestic questions, even on such matters
as this. Kate agreed with Mitton. 'So let it be', Dickens wrote back,
'whatever you and the Decorator think best.'

Now that he would so soon be home with his friends in London again,
he was cheerful and relaxed. His letters became gayer and brighter as he
told Forster how beautiful were the gardens by day and the 'miraculously
splendid fireflies' by night. And so the quarrel with his wife was temporarily patched up.[22]

9

Yet it rankled with him for years, contributing more perhaps to the
increasing unhappiness of his marriage than any other cause.

On returning from a holiday with Wilkie Collins and Augustus Egg in 1853, he referred to it again. His previous letters during the holiday had been cheerful and warmly affectionate. Now that he would soon be back in her company, though, the remembrance of past irritations overclouded the affection he could feel for her when they were not together. He had called on the De La Rues on his way down to Naples, and now wrote to Kate to say 'very seriously':

Nine years have gone by since we were in Genoa. Whatever looked large in that little place may be supposed in such a time to have shrunk to its reasonable and natural proportions. You know my life too, and my character, and what has had its part in making them successful; and the more you see of me, the better perhaps you may understand that the intense pursuit of any idea that takes complete possession of me, is one of the qualities that makes me different—sometimes for good; sometimes I dare say for evil—from other men. Whatever made you unhappy in the Genoa time had no other root, beginning, middle, or end, than whatever has made you proud and honoured in your married life, and given you station better than rank, and surrounded you with many enviable things. This is the plain truth, and here I leave it. . . .

Now I am perfectly clear that your position beside these people is not a good one, is not an amiable one, a generous one—is not worthy of you at all. And I see you have it in your power to set it right at once by writing her a note to say that you have heard from me, with interest, of her sufferings and her cheerfulness—that you couldn't receive her messages of remembrance without a desire to respond to them—and that if you should ever be thrown together again by any circumstances, you hope it will be for a friendly association without any sort of shadow upon it.

I wonder whether you will have done the study mantelpiece by Sunday!—I hope so. Understand that if I come on Sunday I will not write again. My best love to the darlings.[23]

10

The darlings made life at home much easier, of course. They were a distraction and a comforting screen.

To be sure, like many another Victorian father, Dickens reacted to his wife's fecundity with facetiously exaggerated dismay.

What strange Kings those were in the Fairy times [he complained], who, with three thousand wives and four thousand seven hundred and fifty concubines found it necessary to put prayers in all the temples for a prince as beautiful as the day! I have some idea, with only one wife and nothing particular in any other direction, of interceding with the bishop of London to have a little service in Saint Paul's beseeching that I may be considered to have done enough towards my country's population.[24]

Similarly, at the time of Francis's birth Dickens had for a month declined '(on principle)' to look at the 'object'; and when Edward was born he said that he was 'not quite clear that he had particularly wanted him'.

These repeated laments about his wife's recurrent pregnancies did carry more than a hint of genuine distaste and anxiety. Each new baby was proof to the world of a sensual relationship with a woman whom he found increasingly irritating, another tie to that enclosing domesticity which he so much needed and yet from which he so much longed to escape, a fresh financial responsibility when there already were so many others—parents and brothers as well as children—who looked to him for support.

Yet he loved babies and he loved children; and even if, as his daughter, Katey, and his son, Charley, both thought, the children of his imagination were quite as real to him as they themselves and their brothers and sisters were, he seemed a wonderful father to them when they were young.

He had missed them dreadfully when he was in America, and when he arrived home he was quite as delighted to see them, as they were to see him. They, indeed, were almost hysterical with excitement and Charley actually suffered the most violent convulsions which so alarmed his parents that they had to send for the doctor. They had been staying with Charles Macready's family and they had not been happy there. It was a 'prim, gloomy, unjoyful house' whose master, though kind-hearted, was very stern and strict; and to be back home again at Devonshire Terrace was a wonderful relief.

Their father was quite as delighted himself. After breakfast he went out into the garden to play games with them before beginning work, and in the evenings, sitting on the rocking-chair he had brought back with him from America, he sang them funny songs.

They all had nicknames. The baby, Walter, was known as 'Young Skull', because of his high cheekbones, Katey was 'Lucifer Box', because of her temper. The elder two were given new names in honour of their father's return. Mamie, previously known as 'Popem Jee', now became 'Mild Glo'ster', on account of her shy docility, and Charley, once 'the Snodgering Blee', became 'Flaster Floby'. Even the dog had to change its name from 'Timber Doodle' to 'Sniffle Timbery'. Each name had to be pronounced with what Dickens called a 'peculiar drawl'.

Later on, when the other babies were born, they were all given nicknames too. Francis was 'Chickenstalker', Alfred was 'Sampson Brass' or 'Skittles', Sydney, 'The Ocean Spectre', because of the faraway look in his eyes, Henry, 'The Jolly Postboy', and the youngest, Edward, 'evidently the greatest, noblest, finest, cleverest, brightest, and most brilliant of boys', was the beloved 'Plorn', 'Plornish', 'Plornishghenter', 'Plornish-Maroon,' 'May-Roon-Ti-Goon-Ter'.

He loved reading to them, telling them stories and singing them songs; he spent hours, days even, rehearsing plays with them in their schoolroom; he sat by their beds when they were ill; and every Christmas he would take them to a toy-shop in Holborn to buy them presents, and would give them marvellous parties.

There was one memorable Christmas, in particular, the one after he finished the *Christmas Carol*. He had been utterly absorbed in the theme of that book, throwing himself into the writing of it with an enthusiasm that he had scarcely ever felt before, sharing the joys and sorrows of his characters as though they were his own. He had always been liable to do this, being as moved to tears by the tragedy of Little Nell, as to laughter by the comedy of his letters—George Putnam noticed in America how, when he was writing to his friends at home, Dickens's face would be 'convulsed with laughter at his own fun'. Now, over the *Christmas Carol*, he admitted that he 'wept and laughed, and wept again, and excited himself in a most extraordinary manner in the composition; and thinking whereof he walked about the back streets of London fifteen and twenty miles many a night when all sober folks had gone to bed'. He had finished it in less than two months, despite a great deal of unaccustomed rewriting, and then, again in his own words, 'broke out like a madman'.

And so at Christmas that year there were 'such dinings, such dancings, such conjurings, such blind-man's-buffings, such theatregoings, such kissings-out of old years and kissings-in of new ones' as had ever taken place 'in these parts before'. And at a children's party at the Macready's house his excitement was feverish. He performed a country dance with Mrs Macready; he displayed his remarkable skill as a conjuror, producing a plum pudding from an empty saucepan and heating it up over a blazing fire in Clarkson Stanfield's hat, ('without damage to the lining'), changing a box of bran into a live guinea-pig. Jane Carlyle who was at the party and watched him exert himself until 'the perspiration was pouring down', thought that, although he seemed '*drunk*' with his efforts, he was 'the *best* conjuror' she had ever seen.

Thackeray was there, too, and Forster, and they were all 'madder than ever' after supper with the 'pulling of crackers, the drinking of champagne, and the making of speeches'. Then the dancing started and Forster seized Jane Carlyle round the waist and whirled her into the thick of it. 'Oh for the love of heaven let me go,' she cried out. 'You are going to dash my brains out against the folding doors!' 'Your *brains*!' he answered, 'who cares about their brains *here*? *Let them go!*'[25]

Another Christmas, Dickens had galloped round the floor 'for two mortal hours' with Mrs Macready, after entertaining the children with a magic lantern and his conjuring tricks. Mamey and Katey had taught him the polka, and waking up the night before he had suddenly thought that he might have forgotten it, so he jumped out of bed and began hopping and prancing round the floor to remind himself of the step. At the party the next day, he went on dancing until everyone else was exhausted and gave in.[26]

Sometimes their father was cross with the children; and they would feel momentarily afraid of him. But the anger soon cooled and the next moment, so his son Alfred said, would be 'like the sun after a shower'.[27]

Most of the time the children were happy; and most of the time, so it seemed to them, their father was happy too. They loved being with him when he *was* happy, because he loved being with them. And he himself derived such pleasure from their company, for in it he could temporarily succeed in recapturing the savour of his own lost childhood.

EPILOGUE

'You don't object to an aged parent, I hope?'

GAD'S HILL PLACE HIGHAM BY ROCHESTER KENT

The old days—the old days! Shall I ever, I wonder, get the frame of mind back as it used to be then?

Charles Dickens to John Forster

As the years passed, and the children grew older, those who knew their parents best became aware of the underlying tensions in the house. Dickens was not a man who could tolerate clumsiness or incompetence: his eldest son, standing behind him at the rehearsals for some play, could sense the strain even in the back of his father's head as he watched for the actors' mistakes. Occasionally he would break out into what he admitted himself to be 'causeless rages', or at other times he might burst into laughter when, with a more than usual display of her awkwardness, Kate dropped her bracelets into the soup at a dinner party.

But there was no affection in the laughter, no sympathy for her distress. And the more she irritated him with her clumsiness, her slow indolence and nervousness, the less he felt able to tolerate her other weaknesses, the less easy it was for him to forgive or forget her unreasonable jealousy over Mme De La Rue. Even her handwriting was a source of irritation, and her fits of nervousness and post-natal depression assumed in his mind the characteristics of a permanent emotional instability, or—as he was later to put it in published statement—'some peculiarity of her character'.

He could not disguise the intense annoyance she caused him, even in his letters. Though a fundamentally kind and sympathetic man where others were concerned, he wrote of her pregnancies in those facetiously exaggerated letters of his as though he had had nothing to do with them, as though they were yet another example of her lazy ineptitude.

When the family moved from Devonshire Terrace to the larger Tavistock House in Tavistock Square,[1] he told his friend Mrs Watson that during the redecorations, his wife got herself 'all over paint, and seems to think that it is somehow being immensely useful to get into that condition'. When the solid meals that Victorian doctors prescribed for pregnant mothers made her fat, he told Leigh Hunt how her carriage, like a 'little pill box on wheels', staggered about town with her on board. When he had occasion to write a letter to her, he reminded her how much he hated untidiness, how important it was for him to have things kept in the places where he had put them—'keep things in their places. I can't bear to picture them otherwise.'

He made this clear to her in his books, too. The awkwardness of Tilly Slowboy, the sloppy maid in *The Cricket on the Hearth*, is contrasted with the neatness and flair for housekeeping that Little Nell and Little Dorrit, Esther Summerson, Agnes Wickfield, and his other heroines, all shared with his sister-in-law, Georgina, to whom he chose to delegate the running of his household. And in *David Copperfield*, Annie Strong's words, 'There can be no disparity in marriage like unsuitability of mind and purpose', are repeated like a refrain, and are shown to assume for David a peculiar importance.

By April 1856 Dickens was admitting openly to Forster that the skeleton in his domestic closet was 'becoming a pretty big one'. 'Poor Catherine and I are not made for each other and there is no help for it', he wrote the following year when he had definitely decided the marriage had broken down. 'It is not only that she makes me uneasy and unhappy, but that I make her so too—and much more so. . . . Nothing on earth could make her understand me, or suit us to each other.'

He did not confide only in Forster. To Miss Coutts he confessed that he believed 'no people were ever created with such an impossibility of interest, sympathy, confidence, sentiment, tender union of any kind between them' as there was between himself and Kate. And to M. De La Rue he wrote,

> Between ourselves . . . I don't get on better in these later times with a certain poor lady you know of, than I did in the early Peschiere days. Much worse. Much worse! Neither do the children, elder or younger. Neither can she get on with herself or be anything but unhappy. (She has been excruciatingly jealous of, and has obtained positive proof of my being on the most intimate terms with, at least fifteen thousand women of various conditions in life, since we left Genoa. . . .) What we should do, or what the girls would be, without Georgy, I cannot imagine.[2]

He suggested in other letters to Miss Coutts that Kate did not, 'and never did care for the children; and the children do not—and they never did— care for her. The little play that is acted in your Drawing-room is not the truth, and the less the children play it, the better for themselves, because they know it is not the truth. (If I stood before you at this moment and told you what difficulty we had to get Frank, for instance, to go near his mother, or keep near his mother, you would stand amazed.)' It was Georgina, he wanted his friends to believe, to whom the children were more deeply attached. 'She is the active spirit of the house, and the children dote upon her. Enough of this. We put the Skeleton away in the cupboard, and very few people, comparatively, know of its existence.'[3]

And perhaps very few people would have known of its existence, had it not been for Dickens's falling in love with Ellen Ternan, soon after his unfortunate rediscovery of Maria Beadnell had left him in so restless and dissastisfied a state.

Ellen was a pretty, rather sad and wistful-looking young blonde actress, whom he had come to know well while rehearsing one of those plays in which he indulged his passion for acting and theatrical administration, and on which he came increasingly to rely for relief from the pressures of his work. Deeply attracted to her, it seems, from the beginning, the flirtatious manner he adopted with her soon changed into a gnawing passion. And the more intensely he desired her the more repelled he was by Kate, the more firmly gripped by 'grim despair and restlessness'.

For some time now he had been feeling like this and had been repeatedly urging Wilkie Collins to think of 'any tremendous way of passing the night'. 'Any mad proposal you please,' he had urged him. 'I don't care what it is. I give (for that night only) restraint to the Winds!' 'If the mind can devise anything sufficiently in the style of Sybarite Rome in the days of its culminating voluptuousness,' he had written, with characteristic and exaggerated burlesque, in another letter, 'I am your man.'

Now he begged Collins to go with him to write, to 'take any tour—see anything. . . . Will you rattle your head and see if there is any pebble in it which we could wander away and play at marbles with?. . . I want to escape from myself. For when I *do* start up and stare myself seedily in the face . . . my blankness is inconceivable—indescribable—my misery, amazing.'[4]

Soon after his return from a holiday with Collins, towards the end of 1857, he gave instructions for his dressing-room at Tavistock House to be turned into a bedroom, for the doorway between that room and Mrs Dickens's room to be blocked up, and for the washstands to be taken into the bathroom.

As yet he dismissed the idea of a legal separation. 'A dismal failure has to be borne', he told Forster. A strong spirit of abnegation pervades much of the writing that he did at this time, particularly in the scenes in which Lucie Manette appears in *A Tale of Two Cities*.

But then, at the beginning of 1858, events forced Dickens to change his mind. The dismal failure of his marriage, which had cast so dark a shadow over his life, could be borne no longer. A bracelet which he had intended as a present for Ellen was misdirected to Tavistock House. There was nothing unusual in Dickens giving presents to girls who had acted with him in his plays. To Catherine, though, this seemed a final humiliation. Instinctively she felt, as she had felt with Mme De La Rue, that she had just cause for the jealousy she could not control. Tearfully she told her husband of her suspicions and her unhappiness; and he, refusing to be reproached for a sin she had no grounds to believe he had committed, turned on her in indignant anger. He insisted that she must not only accept the fact that there was nothing improper in the relationship between himself and Ellen, but that she must show that she accepted that there was nothing improper in it by going to call on her.

Katey passed her mother's room soon after this new quarrel and heard her crying. She went in and asked her what was the matter. Her mother said, 'Your father has asked me to go and see Ellen Ternan'.

'You shall not go!' Katey said, angrily stamping her foot. But her mother did go. She was frightened of him, Katey said.[5]

Her mother also went to her parents, and told them everything she feared. Neither Mrs Hogarth nor Catherine's sister Helen had any doubt that she should not believe her husband's denials. Ellen Ternan *was* Charles's mistress, they insisted. She must leave him.[6]

And so, in May 1858, after days of uncertainty and agitation, and nights spent dreaming that he was trying to climb over 'a perspective of barriers' with his hands and feet tied, Dickens agreed to the terms of a formal separation. Catherine was to live in a house of her own in Gloucester Terrace, Regent's Park, on an allowance of £600 a year; Charley was to go with her, since that was considered his duty; the other children still living at home were to stay with their father and their aunt Georgina.

While these terms were being negotiated, Dickens, so it seemed to Katey, 'behaved like a madman. This affair brought out all that was worst—all that was weakest in him. He did not care a damn what happened to any of us.'[7]

Furiously denying that Ellen was his mistress, he quarrelled with anyone whom he believed might be taking Kate's side against him; and became wild with indignation when he heard that his mother-in-law and Helen Hogarth—of whose family he had in any case long since decided he could not 'bear the contemplation'—were themselves spreading the rumour of his adultery. Learning that it was also being suggested that a love affair with Georgina was the cause of the separation, he had insisted, against Forster's strong advice, on publishing a denial. And when Mark Lemon declined to publish the embarrassing letter in *Punch*, Dickens turned in rage not only on him but on Bradbury and Evans, the proprietors of the paper. He forbade his children ever to have anything more to do with Frederick Evans with whose family they had formerly been on the closest terms; and they were as vehemently forbidden to utter one word in future to Mrs Hogarth, or their aunt Helen.

He also quarrelled with Thackeray, who explained why in a letter to his mother:

> Last week going into the Garrick [Thackeray wrote] I heard that D. is separated from his wife on account of an intrigue with his sister-in-law. No says I no such thing—it's with an actress—and the other story has not got to Dickens's ears but this has—and he fancies that I am going about abusing him! We shall never be allowed to be friends that's clear. I had mine from a man at Epsom the first I ever heard of the matter, and should have said nothing about it but that I heard the other much worse story whereupon I told mine to counteract it. There is some row about an actress in the case, and he denies with the utmost infuriation any charge against her or himself.[8]

Shortly before Thackeray's death the quarrel was made up. Thackeray was in the Athenaeum talking to Sir Theodore Martin when Dickens walked across the hall to the staircase, ignoring him. Thackeray went up to him and said, 'It is time this foolish estrangement should cease, and that we should be to each other what we used to be. Come; shake hands.' They did shake hands. 'I love the man', Thackeray told Sir Theodore when Dickens had walked on up the stairs, 'and I could not resist the impulse.'[9] When Thackeray told Katey about this reconciliation, she asked him what her father had said; and Thackeray replied airily, 'Oh, your father knew he was wrong and was full of apologies.' But Katey knew that her father would not have been full of apologies. And Thackeray admitted he had not.[10] Dickens never hinted, nor perhaps could even suppose, that any step he had taken was less than just. Never a man to remain uncommitted or indifferent, he had made up his mind that he was in the right, that Catherine and her sympathisers were in the wrong and that was the end of the matter.

For the children old enough to understand what was happening, it was a miserably unhappy time. With their mother crying in her room, their father driven to behave like a frightening stranger by the intolerant vehemence of his hysterical self-will, nothing, so Katey said, 'could surpass the misery and unhappiness' of their home.

2

By the time the terms of their parents' separation had been agreed, this home was Gad's Hill Place, the house which their father had so much admired as a child.

He had been walking past it one day with a friend, the journalist W. H. Wills; and he had told Wills what his father had said to him about it when he was a little boy. That evening at dinner Wills found himself sitting next to the daughter of the old clergyman who owned it. Her father had just died, she said, and she wanted to sell it. Early the following morning Wills rushed round to the hotel where Dickens was staying, to tell him that it was 'written' that he was to have the house. 'You must buy it,' he urged him. 'Now or never.'

Dickens needed no urging. He asked his solicitor to find out how much it would cost to raise the roof and so provide more bedrooms in the attic. Then he offered £1,500 for it, agreed to raise his offer to £1,700 and to pay an additional £90 for the shrubbery on the other side of the road. Soon he was dashing over every day from Waite's Hotel, Gravesend, to hurry up the workmen who never worked hard or fast enough to satisfy his impatience.

> It is old fashioned, plain and comfortable [he reported with satisfaction to Miss Coutts]. On the summit of Gad's Hill, with a noble prospect at the side and behind, looking down into the Valley of the Medway. Lord Darnley's Park at Cobham (a beautiful place with a noble walk through a wood) is close by ... It is only an hour and a quarter from London by the Railway. To crown all, the sign of the Sir John Falstaff is over the way, and I used to look at it as a wonderful Mansion (which God knows it is not), when I was a very odd little child with the first faint shadows of all my books in my head—I suppose.[11]

It was here at Gad's Hill, amidst the scenes of his childhood memories, that most of his later work was written; and it was here that the many guests, who came to visit him during these years, were entertained.[12] When they came by train, they were met at Higham Station by a bright red jaunting car or by a basket-carriage drawn by a pony, Newman Noggs, who, with bells tinkling on his harness, pulled them up the hill to the house. If they were guests whom their host thought would be gratified by such display—he amused Longfellow and several other Americans like this—he would turn out 'a couple of postilions in the old red jacket of the Dover road', and drive them about through the country-side with which his name was by now traditionally associated.

Sometimes they would be taken on long fast walks through the Cobham woods and Cobham Park (to all the gates of which Lord Darnley had given him keys), across the marshes, or past the orchards and hop fields, accompanied by the big dogs which their host kept as a protection against the tramps who wandered up and down the Dover Road.

On summer days he would taken them round the grounds, extending to twenty acres, and show them the horses in the stable, the tunnel he had had built connecting the garden with the land on the other side of the road, the new pet raven, the mastiffs, the field at the back where the local cricket matches were played. Or he would press them to join him in a game of croquet or bowls, or in more energetic games, rounders and battledore, which he still played with all the enthusiasm and determination of his youth.

At dinner, after a shower, he would seem as lively and cheerful as ever, talking with animated gaiety, looking, so an American once said of him in a graphic phrase, like a 'gentlemanly pirate' with eyes in which 'lurked the iron will of a demon and the tender pity of an angel',[13] listening with a flattering and stimulating absorption to the conversation of others, seeming not in the least spoilt by his great fame, often breaking out into a burst of infectious laughter. It was at times like these that Dickens was at his most charming and radiant, glowing with that vitality and cheerful good humour which the Duke of Devonshire found bewitching, which made Lord Redesdale say that his talk had all the sparkle of champagne, and which entranced even those men who could not admire him.

'Of the general charm of his manner', T. A. Trollope despaired of 'giving any idea. . . . Every thought, every fancy, every feeling was expressed with the utmost vivacity and intensity. . . . His enthusiasm was boundless.'[14] George Eliot found him a man one could 'thoroughly enjoy talking to'—there was 'a strain of real seriousness along with his keenness and humour'.[15]

While others could not agree that he was an exceptional conversationalist, no one could deny that he was a wonderful raconteur and mimic, telling a ghost story with as good effect as a funny one. Nor could anyone deny that on occasions he was marvellously, wildly funny. Once in America he had all the guests at a bachelor dinner 'in agonies of laughter', as he played the part of a political campaigner supporting a candidate in an election on the grounds that he had less hair than his rival. 'We roared and writhed', one of the guests remembered, '. . . and the candidates themselves were literally choking and crying.'[16]

In the evenings, after dinner, Mamie would play the piano and the others would join in her songs, the ballads and country airs that her father particularly liked, or he would read to them, or take them into the billiard room. Sometimes there were games and dancing, not card games, which their host disliked, but party games like guessing, and memory ones, or such energetic entertainments as charades and pantomimes at which, of course, he excelled, and in which the younger children could join.

Christmas was still a special time for him, not as a religious festival but as a time in which selfishness was transformed into charity, friends and families were reunited and all brought 'back to the delusions of our childish days'.

At Christmas the house was sometimes so full that guests had to be boarded out in the Falstaff Inn over the way or in a nearby cottage; and their host would take the whole week off from his work to entertain them. On Christmas Day itself they would all sit round the big mahogany table in the dining-room, surrounded by the holly and ivy which covered the walls and dangled from the gas brackets; and when the flaming pudding came in they would greet it by clapping, and Dickens would give his traditional toast: 'Here's to us all! God bless us!'

He gave this toast again on New Year's Eve when, summoned into the hall by the butler beating the gong, the guests would wait for the peal of the village bells; and at the first peal, Dickens, checking the time with his watch, would repeat, 'A happy New Year to us all! God bless us!'

Then Mamie would play the piano and there would be dancing, and the master would lead off with the cook, moving with more excitement than grace and then jigging about and clapping his hands to make everyone join in, and doing little pirouettes behind the backs of those who did not demonstrate the required sense of enjoyment and gaiety. 'A happy New Year to us all! Here's to us! God bless us!'

He did not drink much himself now; and although he insisted on mixing the nightly bowl of gin punch with all the care and traditional ceremony that his father had brought to the ritual, making the same kind of facetious remarks as to its fearful potency, he rarely drank more than one or two small glasses. Nor did he eat much. For breakfast, despite the array of dishes on the sideboard, he usually had just an egg, a slice of bacon, and a cup of tea; and at lunch-time, after a morning's writing in his room, he sometimes contented himself with a piece of bread and cheese and glass of beer, though prepared to discuss the dinner menu which was always put out by the cook on the sideboard.(17)

Meals were served punctually, for Dickens insisted on the highest standards of regularity and order in the running of the household. Indeed, the more his wife had irritated him with her carelessness and clumsiness the more obsessed he had become with neatness and precision, and the more his passion for organisation had increased.[18]

He had always been dressed with scrupulous tidiness and cleanliness, and had always taken great trouble to keep his hair neatly brushed—he would often comb it on sitting down to work, and in America a girl had been shocked to see him, while actually sitting down at the dinner table, take out his comb to straighten a few unruly locks which he had caught sight of in a mirror. Even now in his later years, when he had little hair left on the top of his head, Katey said that if the wind blew a few strands about while he was in the garden, on catching sight of them in one of those big looking-glasses with which he loved to decorate his houses, he would fly upstairs for his hairbrush. The sight of anything out of place in the house, or, for instance, fragments of egg-shell or lobster-shell left on the ground after a picnic, would upset him profoundly.

After the separation he wrote to Mamie to urge her and Georgina to get the household into perfect working order, referring to it as a 'machine'. It had been his habit in London to go on a daily tour of his property—he went round three times a day when the family were on holiday—even inspecting the drawers of the girls' desks, and leaving a note, carefully folded and left on a pincushion in their room, if he had any cause for complaint. He continued this practice of inspecting his property in the country, giving as much attention to the grounds and stables as to the inside of the house, and seeing to it that anything which might have been used the day before in the garden, such as cricket stumps or croquet hoops, were put away in their proper boxes, that the ornaments on his writing table—a pair of bronze frogs, a rabbit on a gilt leaf, an ivory paper-knife, a man with puppies in his pockets, a green cup of fresh flowers—were all in their correct positions so that he could begin work without irritation or distraction. He took particular care to ensure that his boys' hats and coats (which were themselves subject to frequent inspection) were always placed on the particular pegs allotted to them.

What Charley called his father's 'alarming thoroughness', his demanding insistence that his sons must emulate his own hardworking application and tidiness, his obvious exasperation at their lack of determination, all made it difficult for them to live up to his exacting standards. Without confidence in success, they resigned themselves to failure. Only one of them, Henry Fielding, had achieved any notable distinction at school; and he was the only one to be sent to a university. Indeed, his father needed some persuading before he agreed even to Henry's going; and perhaps might not have done so had the son chosen Oxford, of which Dickens was strongly disdainful, rather than Cambridge. Dickens himself wanted Henry to sit for the Indian Civil Service Examination. 'Many of us', he told him strictly, 'have many duties to discharge in life which we do not wish to undertake, and . . . must do the best we can to earn our respective livings and make our way.' And he went on to remind him— although he had only one other son at school at that time—that he was already bearing as heavy a financial strain as could well be 'attached to any one working man'.

It was not only his constant worry about money and his disbelief in prolonged education that made Dickens anxious that his sons should not delay their starting a career. He was beset by the fear that the longer they were allowed to stay at home, the less likely they would be able to do what he repeatedly admonished them to do, 'to hew out their own paths through the world by sheer hard work'. And although a conscientious parent, he seems to have believed they could all do this better abroad than at home. He was firm in his insistence that they should leave home early, and arrangements were made for them to do so: he obtained, for instance, a nomination for an Indian Army cadetship for Walter at the age of eight, sent him to a military crammer when he was ten, to school at Wimbledon when he was thirteen, and off to India before he was seventeen.

'He often lectured his sons, in tones typical of the self-made man, about "when I was your age" ',[19] and so long as they remained at home he made sure that the orderly habits which he felt had regulated his own life as a child should regulate their lives, too.

There were five boys left at home when he came to live at Gad's Hill, and he was anxious that they should not follow the example of their eldest brother, the old Etonian Charley, whose 'indescribable lassitude of character'—which he believed the boy had inherited from his mother —was so painfully distressing, and whose irresponsibility with money preoccupied him at the time of his writing about Pip in *Great Expectations*.

Charley was a failure in his business career; and his marriage to Bessie Evans, the daughter of the publisher Frederick Evans into whose house the family had been forbidden to set foot after the separation, was another sad disappointment to his father, who declined to go to the wedding. Eventually Charley was found a place on the staff of *All the Year Round*, a periodical which his father had started after the row with Bradbury and Evans had stopped the publication of *Household Words*. And Charley did show more promise there, and a 'considerable aptitude in sub-editing work'.[20]

But by then the younger sons were proving more of a worry to their father than even Charley had been. The second son, Walter, who had managed to obtain a commission in the Indian Army, had left for his new career with hopeful prospects, and his father, as he watched him sail away on the *Indus*, thinking how short a time it was since that young man had been a baby, felt that it was like having 'great teeth drawn with a wrench'. But Walter soon proved a disappointment: he found it quite impossible to live within his income, and when he died in India at the age of twenty-two he was deep in debt. The diminutive Sydney, who had become a popular if rather soulful naval officer, was equally extravagant, and his father was so distressed by his reckless spending that he felt obliged to tell him that he must not appear at Gad's Hill when he returned from sea. He, too, died in his early twenties, bequeathing what remained of his money to his mother.

Francis suffered from a fearful stammer which had made him give up hope of becoming a doctor, and he decided that he would like to farm abroad. With a start of fifteen pounds, a horse and a rifle, he thought that in time he would become 'very comfortable'. But his father thought otherwise. 'I perceived', he objected, 'that the first consequence of the fifteen pounds would be that he would be robbed of it—of the horse, that it would throw him—and of the rifle, that it would blow his head off.'[21] So Francis was also found an appointment on *All the Year Round*. But he did not show Charley's aptitude, and his father thought of stopping his allowance. Eventually Francis left to join the Bengal Mounted Police. He died in Canada at the age of forty-two.

Two of the other brothers, Alfred and Edward, went out to Australia. Alfred, who had failed to get into the Royal Military Academy at Woolwich, had gone out leaving behind several unpaid bills, including one from his tailor which listed eleven pairs of best kid gloves. And when Edward went to join him, although he was too young at sixteen to have incurred so many debts, his father had no greater hopes for his future success than for that of any of the others.

Edward had been his favourite child, his little Plornishmaroontigoonter, his darling Plorn. As a baby he had found him 'irresistibly attracting, captivating . . . beating all former babies into what they call in America (I don't know why) sky-blue fits'. But by the time he was fourteen his father confessed himself disillusioned by his 'want of application and continuity of purpose', his 'impracticable torpor'. The best thing for him would be to go out to spend a rough life in Australia where 'his natural abilities' might 'flash up under such conditions'.

When the time came for him to go, his father wrote him a letter:

> I write this note today because your going away is much on my mind, and because I want you to have a few parting words from me to think of now and then at quiet times. I need not tell you that I love you dearly and am very, very sorry in my heart to part with you. But this life is half made up of partings, and these pains must be borne. It is my comfort and my sincere conviction that you are going to try the life for which you are best fitted. . . .(22) What you have always wanted until now has been a set, steady, constant purpose. I therefore exhort you to persevere in a thorough determination to do whatever you do as well as you can do it. I was not so old as you are now when I first had to win my food, and to do it out of this determination, and I have never slackened in it since.23

That was part of the trouble, no doubt: overshadowed by their father's fame, conscious of how hard he had always worked and of their own inferiority, they were always being reminded of how far short they fell of his standards and example. 'Do everything at your best', he frequently enjoined them. 'I can assure you I have taken as great pains with the smallest thing I ever did, as with the biggest.'(24)

Also, there was the barrier of their father's reserve, a reserve which, as he had admitted himself to Maria Winter, attributing it to that painful early love, made him chary of showing his affections, even to his children, except when they were very young.

And now that they were not very young any more, the children became increasingly conscious of their father's remoteness and constraint. They wanted so much to please him yet they could so rarely earn his approbation or his smile. He was not often angry with them: he seemed just saddened, disappointed and resigned. They could not but feel that his anxiety that they should leave home and make their own way in the world was a wish to be rid of them. And although he seemed sad to see them go, he was soon afterwards able to put their problems to the back of his mind. They felt conscious of his love, but conscious, too, that he was holding something back from them.

> There was one feature about my father which we could never quite understand [Henry, the second youngest of his sons wrote] . . . . He was curiously reserved. He did not like to show what he really felt. He was afraid of 'letting himself go'. . . . At the end of my first year

at Cambridge I won the best mathematical scholarship of the year in my College (Trinity Hall). I knew this news would give my father intense pleasure, as, in fact, we know from Forster's *Life*, it did. I met him in the train at Higham Station to tell him what had happened and I gave him the news as he alighted from the train. He said, 'Capital! Capital!' that was all. I was, I must confess, somewhat disappointed at this rather luke-warm treatment of my news; but my father could not for long maintain this apparently cold attitude. Half-way up the road to Gad's Hill he completely broke down. Turning to me with tears in his eyes he gave me a grip of the hand, which I can almost feel now and he said, 'God bless you, my boy, God bless you'.[25]

Dickens had agreed to allow Henry £250 a year to cover all his expenses; but now that he had won this scholarship he reduced the allowance to £200. Anxious that he should not be given the means to become as improvident as his elder brothers, his father was equally anxious to save his own pocket.

His letters are full of this concern. 'I can't get my hat on in consequence of the extent to which my hair stands on end at the costs and charges of these boys', he wrote. 'Why was I ever a father!' He had 'the largest family ever known', he complained on another occasion, 'with the smallest disposition to do anything for themselves'. He looked round his dining-table and saw reflected from every seat at it, 'some horribly well remembered expression of inadaptability to anything'.

It was this constant worrying over the expenses of his 'limp' family as much as the love of acting, the desire for applause, the need to escape from the restrictions of Victorian domesticity, and to have a direct and emotional involvement with his audience, that first drove him to enter upon those readings from his works that became an obsession with him in the last years of his life. And although he did not need the money as urgently as he implied, his family's calls upon his charity, to which he had so often responded, had indeed placed a heavy strain upon his pocket.

3

Dickens's father had died in 1851 after undergoing (without chloroform) a terrible operation on his bladder, and had died, 'O so quietly' and so bravely, 'wonderfully cheerful and strong-hearted'. But his mother lived on until 1863, maintaining to the end, so he said, her demands on him. After her husband's death she had become senile and wandering; and this had irritated her son rather than aroused his pity. She had, he said, a 'strong objection to being considered in the least old' and 'usually appeared on Christmas Day in a juvenile cap' which took 'an immense time in the putting on'. The impossibility of 'getting her to understand what is the matter,' he continued in another letter, 'combined with the desire to be got up in sables like a female Hamlet, illumines the scene with a ghastly absurdity that is the chief relief I can find in it'. One day he visited her and found Letitia poulticing her head, and, 'the instant she saw me', he said, 'she plucked up spirit, and asked me for "a pound" '.[26]

Also, his brother Fred still kept asking him for money. Fred had married Christiana Weller's sister Anna, against the opposition both of her parents and of his brother, who believed his income far too small to support a wife; and he had fallen immediately into deep debt. Before long the marriage broke up; Fred refused to make Anna any allowance, and his brother had found himself once more involved.

Dickens's youngest brother Augustus had also deserted his wife, gone off to America with another woman, and from there written to his brother (who was already doing what he could for his now blind and deserted sister-in-law) for money to help him along. When Augustus died, Dickens sent £50 a month to Chicago for his bereaved mistress and her three children.

Finally, in 1860, the middle brother, Alfred Lambert, died of pleurisy and, as Dickens said, 'died worth nothing, and has left a widow and five children—you may suppose to whom'.[27]

Then there was the £600 a year he had to find for Catherine. And there was Ellen Ternan. He installed Ellen in a cottage at Slough and later in a villa at Peckham, and so had yet another establishment to pay for in addition to Catherine's, his own country house at Gad's Hill, the houses he felt occasionally obliged to rent in London, and the villa he often retired to in France, sometimes, it seems, with Ellen. Nor was this all, for Ellen had a family for whom Dickens assumed responsibility, sending her eldest sister, with her mother, to Italy to study music.

There were also his daughters and Georgina to provide for. Georgina showed no interest in getting married. Augustus Egg had once proposed to her, but she would not think of him. Nor would Mamie have the Irish writer, Percy Fitzgerald, when he proposed to her. Her father had refused to entertain the idea of Mamie marrying another man with whom she had been in love, but he was 'grievously disappointed' when she would not consider the undesirable Fitzgerald, and commented bitterly, returning to a favourite theme: 'What a wonderful instance of the general inanity of Kings, that the Kings in the Fairy Tales should have always been wishing for children! If they had but known when they were well off, having none.'[28]

To be sure, Mamie was completely devoted to him. She had taken his side over the separation and did not visit her mother as the other children did, despite their father's disapproval when he learned that they had done so.[29] But there was something in Mamie that struck him as listless and indecisive: she was too much like her mother, too much like the boys.

Katey was a stronger character. Of all the children, she alone had dared to be occasionally late for breakfast; she alone had dared to sympathise with her mother at the time of the separation. She suggested in conversations towards the end of her life that she was deeply unhappy at home after her mother had gone, and that although she was not in love with him, although her father did not think she should do so, she agreed to marry Wilkie Collins's brother Charles, a tall, neurotic, red-haired artist, eleven years older than herself.

When all the wedding guests had gone, Dickens went up to Katey's room and fell down beside her wedding-dress, the wedding-dress of a girl who but yesterday 'always had a scratched knee'. He held it to his face and burst into tears. Mamie went into the room and found him sobbing. At first he did not notice her. 'When at last he got up and saw her, he said in a broken voice: "But for me, Katey would not have left home", and walked out of the room.'[30]

4

It was at such moments as these that his family recognised the depths of his despair, how far his spirits were capable of sinking.

At those times even the great faith he had in his talents momentarily deserted him. Formerly he had always been confident. 'I *know*', he would write, 'that I could sustain my place . . . though fifty writers started up tomorrow.' Or he would say, 'I wonder, if I went to a new colony . . . I should force myself to the top of the social milk-pot and live upon the cream. . . . Upon my word I believe I should.' But now this confidence often gave way to doubt. And there were many critics, blind to his ever-developing genius, ready to feed these doubts, to suggest that the power that had burned so fiercely in his youth was now exhausted.

'*Our Mutual Friend*', wrote Henry James, for instance, in *The Nation*, on the appearance of Dickens's last completed book, 'is, to our perception,

the poorest of Mr Dickens's works. And it is poor with the poverty not of
momentary embarrassment, but of permanent exhaustion. For the last
ten years it has seemed to us that Mr Dickens has been unmistakably
forcing himself. *Bleak House* was forced; *Little Dorrit* was laboured; the
present work is dug out with a spade and pickaxe.'[31]

This was far from being an isolated opinion. Thackeray, though no
doubt put out by the reflection of himself in the character of Henry
Gowan, was not voicing an isolated view of Dickens's later work when
he told a friend that he thought *Little Dorrit* was 'stupid'. And Trollope
had come to the conclusion that it was impossible to speak in praise of
Dickens's style which was 'jerky, ungrammatical, and created by himself
in defiance of rules'.[32] Other critics noticed a falling off in spontaneity
and vividness.[33]

More recent critics, however, have reversed this opinion, agreeing
with George Bernard Shaw that there is in the later work an 'enormous
increase in strength and intensity', recognising in it a triumph of the
novelist's art and the fulfilment of Dickens's genius. Defects may
certainly be found in him, but these are of small concern when weighed
against his enduring success in stirring people's sympathy, in making
them feel and think as well as in making them laugh. He did not claim
himself to be a pioneer, but

> he shared a great deal of common experience with his public, so that
> it could gratefully and proudly say, 'How true!' . . . He also shared
> with it an attitude to what they both knew, and caught exactly the
> tone which clarified and reinforced the public's sense of right and
> wrong, and flattered its moral feelings. . . . He is still the only one
> of the great English novelists who is read at all widely among simple
> people. Many people maintain this is largely because his reformist
> sentiment is valuable as a permanent statement that it is the goodness
> of individuals in society that matters more than its institutions and
> forms. But goodness itself is relative; its moods and qualities change.
> The particular forms of his goodness were conditioned by his time;
> and it seems more likely that he is now read and will go on being read
> because he made out of Victorian England a complete world, with a
> life and vigour and idiom of its own, quite unlike any other world
> there has ever been.[34]

5

In his heart, Dickens was well aware of all this himself, of his importance
and his stature, the increasing power and artistry of his later work.

But there were days and weeks of depression during which he seemed to be 'always looking for something' he had not found in life, something that he might find 'a few thousand of years hence, in some other part of some other system. God knows'.[35] At these times a deadening sense of *Weltschmerz* overcame him, and he began to feel that he and all men, every day of their lives, were 'instinctively unwilling to be restored to consciousness' when they awoke in the morning.*

This discontent—made all the more wearisome by the angry despair that overcame him at the thought of the dangers and evils in the world around him—seems to have been exacerbated rather than relieved by his affair with Ellen Ternan and all the fresh evasions and concealments it entailed. He had been happy at first, acting with Ellen, flirting with her, making her laugh, making her admire him. But he wanted more from her than that.[36]

He had always hoped to find the ideal love for which he longed in the midst of domesticity. Catherine, he felt, had failed him. And if Estella of *Great Expectations*, Bella Wilfer of *Our Mutual Friend* and Helena Landless of *Edwin Drood* reflect his attitude towards his mistress, it seems that he thought Ellen was failing him in a different way. He had expected more from Catherine than it was in her nature to give him; he had expected more from his love for Ellen than it was in his own nature to supply. He was not, as Katey said, 'a fast man', not a man to enjoy Ellen without a sense of guilt. And a strong sense of propriety, struggling with an impatience with convention, is one of the distinguishing emotions of his later life and of his later work.[(37)]

When he was beginning to fall in love with Ellen, he told Wilkie Collins, 'The domestic unhappiness remains so strong upon me that I can't write, and (waking) can't rest, one minute. I have never known a moment's peace or content, since the last night of *The Frozen Deep*. . . . In this condition, though nothing can alter or soften it, I have a turning notion that the mere physical effort and change of the Readings would be good, as another means of bearing it.'[38]

But since then the readings had become far more than a relief from his personal tensions: they had become an obsession. He could not bring himself to give them up. It was not just that they were highly profitable, it was that they were intoxicatingly exhilarating, bringing him into exciting personal contact with his admirers and filling his ears with their applause. He was constantly warned of the danger to his health, but he

* *Our Mutual Friend*, Bk. III, ch. III.

would not listen; and in the end his doctor, Frank Beard, Thomas's brother, had to tell Charley, 'I have had some steps put up at the side of the platform. You must be there every night, and if you see your father falter in the least, you must run and catch him and bring him off to me, or, by Heaven, he'll die before them all.'[39]

It sometimes seemed almost as though he wished to die. There were still days when he was as effervescent and hilarious as ever—as once when in a train travelling between engagements he suddenly started up from a meal and danced a hornpipe, whistling gaily. But then the concern about money, the worry of his children and his family, the emptiness in his emotional life that Catherine had failed to fill, the secrecy that the guilty relationship with Ellen forced upon him, and his rapidly failing health, would overbear his cheerfulness, and he would sink into that trough of despair characteristic of the manic depressive condition.[40] Yet he would not, and could not, give in. Instead of limiting his repertoire of readings he extended them.

One afternoon Charley was working in the library at Gad's Hill when he heard a succession of violent cries and groans from outside. At first he thought it was a tramp beating his wife and he decided to do nothing about it; but then the screams grew louder and more brutal, and he ran out into the garden. There was his father at the bottom of the meadow enacting, with fearful vehemence, the murder of Nancy in *Oliver Twist*.[41] Despite all the warnings of his family, his friends and his doctor, he determined to perform this horrifying scene on the stage. And although it exhausted him more than all his other readings he insisted on doing it again and again.

One evening in Edinburgh when he returned to his dressing-room utterly worn out, scarcely able to stand up, his manager suggested, while they were having supper, that he really must not do the murder scene so often.

'Have you finished?' Dickens interrupted him furiously, and picking up his knife and fork he threw them down so violently on his plate that he smashed it. 'Dolby!' he shouted at him. 'Your infernal caution will be your ruin one of these days!' Then suddenly he began to cry. 'Forgive me, Dolby,' he said between his sobs, putting his arm round his shoulders. 'I really didn't mean it; and I know you are right. We will talk the matter over calmly in the morning.'[42]

But the readings went on. And in spite of a painfully gouty leg (which he refused to acknowledge *was* gouty), despite insomnia, indigestion, a weakening heart, and high blood pressure, he toured the United States after his tours in England, then gave readings in England again.

He travelled by train, although he had suffered so severe a shock after the train in which he was returning from a holiday in France in 1865 crashed at Staplehurst with heavy loss of life, that he was never able to relax in a train again. Ellen apparently was with him, which added greatly, of course, to his subsequent neurotic disquiet. Slow trains bored and frustrated him, fast trains so alarmed him that he could not bring himself to go on a journey without a bottle of brandy. 'I have seen him sometimes in a railway carriage when there was a slight jolt', his son Henry recalled. 'When this happened he was almost in a state of panic and gripped the seat with both hands. This continued for some time.'[43]

In America he lost his appetite, could only sleep after taking laudanum, could only read after drinking sherry or champagne. There were times between engagements when there were sudden resurgences of his old high spirits and intoxicating cheerfulness; but during the readings it was often painful to watch him as the blood rushed into his hands turning them almost black, and his face changed colour from a deep red to white and then to red again. He was left at the end breathless, with his pulse racing wildly. It was not really acting, as Charley said, but a kind of demonic possession, particularly when he re-enacted the murder of Nancy, an exhibitionistic, frighteningly mesmeric performance which is open to all kinds of psychological interpretations.

When he returned to England (with a profit of nearly £20,000) he felt sick in the mornings, suffered from attacks of giddiness, and on occasions could only read the righthand halves of the signs on shopfronts. 'My weakness and deadness', he confessed to Georgina, 'are all *on the left side*, and if I don't look at anything I try to touch with my hand, I don't know where it is.' He was on the brink of an attack of paralysis of his left side, and possibly of apoplexy, a specialist decided after being called in by Frank Beard. 'The result of extreme hurry, overwork and excitement, incidental to his Readings.'[44]

But still, after a short interval, he went on with these readings, until in the end he could not pronounce Pickwick properly, calling it 'Pickswick', 'Picnic', and 'Peckwicks', and all sorts of names, so Charley said, 'except the right one'.

Charley's daughter was taken to hear her grandfather give the last reading of all, and she remembered how frightened of him she was, how 'wenerables', as she called him, spoke in such strange, far away voices, and how at the end there was 'the dreadful moment when he cried'.[45]

6

Some weeks after this last reading Katey went to stay the night at Gad's Hill to ask her father's advice as to whether she should go on the stage. 'We will talk about it,' he said to her, 'when the others have gone to bed.' And he took her away to see the new conservatory—'positively the last improvement', he assured her, smiling at his own need constantly to alter the house. Ever since he had moved into Gad's Hill he had been having walls pulled down, rooms enlarged, parquet floors laid, new staircases and stables built, new looking-glasses fixed to the walls, dummy books fitted to the back of the library door carrying such heavily humorous titles as *Steele By the Author of 'Ion'*, *Kant's Eminent Humbugs*, *History of a Chancery Suit* (in 21 volumes), *The Wisdom of Our Ancestors* (Vol. 1, *Ignorance*; Vol. 2. *Superstition*; Vol. 3. *The Block*; Vol. 4. *The Stake*; Vol. 5. *The Rack*; Vol. 6. *Dirt*; Vol. 7. *Disease*), Malthus's *Nursery Songs*. But that was all over now.

He was looking very old and grey, Katey thought. His complexion was usually florid, for sunshine and the open air had reddened and coarsened the once pale, smooth skin of his youth. On this day, though, the colour had gone, and the lines that wrinkled the skin between his nose and the grizzled hairs of his beard seemed deep and shadowed.

After dinner he was livelier, and when the others had gone, he said to her, 'Now tell me all about it.'

'I shall never forget that talk,' Katey told a friend not long before her own death. . . . 'With great earnestness my father dissuaded me from going on the stage.'

He told her that she was pretty enough, but too sensitive, clever enough to do something else. If it was money she needed, he would make it up to her; and then he spoke of other things. 'He talked and talked, how he talked, until three o'clock in the morning.' He wished, he said, that he had been a 'better father—a better man'. After this talk Katey felt that she knew things about her father's character 'that no one else ever knew; he was not a good man . . . but he was wonderful! He fell in love with this girl, I did not blame *her*—it is never one person's fault'.

The next morning, she wondered whether or not to go and say goodbye to him. Often she did not because he hated farewells. But on this occasion she decided to go, and she walked through the tunnel to the little Swiss chalet which the actor, Charles Fechter, had given him. She found him at work on *Edwin Drood*; but he looked up when she came in, and instead of turning his cheek to her to be kissed as he usually did, he put out his arms and kissed her with great affection.

On her way back to the house she felt irresistibly drawn to return to him. 'Something said to me, "go back",' she remembered, 'and I immediately ran up the steps, through the shrubbery, into the Chalet and tapped on the door. My father—who was seated with his back to it—called out, "Come in"; turning and seeing me he pushed his chair back from the writing table, opened his arms and took me into them.' As she walked back once more to the house she kept saying to herself, without knowing why she did so, 'I am so glad I went—I am so glad'.[46]

The following Thursday—it was 8 June 1870—he spent all day writing in the chalet, returning to his study in the evening to write a few letters before dinner. At six o'clock Georgina joined him, and noticed with anxiety that his eyes were full of tears. During the meal she watched him with growing concern; and, eventually, alarmed by the colour of his face she asked him if he were feeling ill.

'Yes,' he said, 'very ill for the last hour.'

She suggested calling the doctor. 'No,' he said, blurring the word, and trying to carry on an ordinary conversation. Then he complained of a tooth-ache, and clasping his jaw, asked to have the window shut.

'Come and lie down,' Georgina urged him.

Suddenly he said he must leave immediately for London, pushed back his chair, and struggled to stand up.

He was falling to the floor as Georgina ran round the table. She tried to help him on to a sofa, but he was too heavy, and she had to let him slip to the floor.

'Yes,' he said. 'On the ground.'

After the servants had helped her carry him to a sofa, she called for the local doctor and sent a telegram for Frank Beard. But when they arrived they could do nothing to help him. He had suffered a paralytic stroke and was dying.

For the whole of Friday he lay unconscious, breathing heavily, his eyes closed, while the people in the house, his daughters and Georgina, Charley and the doctors, and Ellen Ternan, waited for the end. At ten past six he sighed deeply, a tear trickled down his cheek, and he died.[47]

7

He left *Edwin Drood* unfinished. But he had always hoped to die in harness. 'I am incapable of rest', he had written some years before. 'I am quite confident that I should rust, break, and die, if I spared myself. Much better to die doing. . . . However strange it is to be never at rest, and never satisfied, and ever trying after something that is never reached . . . how clear it is that it must be, and that one is driven by an irresistible might until the journey is worked out!'[56]

Writing his last book he had been aware of that journey drawing to its close, of the circle of his life being 'very nearly traced'. The striking of the Cathedral clock in Rochester, the cawing of the rooks from the Cathedral tower seemed to him like voices from his nursery time, as 'the beginning and the end were drawing close together'.*

He had been quite clearly conscious, as he wrote, of his earliest impressions, of the 'rustling sounds and fresh scents' of those days long past, of the memories of that 'better world' of his childhood, when there was no distance, and no time.

* *Edwin Drood*, ch. xiv.

REFERENCES AND NOTES

For full titles see Sources

(References to Forster's *Life* are to Dent's Everyman's Library edition, ed. A. J. Hoppé, 1966.)

CHAPTER 1
'The Better World'
Pages 3–34

1. Leslie C. Staples, 'The Dickensian Ancestry', *The Dickensian*, vol. 45, nos. 290, 292; William J. Carlton, 'More About the Dickens Ancestry', vol. 57, no. 55.
(2) The house where Dickens was born is now 393 Commercial Road, Portsmouth, and a Dickens Museum.
(3) This house has sometimes been provided with a number—16—but, as William J. Carlton has pointed out to me, there is no sound evidence for this. For a time the family seem to have occupied another house in Portsea not mentioned by previous biographers. Local newspapers show that John Dickens's second son, Alfred Allen Dickens, was born at Wish Street on 28 March 1814 and died there the following 6 September.
(4) In 1817, £200 a year was a very respectable income. According to a book published a few years later, *A New System of Practical Domestic Economy* (1824), a man earning only £150 a year was entitled to call himself a 'gentleman'. And £400 was considered sufficient not only for the employment of two maidservants but also for the keep of a horse and a groom.

   Here is the recommended outlay for a man earning an income roughly comparable to John Dickens's, and having a wife, three children and a maid:

Weekly housekeeping: Bread	6s	0d
Butter, cheese, milk	6s	3d
(butter 1s a lb., cheese 6½d a lb.)		
Tea, coffee (tea 8s a lb)	2s	6d
Sugar (8d a lb)	3s	0d
Other groceries	3s	0d

	s	d
Meat (7*d* a lb)	10*s*	6*d*
Fish	3*s*	6*d*
Fruit and vegetables	3*s*	0*d*
Beer and other liquors	7*s*	0*d*
Coal, wood, soap, sundries	6*s*	10*d*

£2 11*s* 7*d*

	£	s	d
Annual housekeeping	134	2	4
Entertainment, Medicine	7	11	0
Clothes (husband, £15, Wife, £12, Children £9)	36	0	0
Rent and taxes	25	0	0
Education, extras, personal	10	10	0
Maid	16	0	0
TOTAL	229	3	4
Savings (1/12th)	20	16	8

£250 a year

The same book also shows how it was possible for a couple with three children to live quite comfortably on 48*s* a week. It is clear from this how very improvident John Dickens was.

(5) The house in Ordnance Terrace is now numbered 11.

(6) Lucy Stroughill served as a model for the Golden Lucy in 'The Wreck of the Golden Mary' (*Household Words*, Christmas Number, 1856); and George as a model for Steerforth in *David Copperfield*.

7. Langton, 25.

8. *Ibid.*, 106.

9. K. J. Fielding's edition of *The Speeches*, 323.

10. Nonesuch edition of *The Letters*, i, 807.

(11) According to a guidebook, published in 1886, Chatham had not changed much fifty years later: 'Its streets are narrow and squalid; and its only productions are soldiers, sailors, marines, and shell-fish. The shops are filled with those commodities peculiarly favoured by

seafaring people; and the "children of Israel" are here established in the various capacities of "salesmen, outfitters, tailors, old clothesmen, army and navy accoutrement makers, and bill-discounters".' *Black's Guide to Kent* (1886), 101.

(12) The Mitre appears as the Holly Tree in *Household Words* (Christmas Number, 1855) and as The Crozier in *Edwin Drood*, ch. XVIII. James Budden, the son of the proprietor of the Red Lion, was recognised as being Joe, the Fat Boy, page to Mr Wardle of Manor Farm, Dingley Dell, in *Pickwick*.

13. Langton, 22.

14. Forster, ii, 103–4.

(15) The fifth child (Harriet Ellen, born in 1819) had not survived.

(16) These attacks of 'spasm' have been diagnosed as renal colic, although Lord Brain has written to me to say that he thinks 'they could as well have been some form of intestinal colic'. The complaint, whatever it was, troubled him intermittently for the rest of his life, and may have contributed to premature arteriosclerosis and the resultant heart failure and incipient paralysis which characterised the illness of his last years—see 'The Medical History of Charles Dickens' in W. H. Bowen's *Charles Dickens and His Family* (Heffer, Cambridge, 1956). Some symptoms of his attacks—dizziness, misting sight and violent headaches—suggest that a concomitant complaint may have been acute migraine. His sister, Letitia, suffered from 'prolonged fainting fits'.

17. Langton, 25.

(18) This reference to *Robinson Crusoe* and the *Arabian Nights* (*Martin Chuzzlewitt*, ch. v) is just one of numerous specific allusions to these childhood readings in his work. 'We have never grown the thousandth part of an inch out of Robinson Crusoe', he confessed when himself the father of nine children. 'He fits us just as well, and in exactly the same way, as when we were among the smallest of the small. We have never grown out of his parrot, or his dog, or his fowling-piece, or the horrible old staring goat he came upon in the cave, or his cap, or umbrella. . . . Our growth stopped, when the great Haroun Alraschid spelt his name so, and when nobody had ever heard of a Jin. When the Sultan of the Indies was a mighty personage, to be approached respectfully even on the stage; and when all the dazzling wonders of those many nights held far too high a place in the imagination to be burlesqued and parodied.' 'Where

We Stopped Growing', *Household Words*. See also 'Frauds on the Fairies' (October 1853).

(19) Forster, 5–6. As well as the books and the Fielding and Smollett, Defoe and Cervantes in the small attic in St Mary's Place, there were volumes of the *Tatler* and the *Spectator*, Goldsmith's *Citizen of the World* and Johnson's *Idler*. And, as Professor Edgar Johnson has said, 'it is impossible to calculate the entire extent of their effect upon him, but the nature and direction of their stimulus is unmistakable. No writer so intimately fuses the familiar and the strange as Dickens does'. Johnson, i, 22.

Dickens himself gave one example of this. As a 'not very robust child, sitting in bye-places near Rochester-castle, with a head full of Partridge, Strap, Tom Pipes and Sancho Panza', he was told of a master at one of the notorious Yorkshire schools who had ripped open a pupil's suppurating abscess with an inky penknife. Years later these childhood memories found expression in Dotheboys Hall and its proprietor, Wackford Squeers.

Nor is it only this mingling of realism with fantasy in a constantly developing imagination that can be seen as an outgrowth of his childhood reading. Dickens's characters themselves have recognisable counterparts in the classics of eighteenth-century English comedy, as several critics have observed.

The constructions of the novels, too, have the same affinities and antecedents; *Pickwick*, in particular, carries persistent echoes of such novels as *Peregrine Pickle* and *Humphry Clinker* (Dickens's favourite novel), *Jorrock's Jaunts and Jollities* and *The Vicar of Wakefield*. Dickens himself remarked that 'if it be objected to the *Pickwick Papers*, that they are a mere series of adventures, in which the scenes are ever changing [the author] can only content himself with the reflection, that . . . the same objection has been made to the works of some of the greatest novelists in the English language'. But while the *Pickwick Papers* is the most obvious example of Dickens's continuation of the classical eighteenth-century tradition, the later works—though their increasingly firm and unequivocal moral intention brings them closer to the works of his greatest contemporaries and successors— still bear the unmistakable marks of this early influence so ineradicably planted in his young mind in the attic of St Mary's Place.

For although the *Pickwick Papers* is clearly influenced by Dickens's early devotion to Smollett, the influences of Goldsmith and Sterne may equally well be seen in *The Old Curiosity Shop* and *A Christmas Carol*, while *David Copperfield* is quite consciously modelled on Fielding's *Tom Jones*.

As the story of *David Copperfield* took shape in Dickens's mind, he returned to Fielding's novel to discover the secrets of its greatness and, in 'a kind of homage to the style of work he was now so bent on beginning', so John Forster put it, he christened his new baby Henry Fielding.

As in later life, so in the garret at Chatham, these works of the eighteenth-century masters were not merely read, admired and imitated, but imbued with that special inner light that his vivid imagination brought to play upon them.

(20) Although Dickens retained his detestation of such advocates of Christianity, refusing at the end of his life to go to his village church because he could not 'sit under a clergyman who addresses his congregation as though he had taken a return ticket to heaven and back', he remained a believer in a Christian God. His religion, as A. O. J. Cockshut has well described it, was 'a kind of loose, moralistic Anglicanism-cum-unitarianism' (*The Imagination of Charles Dickens*, 13, 154), yet it was perfectly sincere.

He recommended his children to read the New Testament 'as the one unfailing guide in life'—not the Old Testament, the 'injudicious use' of which in schools did much harm. He wrote, as well as prayers for them, a little book about Jesus which they knew well, he said, 'from having it repeated to them, long before they could read'; and he advised them never to abandon 'the wholesome practise of saying your own private prayers, night and morning. I have never abandoned it, and I know the comfort of it.'

21. Langton, 58

(22) These manœuvres also took place behind Fort Pitt fields around Tom-All-Alone's, a group of semi-derelict houses whose strange history fascinated Charles. A long time ago, he was told, Thomas Clark, an odd recluse, had lived there alone for twenty-five years. He had called out mournfully 'Tom's all alone!' on his way home each evening. One day, to the astonishment of Chatham, Tom got married. He had a big family, followed by numerous grandchildren, who all settled down at Tom-All-Alone's in an exclusive colony of Clarks.

But the waste ground on which the crumbling houses were built was needed in the 1820s for a prison, and Charles was taken to see the soldiers mine them and blow them up. It was a sight he never forgot. The first title he thought of for his tenth novel was *Tom-All-Alone's: The Ruined House*. And it is amongst the ruins of Tom-All-Alone's, where 'there has bred a crowd of foul existence that crawls in and out of gaps in walls and boards', that Jo the little crossing-sweeper finds his unsavoury shelter, where 'twice lately there has been a crash and a cloud of dust, like the springing of a mine, and each time a house has fallen. . . .' *Bleak House*, ch. XVI.

CHAPTER 2
Warren's Blacking
Pages 37–80

(1) Willoughby Matchett, 'Dickens in Bayham Street', *The Dickensian*, vol. 5, nos. 6 and 7. The house in Bayham Street was demolished before the First World War. The window of Dickens's little room in the garret is now preserved at The Dickens House, 48 Doughty Street.

2. K. J. Fielding's edition of *The Speeches*, 326.

3. Forster, i, 13.

4. Foster, i, 15; Lindsay, 47.

5. William J. Carlton, 'The Barber of Dean Street', *The Dickensian*, vol. 48, no. 301.

6. Arnold Kettle, 'Our Mutual Friend', *Dickens and the 20th Century*, 223.

7. William J. Carlton, ' "The Deed" in *David Copperfield*', *The Dickensian*, vol. 48, no. 302.

(8) The house in Gower Street North has since been demolished; part of Maple's store covers the site.

(9) Mrs Micawber resembled her husband in other respects, too. Evidently she found his manner of talking infectious: 'The truth is,' said Mrs Micawber, 'talent is not wanted in the Custom House. The local influence of my family was quite unavailing to obtain any employment in that department, for a man of Mr Micawber's abilities. He would only show the deficiency of the others. Apart from which,' said Mrs Micawber, 'I will not disguise from you, my dear Master Copperfield, that when that branch of my family which is settled in Plymouth became aware that Mr Micawber was accompanied by myself, and by little Wilkins and his sister, and by the twins, they did not receive him with that ardour which he might have expected, being so newly released from captivity. In fact,' said

Mrs Micawber, lowering her voice,—'this is between ourselves—
our reception was cool.' (*David Copperfield*, ch. XVII.)

As well as containing echoes of Mr Micawber's style, this is
reminiscent, too, of Mrs Nickleby's. It is, moreover, clear from this
passage that like Mrs Nickleby (whose family also comes from
Devon) Mrs Micawber considers her social background rather
superior to her husband's, as Mrs Dickens did.

(10) All the titles were replaced by Dickens as soon as he could afford
them, and were in his library at the time of his death.

(11) 'Taking the country as a whole, regular work generally began
between the ages of seven and eight.' *Early Victorian England, 1830–
1865* (Oxford University Press, 1934), i, 45.

12. Forster, i, 21.

13. *Ibid.*, cf. *David Copperfield*, ch. XI.

(14) Day and Martin's blacking which Sam Weller uses at the White
Hart to bestow a polish that would have 'struck envy to the soul
of the amiable Mr Warren', was, in fact, a better known make by
the time Dickens had begun to write.

15. *Recollections of Sir Henry Dickens*, 45.

(16) In later years, although he never made any pretence to distinguished
lineage, he had this crest engraved on his silver plate, painted upon
various pieces of a china dinner service which Copelands made for
him, and he used it as a book-plate. See T. P. Cooper (who refers to
it as 'a sham heraldic device'), 'Dickens and His Heraldic Crest',
The Dickensian, vol. XVIII, No. 4.

(17) Dickens's child heroes and heroines, with whom he so often identified
himself—one reason, as Philip Collins says, why he so rarely presents
them comically—are always made to talk as though they had been
quite uninfluenced by the accents of their families or companions.
There is nothing of the Cockney in Oliver Twist's speech, nor of the
country blacksmith in the young Pip's. Little Dorrit, Cissy Jupe and
Lizzie Hexam all talk like young ladies. And David Copperfield
himself is very conscious of being a 'young gentleman'.

18. Forster, i, 22–3.

19. *Ibid*, i, 30–1.

20. Edmund Wilson, 'Charles Dickens: The Two Scrooges' in *The
Wound and the Bow*.

(21) The site of Lowther Arcade, then famous for its toy shops, is now
occupied by Coutts's Bank.

(22) Forster, i, 23. Waiters, naturally, make frequent appearances in the
novels, and are scarcely ever described with favour.

They 'always speak in hints', we are told, 'and never with complete
sentences' (*Sketches*, 'The Steam Excursion'). They 'never walk or
run. They have a peculiar and mysterious power of skimming out
of rooms, which other mortals possess not' (*Pickwick*, ch. XLIX).
They are, in addition, either rude ('Refreshments for Travellers',
The Uncommercial Traveller), or gloomy (*Great Expectations*, ch.
XXXIII), disdainfully familiar or outrageously fraudulent (*David
Copperfield*, chs. V and XIX), immoveable (*Edwin Drood*, ch. XI), or
tiresomely watchful: 'Rounding his mouth and both his eyes, as he
stepped backward from the table, the waiter shifted his napkin from
his right arm to his left, dropped into a comfortable attitude, and
stood surveying the guest while he ate and drank, as from an observatory or watch-tower. According to the immemorial usage of waiters
in all ages.' (*Tale of Two Cities*, Bk. I, ch. IV). It may be, then, that
the scene in the inn at Yarmouth where the waiter drinks David's
ale because the same brew poisoned Mr Topsawyer, and eats his
chop 'to take off the bad effects', is not altogether fictitious, although
Thomas Holcroft recalls a similar experience with a waiter in his
Memoirs published in 1816.

23. Forster, i, 29.
24. *Ibid.*, i, 25.
25. *Ibid.*
26. *Ibid.*, i, 28.

(27) Allusions to Punch are almost as frequent in his work as allusions to
the theatre and to Shakespeare; and it is surprising that no ardent
Dickensian such as the one who published in *The Dickensian* (vol. 22,
no. 4) his findings as to the number of times various foods and drinks
are mentioned in *Pickwick*, has not turned his attention to them. The
policemen at the rowdy meeting of the United Metropolitan
Improved Hot Muffin and Crumpet Baking and Punctual Delivery
Company wield their truncheons like Punch. Mr Pecksniff, spying
on Mary Graham in church, 'was constantly diving down into the
state pew and coming up again, like the intelligent householder in
Punch's show, who avoids being knocked on the head with a cudgel'.
Mr Spenlow is so stiff and starched that when seated at his desk he is
obliged, if he wants to look down at the papers on it, 'to move his
whole body, from the bottom of his spine, like Punch'. The street

outside Mr Dombey's house is visited by 'straggling Punch's shows'. The itinerant showmen whom Little Nell meets in the church-yard are 'exhibitors of the freaks of Punch'. *Nicholas Nickleby*, ch. II; *Martin Chuzzlewit*, ch. XXXI; *David Copperfield*, ch. XXIII; *Dombey and Son*, ch. III; *Old Curiosity Shop*, ch. XVI.

(28) Johnson Street was renamed Cranleigh Street in 1937.

(29) The site of Warren's new premises is now occupied by the Civil Service Stores.

30. Forster, i, 32.

31. Johnson, i, 27-44; Forster, i, 19-23.

(32) Charles Wentworth Dilke (1789-1864) was at this time a clerk in the Navy Pay Office. Like John Dickens he had literary interests and was a frequent contributor to the *Quarterly*. In 1830, in the words of his grandson (the Radical politician whose career was shattered by a sensational divorce scandal), 'he bought the but-just-born yet nevertheless dying *Athenaeum* . . . and restored its fortunes and his own'. For a time he acted as manager of the *Daily News*, the newspaper which Charles Dickens was to found in 1846 and which was to employ John Dickens as supervisor of the reporting staff.

(33) 'All the while in his work, he is consciously or unconsciously moving over the narrow ground of certain key experiences of childhood'. Lindsay, 25.

His novels take shape, in the words of another critic, Steven Marcus, 'largely under the pressure of a progressive returning into consciousness of urgent and crucial events from his past. . . . His creative intelligence was, in its highest function, always connected with explicit recollections of his early life.' Marcus, 44, 124.

To Edmund Wilson, Dickens's whole career seems an attempt to digest these early shocks and hardships, to explain them to himself, to justify himself in relation to them, to give an intelligible picture of a world in which such things could occur. To men of spirit whose childhood has been crushed by the cruelty of organised society, Mr Wilson goes on to argue, two attitudes of mind are possible—the criminal and the rebel. In his imagination, Dickens was to play the roles of both. Edmund Wilson, 8,13.

(34) For a fuller description of Dickens's heroes as seen in this light see Hillis Miller, 251, 328-9.

35. Nonesuch edition of *The Letters*, i, 490.

36. Lionel Trilling, Introduction to *Little Dorrit* (Oxford Illustrated Dickens).

37. Bernard Bergonzi, 'Nicholas Nickleby', *Dickens and the 20th Century*, ed. John Gross and Gabriel Pearson.

38. Dorothy van Ghent, 'The Dickens World: A View from Todgers's', in *The Dickens Critics*.

39. Steven Marcus, 43.

40. Humphry House, *The Dickens World*, 21.

(41) These Spanish refugees were exiles of the Torrijos party. Smoking paper cigars, as cigarettes were at first called, was unknown in England until after the Crimean War. The English soldiers picked up the habit from the French who were themselves picking it up from the Spanish at about this time.

42. House, *The Dickens World*, 21.

(43) John Bayley, 'Oliver Twist', *Dickens and the 20th Century*, 53. Steven Marcus has also commented on this: 'Friendship with Bob Fagin, the brother-in-law of a waterman, would in Charles's condition have been equivalent to an admission that his lostness and desolation were not merely real but somehow permanent. . . . Oliver Twist, the workhouse boy, is the son of a gentleman; and it is Fagin's task to prevent him from discovering that secret and entering upon that salvation. In life, young Charles Dickens was the son of a gentleman who was at that time inhabiting comfortable but close apartments in the Marshalsea prison; and it is *he* who keeps the secret from Fagin. The shame of admitting this secret is, in part, transformed in the novel into Oliver's incorruptibility and innocence, his instinctive repugnance for lying or stealing: so strangely are some of our virtues derived. In both instances, however, the danger is connected with a companionship or affection which is at once needed and intolerable; Bob Fagin's protectiveness is transformed into Fagin's treacherous maternal care.' Marcus, 367.

CHAPTER 3
Wellington House Academy
Pages 83–94

(1) Part of the buildings were cut off by the construction of the London and Birmingham Railway in Dickens's lifetime. The rest are now demolished.

2. Fielding's edition of *The Speeches*, 240-1.

(3) Fielding's edition of *The Speeches*, 336. Despite this commendation only Charley, his eldest son (1837-96), was sent to a public school. At the expense and at the wish of his father's friend, Miss Coutts, Charley went to Eton, though Dickens himself would have preferred him to go to Harrow, and had first thought of the recently established Marlborough. In any event, he took him away from Eton before he was sixteen and sent him to Leipzig to learn German as a prelude to a business career.

Charley's brothers, Walter Landor (1841-63), Francis Jeffrey (1844-86), Alfred D'Orsay Tennyson (1845-1912), Sydney Smith Haldimand (1847-72), Henry Fielding (1849-1913), and Edward Bulwer Lytton (1852-1902) all attended either a private boarding school for English boys run by two clergymen at Boulogne, where it was hoped they would learn to speak perfect French, or a private school at Wimbledon, which had been founded in 1850 to train boys for a military career in one or other of the technical branches, or, in the case of the youngest boy—who was unhappy at Wimbledon—Rochester Grammar School.

The two girls were educated at home by governesses, though the second one, Katey, went to art classes at Bedford College when she was thirteen.

(4) *The Dickensian*, vol. 22, no. 1. Walter Dexter, 'Dickens's Schooldays in London'. This former pupil at the school, Dr Henry Danson, is wrong in supposing that Dickens never learned Latin there. All the senior boys, in fact, did so, and Charles seems to have won a Latin prize. But it is certainly true that he was never inspired by the classics or remembered much about them in later life.

5. 'Recollections of Charles Dickens by a Schoolfellow', *The Dickensian*, vol. 7, no. 9; Willoughby Matchett, 'Dickens at Wellington House Academy', *The Dickensian*, vol. 7, nos. 6, 7, 8.

6. *Ibid*.

(7) He never lost his fascination for *The Miller and His Men* to which there are many references in his books and letters. He knew most of it by heart; and was so disappointed by a revival in the 1850s that he got up in the second act, saying he could 'stand it no longer'— ' "The Miller and His Men": a Reminiscence' by Percy Fitzgerald, *The Dickensian*, vol. 4, no. 12.

8. Forster, i, 42.

(9) Clarendon Square has been renamed Chatton Street (east side), Polygon Road (north side), Phoenix Road (south side), and Warrington Street (west side). The Polygon itself has been demolished.

(10) Holborn Court was renamed South Square in 1829.

CHAPTER 4
Messrs Ellis & Blackmore
Pages 97–119

1. W. J. Carlton, 'Mr Blackmore Engages an Office Boy', *The Dickensian*, vol. 48, no. 302.

(2) He became a student of the Middle Temple, after his first successes as a writer in 1839; but he was never called to the Bar.

(3) These chambers are now the offices of Messrs Wood, Nash & Co.

4. V. S. Pritchett, *The Living Novel*, 77.

(5) It has been suggested that the original of Crummles was T. D. Davenport, described by *Figaro in London*, a satirical journal of the day, as 'a man of about 20 stone with lungs *en suite* and a face of alarming fatness which he screwed into the most distorted shape, presenting a series of grimaces equally unmeaning and horrible'. Davenport, formerly a lawyer, was the actor-manager of the Westminster Subscription Theatre which was the one Dickens was most likely to have attended, it being so close to his office. *The Dickensian*, vol. 58, no. 336; vol. 59, no. 340; Malcolm Morley, 'Where Crummles Played' and 'Private Theatres and Boz'.

6. Allardyce Nicholl, 'The Theatre', *Early Victorian England*, ii, 267–82.

(7) 'The first impression, and a continuing one, in Dickens's prose,' as Robert Garis has emphasised, 'is of a voice manipulating language with pleasure and pride in its own skill . . . there is the constant and overt intention to dazzle us with verbal devices, leading us to applaud . . . a self-exhibiting master of language. . . . Dickens is a performing artist, displaying his verbal skills in familiar modes and in a theatre created by the insistent and self-delighting rhetoric of his voice.' Garis, 16, 24, 63.

8. Nonesuch edition of *The Letters*, ii, 274.

(9) 'Whenever Dickens came to a scene in which right triumphed and villainy met its just reward,' Earle Davis suggests, 'he instinctively

imitated on paper the stage mannerisms of Macready, just as he mimicked Charles Mathews in comedy and farce.' Davis, 60–1.

(10) Sam Weller's taste for such comments as 'It's a great deal more in your way than mine, as the gen'lm'n on the right side o' the garden wall said to the man on the wrong 'un, ven the mad bull wos a cummin' up the lane', was one shared by many comedians of his time, professional and amateur alike. One comedian who was famous for the delivery of such lines at the time that Dickens was at Ellis & Blackmore's, was Sam Vale—and since Sam Weller pronounces his name Veller, the choice of name seems all the more significant. Vale scored a great success as Simon Splatterdash in the farce, *The Boarding House*, at the Surrey Theatre, and delighted his audiences with such 'Wellerisms' as 'Let everyone take care of himself, as the jackass said when he danced among the chickens', and 'I know the world, as the monkey said when he cut off his tail' (see Edwin Pugh, *The Charles Dickens Originals*, London, 1912, 86–90).

11. Quoted by Earle Davis, 45.

12. Quoted by Humphry House, *All in Due Time*.

13. Mary Dickens, *My Father*, 47–8.

(14) John Payne Collier, *An Old Man's Diary* (Privately printed, 1872). Dickens never lost his taste for such clothes. At a banquet given in honour of the actor William Charles Macready in 1851, he appeared 'in a blue dress coat, faced with silk and aflame with gorgeous brass buttons, a [waistcoat] of black satin, with a white satin collar, and a wonderfully embroidered shirt. When he got up to speak, his long curly hair [his 'ringlets', Thackeray called them], his bright eyes, and his general aspect of geniality and *bonhomie* presented a delightful picture.' The actor John Coleman, who was present, 'made some ingenuous remark upon the subject to Thackeray who rejoined, "Yes, the beggar is as beautiful as a butterfly, especially about the shirt-front." ' John Coleman, *Fifty Years of an Actor's Life* (1904), ii, 23–4, quoted in K. J. Fielding's edition of *The Speeches*, 114.

(15) John Dickens had some experience as a writer, and years before at Chatham he had sent up to *The Times* an account of one of the worst fires in the town's history, and had been gratified to see it printed under his name in two long columns. As City Correspondent of the *British Press* he wrote a series of articles on marine insurance which were marked by his peculiarly grandiloquent style. In the opinion of a journalist on the staff of the same paper, Samuel Carter Hall,

John Dickens was 'a gentleman of no great intellectual capacity'; but Charles (who did not deny the general belief that he had modelled the hypocritical Pecksniff on Hall) said that his father was 'a first-rate shorthand writer on Gurney's system, and a capital reporter'. In 1846 Charles found him an appointment with *The Daily News* where, according to one of the reporters, he 'revelled in his work' as manager of the parliamentary staff, as much as he revelled in mixing a bowl of gin punch at the Rainbow in Fleet Street. Another journalist, however, thought that the job was 'something that "turned up" in conjunction with his illustrious son's prosperity, and he took it with an airy grace which did not hide his inefficiency from the eyes of his young staff'.

John Dickens's articles for the *British Press* provided him with an excuse to raise money in a characteristic way. When the newspaper failed, he wrote to Lloyds whom he had supported in its columns against newly-founded companies which were offering to undertake marine insurance. He spoke of his 'serious pecuniary inconveniences' and was pleased to accept a gratuity of ten guineas. William J. Carlton, 'John Dickens, Journalist', *The Dickensian*, vol. LIII, no. 321.

(16) This description of the difficulties of learning Gurney's system was used in advertisements by Isaac Pitman whose less complicated system was put before the public in 1837.

(17) Although Dickens did not make use of his acquired skill at shorthand in writing his novels, he did not lose it. And Forster noticed that it was 'quite an ordinary habit' with him when listening to an after-dinner speech to draw his hand across the table, tracing the shorthand symbols with his finger on the cloth.

CHAPTER 5
Miss Maria Beadnell
Pages 123–148

(1) The premises of Doctors' Commons were pulled down in 1867.

(2) In the second chapter of their absorbing book *Dickens at Work* (Methuen, 1957), John Butt and Kathleen Tillotson have indicated how much of the original sketches, as they were first printed, Dickens cut out or altered for publication in book form. Personal and topical allusions, rebellious or impertinent attitudes, occasional indelicacies,

were either softened or deleted, so that on their first appearance several of his articles would have struck home as hard as this attack on Dr Joseph Phillimore, Regius Professor of Civil Law at Oxford and, at the time Dickens wrote, a judge.

When the *Sketches* first appeared in book form 'Dickens was established as a popular "family" author . . . he had a keener sense of his audience and of his responsibilities towards it; he was rising socially, and possibly especially sensitive to imputations of vulgarity.' Butt and Tillotson, 57.

(3) This house and the bank at Number 1, Lombard Street, have now been rebuilt and form part of the Scottish Provident Institution buildings. Edwin Pugh believed that Dickens had Smith, Payne and Smith's in mind when describing Tellson's Bank in *A Tale of Two Cities*, 'an old fashioned place . . . very small, very dark, very ugly, very incommodious. . . . After bursting open a door of idiotic obstinacy with a weak rattle in its throat, you fell into Tellson's down two steps, and came to your senses in a miserable little shop, with two little counters, where the oldest of men made your cheque shake as if the wind rustled it, while they examined the signature by the dingiest of windows, which . . . were made the dingier by their own iron bars' (Bk. II, ch. 1).

Dickens himself did not bank here, but with Coutts, where he opened an account in November 1837 with £500 of the additional money which Chapman and Hall gave him out of their profits on *Pickwick*. Lady Pansy Pakenham thinks that the old Coutts building was a more likely inspiration for Tellson's, although she was brought up in the belief that Tellson's was Child's bank—her mother was a descendant of Child. Clearly there were several banks in early nineteenth-century London which resembled Tellson's.

(4) George Beadnell died in 1862, leaving £40,000. 'Of course I could not be surprised, knowing his great age, by the wearing out of his vitality', Dickens wrote to Maria in a letter of sympathy, 'but—almost equally of course—it was a shock too, for all the old Past comes out of its grave when I think of him, and the Ghosts of a good many years stand about his memory.' Nonesuch edition of *The Letters*, iii, 320.

5. Pilgrim edition of *The Letters*, i, 16; Nonesuch edition of *The Letters*, ii, 628–34; Johnson, 1, 67–70.

6. Forster, i, 50.

7. Gerald G. Grubb, 'Dickens's First Experiences as a Parliamentary Reporter', *The Dickensian*, vol. 36, no. 256.

8. Johnson, i, 62–4.

9. Leslie C. Staples, 'Two Early London Homes of Charles Dickens', *The Dickensian*, vol. 47, no. 300.

10. Nonesuch edition of *The Letters*, i, 627.

11. *Ibid.*, 782.

12. Pilgrim edition of *The Letters*, i, 16–17.

13. *Ibid.*, i, 28–9.

14. Nonesuch edition of *The Letters*, ii, 633.

15. *Ibid.*, ii, 596.

16. *Ibid.*, ii, 620.

17. *Ibid.*, ii, 626–7.

18. *Ibid.*, ii, 629.

19. *Ibid.*, ii, 634–5.

20. *Ibid.*, ii, 649.

21. *Ibid.*, ii, 661; Johnson, ii, 830–9.

CHAPTER 6

The *Chronicle* Reporter

Pages 151–162

(1) Lady Pansy Pakenham doubts this story of Collier's. Collier's memoirs were published after the first volume of Forster's *Life*, in which the blacking episode was made public for the first time.

2. Collier, 12–14; Johnson, i, 90–1.

3. Collier, 15.

(4) The competition between the papers was intense, and they hurled insults at each other with abandon. According to *The Times*, the *Morning Chronicle* was 'a squirt of filthy water'. See E. E. Kettett's article 'The Press' in *Early Victorian England, 1830–1865* (Oxford University Press, 1934), ii, 3–97.

5. Forster, i, 52–54; Johnson, i, 10–68; Pilgrim edition of *The Letters*, i, 106–7, 109; Dexter, *Mr and Mrs Dickens*, 31–45.

6. Forster, i, 51.

(7) Forster, i, 52; *The Speeches*, 348. To the end of his life, as readers of *Barnaby Rudge*, *A Tale of Two Cities* and chapter XLV of *The Old Curiosity Shop* cannot fail to notice, Dickens was at once

fascinated and horrified by the behaviour of the mob which these days as a parliamentary reporter enabled, indeed forced, him to study. The evident ambivalence of his attitude was the result not only of the clash between his instinctive radicalism and his characteristically Victorian fear of the strange and alien, but also, as Humphry House has suggested, of his emotional need to 'work off something of his own neurotic impatience and anger'.

John Gross has put the point well: 'Dickens dances the Carmagnole, and howls for blood with the mob. Frightened by the forces which he has released, he views the revolution with hatred and disgust. . . . Confronted with the crowd, Dickens reaches for his gun . . .' John Gross, *'A Tale of Two Cities'* in *Dickens and the 20th Century* (ed. John Gross and Gabriel Pearson, 1962), 192.

(8) F. G. Kitton, *The Minor Writings of Charles Dickens* (London, 1900), 7–9; Johnson, *op. cit.*, i, 103–4. £150 was a generous sum, the equivalent of which most young authors would be delighted to accept today for a first book of this type. Thirty-four years later, however, in 1869, Dickens was able to demand and obtain £7,500 for the profits on the first 25,000 copies of his last book, and an equal share with the publishers on the profits of all subsequent copies. At that time he had no difficulty in selling a short story for £1,000.

9. Forster, i, 51.

(10) John Westlock, who marries Ruth, the sister of Martin's friend, Tom Pinch, lives there. 'A handsome pile of buildings . . . four stories in height', according to *Tallis's Illustrated London*, it had been built in 1819. Now demolished, the offices of the Prudential Insurance Company cover its site.

11. Pilgrim edition of *The Letters*, i, 47.

12. Forster, i, 456.

13. Pilgrim edition of *The Letters*, i, 33–34; Johnson, i, 98–100; Forster, i, 13.

(14) See John Malcolm Bullock, 'The Ancestry of Mrs Charles Dickens', *The Dickensian*, vol. 31, no. 235, and Arthur A. Adrian, *Georgina Hogarth and the Dickens Circle* (Oxford University Press, 1957), 4–6. Dickens's high opinion of George Hogarth did not endure. His untidiness, which had at first seemed rather endearing, later irritated his son-in-law beyond measure when its effects were seen in his own house. He was enraged to discover on returning from a holiday or a visit to the Continent that the Hogarths, who

sometimes lived in the house in his absences, had left it with dust an 'inch thick' on the floors, with books and papers in their wrong places in his study, with windows uncleaned and bills unpaid. Eventually he grew 'dead sick' of Hogarth's Scottish accent, and decided that his constitution was completely undermined by the sight of the man at breakfast. Walter Dexter, *Mr and Mrs Dickens*, 239, 249; Nonesuch edition of *The Letters*, ii, 646, 764.

CHAPTER 7
Miss Catherine Hogarth
Pages 165–170

1. Pilgrim edition of *The Letters*, i, 61–2.
2. *Ibid.*, i, 104.
3. *Ibid.*, i, 97, 110.
4. *Ibid.*, i, 133.
5. *Ibid.*, i, 86.
(6) The work for the *Chronicle*, in fact, provided him with material for his other work. For instance, his attendance at the Norton–Melbourne case, in which George Norton accused Lord Melbourne of having had a criminal connection with his wife, resulted not only in twenty-six columns of newsprint in the 23 June issue of the *Morning Chronicle*, but is the basis for the splendid thirty-third chapter of *Pickwick*, in which occurs 'the full and faithful Report of the Memorable Trial of Bardell against Pickwick'.
7. Walter Dexter, 'The Reception of Dickens's First Book', *The Dickensian*, vol. 32, no. 237.
8. Johnson, i, 107–9, 116–18; Forster, i, 58–62.
(9) The name he borrowed from Moses Pickwick, whose coaches were a familiar sight in the West Country, and whose White Hart Hotel stood opposite the Pump Room in Bath.

Dickens always found it difficult to start a book until he had hit upon the names for its leading characters; and he spent a great deal of time composing suitable ones. Sweezlewag, Sweezleden, Sweezleback, Chuzzletoe, Chuzzleboy, Chubblewig, Chuzzlewig, were all considered before he decided on Chuzzlewit; and Wrychin, Tipchin, Alchin, Somching, were all considered before he settled on Pipchin. Many of his most famous names have associations with his youth.

Weller, for instance, as well as being the name of his nurse and a name often to be seen inscribed on the tombstones of churchyards round Chatham, also appears in Ellis & Blackmore's account book which it was one of his clerkly duties to keep up to date.

This account book, indeed, provided him with several of his more curious names. But, in fact, most of his best are inspired inventions or adaptations, and, as George Gissing said, even though there are many—like Gamp, Micawber, Bumble, Murdstone—which are so familiar we associate them inevitably with certain characteristics, 'one recognises their exquisite rightness'.

All these descriptive names come from a single book, *Little Dorrit*: Flintwich, Barnacle, Plornish, Stiltstalking, Wobbler, Meagles, Pancks, Mrs Captain Barbary, Captain Maroon, Finching, Ticket, Bilberry, Toozellem, Joddleby, Chivery, Cripples, Merdle, Sparkler, Tinkler, Nandy, Mrs General, and Messrs Peddle and Pool.

10. Pilgrim edition of *The Letters*, i, 106, 118, 133, 140, 145.
11. Walter Dexter, *Mr and Mrs Charles Dickens*, 65–6; F. G. Kitton, *Charles Dickens by Pen and Pencil*, 109.

CHAPTER 8
The Inimitable Boz
Pages 173–184

1. Pilgrim edition of *The Letters*, i, 95–134.
2. *Ibid.*, i, 259.
3. *Ibid.*, i, 689.
4. *Ibid.*, i, 630.
(5) Edward Bulwer (1803–73), the novelist and politician, was shortly to be created a baronet, and on succeeding to the Knebworth estate added Lytton to his surname under the terms of his mother's will. He was raised to the peerage as Lord Lytton in 1866. He immediately recognised Dickens's great qualities, and although many other writers did not very much like Bulwer, he and Dickens eventually became close friends.
6. Johnson, i, 117–18, 135–8, 140–1, 148–55.
7. Pilgrim edition of *The Letters*, i, 189.
8. *Ibid.*, i, 183.

9. *Ibid.*, i, 165.

10. Johnson, i, 184–5.

11. Percy Fitzgerald, *John Forster*; Renton, *John Forster*; Ley's Introduction to his edition of Forster's *Life*; Johnson, i, 186–7; Fielding, *Dickens*, 30–1.

(12) This at least is what Charles Culliford Boz Dickens later told Lord Redesdale when they were boys together at Eton. Lord Redesdale, *Memoirs* (London, 1915), i, 65.

CHAPTER 9
Miss Mary Hogarth
Pages 187–201

1. Quoted by Kitton, *The Dickens Country*, 53.

(2) Leslie C. Staples, '48 Doughty Street: Dickens Negotiates', *The Dickensian*, vol. 58, no. 336. 48 Doughty Street, now known as The Dickens House, was bought by the Dickens Fellowship in 1924. It contains an interesting collection of Dickensiana.

3. Kitton, *The Novels*, 29.

4. Pilgrim edition of *The Letters*, i, 268.

5. *Ibid.*, i, 257.

6. *Ibid.*, i, 256–260.

7. Nonesuch edition of *The Letters*, i, 519.

(8) This certainly does not indicate, as Dr K. J. Fielding has said, 'any strong leaning to Roman Catholicism, of which he strongly disapproved. It was probably influenced by the very natural association between the name, Mary, and the Virgin; and it is strange to notice, what seems to have caught no one's attention before, that on the head of Little Nell's deathbed, also associated with Mary Hogarth, Dickens's artist had pictured the Virgin and Child'. K. J. Fielding, *Charles Dickens: A Critical Introduction*, 106.

9. *Ibid.*, i, 359–60.

10. K. J. Fielding, 'Charles Dickens and His Wife', *Études Anglaises*, 1955, quoted by Adrian, 14.

11. Nonesuch edition of *The Letters*, i, 519.

(12) It is interesting to notice, too, that both Mr Dick of *David Copperfield* and Dick Swiveller of *The Old Curiosity Shop* are given a name which indicates that Dickens was playing a similar game with them, too.

Mr Dick (whose real name is Mr Babley) can be seen as yet another refraction of his creator's attitude towards his own garrulous parent; while Dick Swiveller, a kindly stage-struck youth who had been 'cast upon the world in [his] tenderest period' has within him much of Dickens's own feelings about himself.

13. Steven Marcus, *Dickens*, 289–92.

14. George Orwell, 'Charles Dickens' in *Inside the Whale*.

(15) Two striking passages in the book—in chs. xxv and xxxix—, as J. Hillis Miller has noticed, both of them describing experiences of *déjà vu*, the strange sensation in which one feels oneself to be re-enacting a scene that has occurred before, long ago in the past, or in another life, 'assert covertly that Agnes has been all along secretly designed' for David. 'Both experiences are covert premonitions of the place Agnes is to have in David's life.' J. Hillis Miller, *Charles Dickens: The World of His Novels* (O.U.P., 1959), 158.

The notes (reproduced by Butt and Tillotson, *op. cit.*, p. 120) which Dickens made for the fifth number of the book, in which he refers to the 'introduction of the real heroine', provide evidence of Dickens's immediate intention that the 'sister' shall become the wife.

(16) His short piece, 'A Child's Dream of a Star', written for *Household Words* some time after her death, and recalling their childhood in Chatham together when they used to wander at night about St Mary's churchyard looking at the stars, is an intensely felt and highly sentimental evocation of his childish devotion to her. In this story, the sister of the 'child' of the title dies when she is 'still very young, oh very very young'; and the brother keeps dreaming of the star to which his 'angel sister' has gone and to which he longs to go, too, to join her. He does not do so until he is old, but then his age falls from him like a garment and he moves 'towards the star as a child'.

17. Johnson, ii, 650–3.

CHAPTER 10
The Novelist Triumphant
Pages 205–219

1. Pilgrim edition of *The Letters*, i, 312, 317, 350, 353, 364.

(2) Copyright at this time expired with the death of the author who had scant redress against piracies of his work, as against foreign publishers

who appropriated it. Dickens, who suffered more from pirates than any other author of his day, was always highly indignant that his work should be the means of putting 'a few shillings in the vermin-eaten pockets' of these 'miserable creatures'. While *Oliver Twist* was still running in *Bentley's Miscellany* it was adapted for the stage of the Surrey Theatre. Dickens went to see it and by the middle of the first scene had found it so unbearably bad that he lay down on the floor and stayed there until it was over.

3. Pilgrim edition of *The Letters*, i, 304.

4. Cockshut, 14.

(5) Pilgrim edition of *The Letters*, i, 311. The way in which Dickens incorporated his experiences (and the curious people he chanced to meet) into his novels may be seen by comparing this letter to his wife with the early chapters of *Nicholas Nickleby*. In these chapters Nicholas is described as going to Yorkshire in a heavy snow storm and stopping on the way at the George, Grantham, 'one of the best inns in England'. One of his fellow travellers is a lady who asks that the others keep a sharp look out for a green chariot driven by a coachman 'with a gold-laced hat on the box, and a footman most probably in silk stockings, behind'. He is put down at the George and New Inn, Greta Bridge. And Mr Squeers, the headmaster of Dotheboys Hall, brings back to the school from London a letter from one of the boys' step-parents who had taken to her bed 'on hearing that her stepson would not eat fat, and has been very ill ever since'. *Nicholas Nickleby*, chs. v, vi and viii.

6. Pilgrim edition of *The Letters*, i, 366.

7. *Ibid.*, i, 263.

8. Forster, i, 85, 131.

(9) The Sunday was 2 April 1838, and the next day was the anniversary both of their wedding and Forster's birthday. They celebrated this together at the Star and Garter and for the next twenty years, so Forster said, they continued to do so 'at the same place, except when they were living out of England. It was part of his love of regularity and order, as well as of his kindliness of nature, to place such friendly meetings as these under rites of habit and continuance.' Forster, i, 86.

(10) This was the London local postage rate until Sir Rowland Hill's introduction of the penny postage at the end of the following year.

11. Pilgrim edition of *The Letters*, i, 392–3.

12. Forster, i, 85.

13. Johnson, i, 230; Pearson, 72–3.

(14) Lord Ilchester, *Chronicles of Holland House* (London, 1837), 240; a year or so later another observer described Dickens as a 'little slender, pale-faced, boyish-looking individual, and perhaps the very last man in the room whom a stranger to his portrait could have picked out as being the author of *Pickwick*'. (From a private letter in R. Shelton Mackenzie's *Life of Charles Dickens* (Philadelphia, 1870), quoted by K. J. Fielding in his edition of the *Speeches*.) To T. A. Trollope, Anthony's brother, he seemed at first sight 'a dandified, pretty-boy-looking sort of figure, singularly young looking . . . with a slight flavour of the whipper-snapper'. T. A. Trollope, *What I Remember* (London, 1887), i, 110. To Forster it was the eagerness in Dickens's expression which was most striking. He had 'a firm nose with full wide nostrils, eyes wonderfully beaming with intellect and running over with humour and cheerfulness, and a rather prominent mouth strongly marked with sensibility'. His face was marked by a 'quickness, keenness, and practical power, the eager, restless, energetic outlook on each several feature, that seemed to tell so little of the student or writer, and so much of the man of action and business in the world. Light and motion flashed from every part of it'. Jane Carlyle said that it was as though his face were made of steel; and Leigh Hunt thought it had 'the life and soul in it of fifty human beings'. Forster, i, 65–66.

15. Johnson, i, 227–9.

(16) 1 Devonshire Terrace was demolished in 1960. A block of offices now covers the site.

(17) Dickens's first groom, Henry, was dismissed for being rude to Kate, and his place had been taken by William Topping, a Cockney whom his master described as 'a very small man, with fiery red hair', and elsewhere as 'trusty' and 'gentle'. He stayed with the family for about twelve years. In Forster's opinion he was 'a highly absurd little man'. He so complicated the disputes that his master had with his neighbours about the smoking of the stable chimney, 'meaning, by secret devices of his own, to conciliate each complainant alternately but succeeding only in aggravating them both, that law proceedings were only barely avoided'. Forster, i, 130.

18. Pilgrim edition of *The Letters*, i, 493–4.

19. Johnson, i, 234–53; Forster, i, 92–4, 112–15.

20. *The Observer*, 14 February 1965.

CHAPTER 11
Mrs Charles Dickens
Pages 223-246

(1) Forster, i, 105. Despite this excess of energy, Dickens never seems to have felt the need to do any physical work. We do not hear of him wanting to use his hands, to dig in his garden (as Carlyle did) or to make or build anything.

2. Nonesuch edition of *The Letters*, i, 259, 260, 271.

3. Toynbee, Macready's entry for 16 August 1840.

(4) Indeed, it sometimes appeared that the behaviour was compulsive. During his first visit to America, he amazed his companions on a walk, or rather a kind of jerky, excited run, through the streets of Boston, by suddenly—after having entertained them with a stream of talk, punctuated by outbursts of laughter—letting out a sudden howl. And once at a dinner party, overhearing a woman calling her husband 'darling', then an unusual endearment to use in public, he slid out of his chair on to the floor, raised one foot in the air, and cried out in tones of anguish, 'Did she call him darling?' When he got up and sat back in his chair, he carried on the conversation as though nothing had happened. See Edgar Johnson, *Dickens*, i, 366, 455.

(5) Three years later another observer was struck by these mannerisms when Dickens was making a visit to Manchester. Dickens was not 'strictly speaking *handsome*', this man thought. But his eyes were 'dark and full of fire, and, when turned upon you give a light . . . such as I have seldom seen before.' He had a good deal 'of the eye-brow elevating, shoulder-shrugging, and head nodding peculiar to people who have travelled a good deal'. E. W. Watkins, *Alderman Cobden of Manchester* (1891), 123–30, quoted by K. J. Fielding in his edition of *The Speeches*, 44.

6. Nonesuch edition of *The Letters*, i, 247, 248.

(7) The rumours persisted; and when Dickens wanted to take out a life insurance policy before his departure for America, the company insisted on a confirmation that they were false. Nonesuch edition of *The Letters*, i, 362.

8. Eleanor E. Christian, 'Recollections of Charles Dickens, *Temple Bar*, April 1888.

(9) *Ibid*. In later life, according to one of her nephews, Letitia was 'Betsey

'Trotwood all over, both in looks and manner'. Sir Henry Fielding
Dickens, *Recollections*, 28.

10. Eleanor E. Christian, *op. cit.*

11. *Ibid.*

12. *Ibid.*

(13) 'Undoubtedly, the death of Mary Hogarth was something like a
religious crisis', Gabriel Pearson has written. 'Nell was an unsuccessful
attempt to grope and feel a way through this crisis, to locate death
as a human event. Dickens probes and rummages around the grave.
He attempts to feel what it is like being dead. But this exploration
yields only two sorts of imagery: the shadowy remembrance of
pre-London Rochester and Victorian funereal decoration. Blank
verse and pathetic fallacy meanwhile secretly give the game away.
Dickens could not after all feel what death is like. He could only
feel what it was like to try to feel it. . . . The whole novel can be
read as an immense, unruly wreath laid on the clammy marble of
Kensal Green Cemetery.' Gabriel Pearson, 'The Old Curiosity Shop',
Dickens and the Twentieth Century, 79, 78.

14. Gabriel Pearson, *op. cit.*

(15) In Gabriel Pearson's view this scene is 'the closest we get to downright
copulation in early-Victorian fiction', *op. cit.*, 84.

(16) Arthur Gride has a similar relish for Madeline Bray who is 'fresh,
lovely, bewitching, and not nineteen. Dark eyes, long eyelashes, ripe
and ruddy lips that to look at it is to long to kiss, beautiful clustering
hair that one's fingers itch to play with.' *Nicholas Nickleby*, ch. XLVII.

17. Thomas Wright, *Life of Charles Dickens* (1935), 131.

18. Morgan MS., quoted by Johnson, ii, 726.

19. Nonesuch edition of *The Letters*, i, 443.

(20) He had frequently been irritated by Kate's carelessness or clumsiness
while in the United States. He complained to Forster that she had
fallen over no less than 743 times. 'She falls into, or out of every
coach or boat we enter; scrapes the skin off her legs; brings great
sores and swellings on her feet; chips large fragments out of her
ankle-bones; and makes herself blue with bruises.'

But George Putnam, the American whom her husband had
employed as his secretary, could not but admire her calmness and
gentle dignity, knowing how unwell she felt for most of the time—
her face kept swelling—how homesick she was, and how worried
about the children she had so unwillingly left behind. George W.

Putnam 'Four Months with Charles Dickens' in the *Atlantic Monthly*, October, November, 1870, quoted by Johnson, i, 417.

Dickens, who was almost as homesick as she was herself, and played 'Home, Sweet Home!' on an accordion night after night, had to admit, in the end, that Kate had made 'a *most admirable* traveller in every respect. She has never screamed or expressed alarm under circumstances that would have justified her in doing so, even in my eyes.' Nonesuch edition of *The Letters*, i, 436–7.

(21) Nonesuch edition of *The Letters*, i, 593. In the end, after a second broken engagement, Thompson and Christiana Weller were married in October 1845. Dickens attended the wedding in a dazzling waistcoat with 'broad stripes of blue or purple' which he had copied from one of Macready's. 'Let me show [my tailor that waistcoat],' he had asked Macready, 'as a sample of my taste and wishes; and—ha, ha, ha, ha!—eclipse the bridegroom!'

After the Thompsons were married, Dickens wondered why he had found Christiana so disturbingly attractive. She became, in his eyes, 'a mere spoiled child . . . with a devil of a whimpering, pouting temper'. The Thompsons spent most of their early married life in Italy where their daughters (one of whom became Alice Meynell and the other the painter of battle-scenes Lady Butler) were brought up, being taught by their father whose acceptance of his grandfather's fortune was conditional upon his not adopting a profession.

22. Johnson, i, 541–4, 551–7; Nonesuch edition of *The Letters*, i, 669–79.

23. Walter Dexter, *Mr and Mrs Dickens*, 228–9.

24. Nonesuch edition of *The Letters*, ii, 416.

25. Carlyle, *Letters to Family*, 169–71.

26. Morgan MS., quoted Johnson, ii, 662.

27. Alfred Tennyson Dickens, 'My Father and His Friends', *Nash's Magazine*, September, 1911.

EPILOGUE

Pages 249–270

(1) Like the Devonshire Terrace house, Tavistock House has been demolished. The British Medical Association Building now occupies the site.

2. Nonesuch edition of *The Letters*, ii, 765, 887; Berg MS., quoted by Johnson, ii, 905, 907.

3. Berg MS., quoted by Johnson, ii, 907, 909; Nonesuch *Letters*, ii, 873.

4. Nonesuch edition of *The Letters*, ii, 846, 848; Morgan MS., quoted by Johnson, ii, 878.

5. Storey, 94.

6. Johnson, ii, 918.

7. Storey, 94.

(8) *Letters and Private Papers of W. M. Thackeray* (ed. Gordon N. Ray, 1945). It seems unlikely that Ellen Ternan *was* Dickens's mistress before the separation. It is conceivable, of course, that the relationship remained platonic afterwards. Many distinguished Dickensians continue to suggest that it did remain so (as, for instance, Professor Edward Wagenknecht: *Dickens and the Scandalmongers*, University of Oklahoma Press, 1964). Certainly no evidence has been found to support the assertion, made by his daughter Katey amongst others, that Dickens and Ellen had a child. But if Dickens took houses for her under a false name (Tringham) and frequently visited her under that name, as he seems to have done, and if he did not then make her his mistress, he must have been, as Edmund Wilson suggests, an even more unusual man than we suppose.

9. Ley, *The Dickens Circle*, 95; Johnson, ii, 1013.

10. Perugini, *Thackeray and my Father*, 215.

11. Nonesuch edition of *The Letters*, ii, 743.

(12) Gad's Hill Place is now a girls' school.

13. Dolby, 30.

14. Trollope, ii, 112, 114.

15. G. S. Haight, ed. *The George Eliot Letters*, iii, 200.

16. Fields, quoted by Johnson, ii, 1089.

(17) Johnson, ii, 1053-8; Adrian, 71-2; Mary Dickens, *passim*; Forster, ii, 207-16; Yates, ii, 102-6. The food was good, although in the days when Mrs Dickens was hostess at Devonshire Terrace, Jane Carlyle had found the manner of its serving and the decorations on the table pretentious and vulgar. 'Such getting up of the steam is unbecoming to a literary man. The dinner was served up in the new fashion—not placed on the table at all—but handed round—only the dessert on the table and quantities of *artificial* flowers—but such an overloaded dessert! Pyramids of figs, raisins, oranges—ach!' *Jane Welsh Carlyle: A New Selection of Her Letters* (ed. Trudy Bliss, 188-9).

Mrs Dickens, under the name of Lady Maria Clutterbuck (a character she had played in a farce her husband had produced when

staying with the Richard Watsons at Rockingham Castle), had published a cookery book in 1852. Based on the stodgy dinners served
at Devonshire Terrace, it claims to have paid close attention to the
requirements of Sir Joseph Clutterbuck's appetite, and suggests how
often Dickens was served with cooked cheese, potatoes and bloaters.

The menus at Gad's Hill, under the direction of Georgina and
Mamie, were less monotonous; and the wines were excellent. In a
sale at Gad's Hill, after Dickens's death, the contents of his carefully
selected cellar fetched over £600.

(18) He seems to have been quite as concerned with the detailed organisation of Miss Coutts's reformatory home for prostitutes as with the
girls themselves. (Certainly, the prostitutes in the novels written after
he began working for this home are as melodramatically treated as
the earlier ones.) His fascination with police work displays not only
an 'inquisitively morbid interest in all forms of crime and death',
but also 'a kind of clerical satisfaction in the functioning of a well-run
organization.' Even his devotion to the theatre was almost as much a
love of administration as of acting. What he would really like to do,
he said close to the end of his life, would be to settle down near a
great theatre in the 'direction' of which he would have supreme
authority—Johnson, ii, 1151; House, 202–3; Fielding, 125–6.

(19) Collins, *Dickens and Education*, 50. Dickens 'doubtless meant well in
trying to instil these orderly habits', Philip Collins continues, 'and one
must remember that he was always conscious of the ancestral failings
of laxity and fecklessness, from which he hoped to save his own
progeny. But his efforts failed. Perhaps he had tried too hard, so
that the boys, once free from his surveillance, reacted strongly against
the parental virtue that had never become part of themselves. . . . He
may be criticised both for having hoped too much and for being too
vocal about his disillusion. . . . Towards the end of his life, two of his
intimate friends were discussing him. "Yes, yes," said one, "all his
fame goes for nothing since he has not got the one thing. He is
very unhappy in his children . . ." The other commented: "Nobody
can say how much too much of this the children have to bear." '

20. Morgan MS., quoted by Johnson, ii, 1111.

21. Nonesuch edition of *The Letters*, iii, 104.

(22) Dickens stuck to this conviction even when Plorn proved himself
incapable of settling down happily on a sheep station. It was clear
that he wanted to come home; but his father, whose normal reserve

had been broken down by grief when he had said goodbye to the nervous, sensitive, tearful boy on the platform at Paddington Station, would not consider it until the experiment had been made to 'try him fully'.

23. Quoted by Henry Fielding Dickens, 37.

(24) The same tone of vaguely accusatory self-congratulation is apparent in one of the only three notes Dickens wrote to his wife after the separation: 'I am glad to receive your letters'—she had written him to wish him well on a reading tour—'and to accept and reciprocate your best wishes. Severely hard work lies before me; but that is not a new thing in my life, and I am content to go my way and do it.' Dexter, *Mr and Mrs Dickens*, 265.

25. Henry Fielding Dickens, 36.

26. Nonesuch edition of *The Letters*, iii, 192.

27. *Ibid.*, iii, 172.

28. *Ibid.*, iii, 478.

(29) He had wanted to cut himself off completely from Catherine, and hoped that the children would do the same without pressure from himself. He wrote to her only to acknowledge notes of sympathy or wishes of goodwill, and refused to go to advise her when she ran into some difficulties over her house. Even when their son Walter died, and his mother was profoundly upset, he did not take 'any notice of the event to her, either by letter or otherwise', according to Sir William Hardman. 'If anything were wanting to sink Charles Dickens to the lowest depths of my esteem, this fills up the measure of his iniquity. As a writer I admire him; as a man I despise him.' Ada Nisbet, *Dickens and Ellen Ternan* (University of California Press, 1952), 41–2.

One day when Katey went to call at the house in Gloucester Terrace, her mother said sadly, although they had agreed not to talk about him, for it upset them both so, 'Do you think he is sorry for me?' And as she lay dying she gave the letters she had had from him to her daughter with the request made with 'great earnestness', that they should be given to the British Museum so that 'the world may know that he loved me once'. Storey, 131, 164. Catherine Dickens died nine years after her husband, in 1879.

30. Storey, 106.

31. Quoted in *The Dickens Critics* (ed. Ford and Lane), 48.

(32) A flatly contradictory opinion of Dickens's style was given by Alice

Meynell, writing in the *Atlantic Monthly* a few years later: 'On the point of grammar Dickens is above criticism. Ignorant of those languages which are held to furnish the foundations of grammatical construction he assuredly was. Nevertheless, he knew how to construct. He grasped the language, as it were, from within. I believe that throughout all those volumes of his there is not one example of . . . weak grammar. Hardly another author is thus infallible. Those authors who think Thackeray to be, in some sort, more literary than Dickens, would be dismayed if they compared the two authors upon this point.' Ford and Lane, *The Dickens Critics*, 106.

(33) It was also often objected that in the later novels, Dickens, increasingly absorbed with social criticism, had begun to lose that satirical touch which had been the hallmark of his genius. There was some truth in this. The satire 'becomes harsher and I think cruder as Dickens grows older,' V. S. Pritchett had observed, 'as his nerves become exacerbated by domestic unhappiness, by overwork, by straining after money, and as Victorianism became more vulgar and more blatant. There is an increase in hatred and violence as the years go by. These are dulling to the poetic genius and the comic portrait of Mr Gradgrind, for example, is actually dull.' 'The Comic World of Dickens' in *The Dickens Critics*, 322.

Such comic portraits in the earlier books were never dull; and although the satire on the running of the workhouse and the indictment of the 1834 Poor Law in *Oliver Twist* are finished with at the end of chapter VII, the reader is nevertheless constantly aware that it is Dickens himself talking when he allows Nancy to protest against Oliver's ill-treatment, a protest that occurs again, in exactly the same words, in *Nicholas Nickleby*—'I will not stand by and see it done'.

There was the objection, too, that in the social criticism which pervades the later writings Dickens was often prejudiced, amateurish and unfair, more ready to follow public opinion than to form it.

'Even without any external evidence showing that Dickens habitually read *The Times*, the internal evidence would be strong enough', John Butt and Kathleen Tillotson have noticed. 'Of the five subjects to which *The Times* kept recurring during the months immediately preceding the inception of *Bleak House*, three [the ineffectuality of Parliament, the unhealthiness of towns, and Chancery reform] take a prominent place in the novel, and one of the remaining two is memorably represented. What is of greater significance is that both the policy of the newspaper and its interpretation of facts are represented without much distortion in the novel.' Butt and Tillotson, 193. See also Philip Collins, *Dickens and Crime*.

Moreover, as other critics such as George Orwell have suggested, there are not in these later works—nor indeed in any of the works— any constructive suggestions. Institutions and systems are attacked, but no clear suggestions are ever made as to what should be put in their places. They are attacked with marvellous intensity and anger; but the anger displays an emotional dependence on the institutions assaulted. Many of the bitterest attacks, indeed, remarks A. O. J. Cockshut in a striking analogy, 'are reminiscent of a man trying to burst through a locked door with his shoulder. If he succeeds he is in danger of collapsing.' (Cockshut, 53). 'Of course it is not necessarily the business of a novelist, or a satirist, to make constructive suggestions,' as Orwell said, 'but the point is that Dickens's attitude is at bottom not even destructive. There is no clear sign that he wants the existing order to be overthrown, or that he believes it would make very much difference if it were overthrown.' ('Charles Dickens' in *Inside the Whale*).

Yet other critics have gone on to demonstrate Dickens's fundamental jejuneness: 'the meagreness of his intellectual comment on what he had seen' when contrasted with 'the incomparable power of his imaginative observation' (Cockshut, 65); the scrappiness of his knowledge: 'G. H. Lewes was right—Dickens was and remained, "outside philosophy, science, and the higher literature." When he had read anything on the subject it was usually the wrong books' (Philip Collins, *Dickens and Education*, 17); the narrowness of his aesthetic sensibility: 'his powers of appreciation of any art were probably more limited and his taste more set and conventional than those of any man of comparable genius' (Humphry House, *The Dickens World*, 129); the inability to construct, the lack of unity of tone, the conventionality of most of his serious characters and his 'uncertain grasp of psychological essentials' in portraying the more memorable ones (Lord David Cecil, 'Charles Dickens' in *Early Victorian Novelists*).

But all modern critics agree that despite his manifest faults, Dickens was a very great novelist. For whatever truth there may be in the objections which have been raised against him, his novels are not only among the most powerfully imaginative in any language,

they are unique. There is no other major novelist comparable with
him; he cannot be judged in conventional terms of criticism.

34. Humphry House, *The Dickens World*, 224.

35. Nonesuch edition of *The Letters*, ii, 403.

(36) A man of little self-knowledge, he was, as Angus Wilson has said
in an understanding essay, 'a strongly sensual man, he had a deep
social and emotional need for family life and love, he had a compen-
sating claustrophobic dislike of the domestic scene, and he woke up
to these contradictions in his sexual make-up very late'. Angus
Wilson, 'The Heroes and Heroines of Dickens', reprinted in *Dickens
and the 20th Century* (ed. John Gross and Gabriel Pearson, 1962).

(37) One might almost suppose that his gratuitous naming of Ellen
Ternan in his will—when he could have provided for her without
doing so, and no doubt did make other provisions for her, since
he left her only £1,000—was a direct provocation to the type of
smugly self-satisfied, conventional burgher he attacked in his last
book in the form of Mr Sapsea, auctioneer and mayor.

38. Nonesuch edition of *The Letters*, iii, 7.

39. Charles Dickens, Junior, 'Reminiscences of my Father', *Windsor
Magazine*, September 1934.

(40) The form of insanity which is most closely related to genius,
Lord Brain has said, is cyclothymia, the manic depressive state.
'Dickens manifested some obsessional traits, but his general mood
of elation, associated with hyperactivity and broken by short
recurrent periods of depression, suggest that he was cycloid. . . . The
untiring energy and flight of ideas of the phase of elation may
persist as a milder enduring state without disorder of thought, and
add greatly to the productivity of the artist, as was the case with
Dickens.' Russell Brain, *Some Reflections on Genius* (Pitman Medical
Publishing Co., 1960), 21.

41. Charles Dickens, Junior, *op. cit.*

42. Dolby, 388.

43. Henry Fielding Dickens, 27.

44. Forster, ii, 363.

45. Mary Angela Dickens, 110.

46. Storey, 133–4; Kate Perugini, 'Edwin Drood and the Last Days of
Charles Dickens', *Pall Mall Magazine*, June 1906.

47. Johnson, ii, 1153–4; Adrian, 136–7; Forster, ii, 415–16.

48. Nonesuch edition of *The Letters*, ii, 765.

SOURCES

Fuller bibliographies will be found in the second volume of Edgar Johnson's biography and in *The Dickens Critics*, ed. Ford and Lane.

ADRIAN, ARTHUR A. *Georgina Hogarth and the Dickens Circle* (O.U.P., 1957)

ALDINGTON, RICHARD. 'The Underworld of Young Dickens' in *Four English Portraits* (1948)

AYLMER, FELIX. *Dickens Incognito* (Hart-Davis, 1959)

BAYLEY, JOHN. Essay on *Oliver Twist* in *Dickens and the 20th Century* (ed. John Gross and Gabriel Pearson, 1962)

BEERS, HENRY A. *Nathaniel Parker Willis* (1885)

BERGONZI, BERNARD. Essay on *Nicholas Nickleby* in *Dickens and the 20th Century* (ed. John Gross and Gabriel Pearson, 1962)

BIGELOW, JOHN. *Retrospections of an Active Life* (1909)

BOWEN, W. H. *Charles Dickens and his Family* (Heffer, Cambridge, 1956)

BRAIN, LORD. 'Authors and Psychopaths' in *British Medical Journal* (1949, vol. ii, p. 1427)

—— 'Diagnosis of Genius' in *Doctors Past and Present* (1949)

—— *Some Reflections on Genius* (Lippincott, 1962)

BROWN, IVOR. *Dickens in his Time* (Nelson, 1963)

BUTT, JOHN and TILLOTSON, KATHLEEN. *Dickens at Work* (Methuen, 1957)

CARLTON, W. J. *Charles Dickens: Shorthand Writer* (1926)

CECIL, LORD DAVID. *Early Victorian Novelists* (Constable, 1934)

CHESTERTON, G. K. *Charles Dickens* (1906)

CHRISTIAN, ELEANOR. 'Recollections of Charles Dickens' in *Temple Bar*, LXXXII (1888), 483

CRUIKSHANK, R. J. *Charles Dickens and Early Victorian England* (Chanticleer, 1950)

CLARKE, CHARLES and CLARKE, MARY COWDEN. *Recollections of Writers* (1878)

COCKSHUT, A. O. J. *The Imagination of Charles Dickens* (N.Y. Univ. Press, 1962); Essay on *Edwin Drood* in *Dickens and the 20th Century*. (ed. John Gross and Gabriel Pearson, 1962)

COLEMAN, JOHN. *Fifty Years of an Actor's Life* (1904)

COLLIER, JOHN PAYNE. *An Old Man's Diary, Forty Years Ago* (1872)

COLLINS, PHILIP. *Dickens and Crime* (St. Martins, 1962)

—— *Dickens and Education* (St. Martins, 1963)

DAVIS, EARLE. *The Flint and the Flame: The Artistry of Charles Dickens* (Univ. of Mo. Press, 1963)

DEXTER, WALTER. *The England of Dickens* (1925)

—— *The Kent of Dickens* (1924)

—— *The London of Dickens* (1930)

—— (ed.) *Mr and Mrs Charles Dickens: His Letters to Her* (Constable, 1935)

—— With J. W. T. Ley *The Origin of Pickwick* (Chapman and Hall, 1936)

DICKENS, ALFRED TENNYSON. 'My Father and his Friends', *Nash's Magazine* (September, 1911)

DICKENS, CHARLES. *Letters*, ed. A. Waugh, Hugh Walpole, W. Dexter and T. Hatton (Nonesuch edition, 1938)

—— *Letters*, ed. Madeline House and Graham Storey (Pilgrim edition, Vol. 1, Clarendon Press, Oxford, 1965)

—— *The Speeches*, ed. K. J. Fielding (Oxford University Press, 1960)

DICKENS, CHARLES (the Younger). 'Reminiscences of my Father' in *Windsor Magazine* (Christmas Supplement, 1934)

DICKENS, HENRY FIELDING. *Memories of my Father* (Duffield, 1929)

—— *Recollections* (Ryerson Press, 1934)

DICKENS, MARY. *My Father as I recall Him* (1900)

DICKENS, MARY ANGELA. 'A Child's Recollections of Gad's Hill', *Strand Magazine* (January, 1897)

—— 'My Grandfather as I knew Him', *Nash's Magazine* (October, 1911)

Dickensian, The, particularly articles by:

Leslie C. Staples, Philip Collins, William J. Carlton, Percy Fitzgerald, Willoughby Matchett, Malcolm Morley, Walter Dexter, A. E. Brookes Cross, Nancy Stewart Parnell, Florence Tylee, Sir Henry Fielding Dickens, A. de Suzannet, John Malcolm Bullock, Gerald G. Grubb, Arthur Waugh, T. W. Hill, J. H. McNulty, John Greaves, J. Leslie Dunstan, in these issues:

Vol. 4, nos. 3 and 12; vol. 5, nos. 6 and 7; vol. 7, nos. 5, 6, 7, 8 and 9; vol. 22, nos. 1 and 4; vol. 23, no. 202; vol. 25, nos. 210, 211 and 212; vol. 30, no. 232; vol. 31, nos. 233, 234 and 235; vol. 32, nos. 237 and 239; vol. 33, no. 241; vol. 36, no. 256; vol. 38, no. 262; vol. 45, nos. 290, 291 and 292; vol. 47, no. 300; vol. 48, nos. 301, 302; vol. 49, no. 306; vol. 50, nos. 309 and 311; vol. 53, nos. 321 and 323; vol. 56, nos.

330 and 331; vol. 57, no. 333; vol. 58, nos. 336 and 337; vol. 59, no. 340; vol. 60, nos. 342 and 343; vol. 61, no. 345; vol. 62, no. 349.

DOLBY, GEORGE. *Charles Dickens as I Knew Him* (1912)

ENGEL, MONROE. *The Maturity of Dickens* (Harvard Univ. Press, 1959)

FIELDING, K. J. *Charles Dickens* (Longmans, new enlarged edition, 1965)

—— ed. *The Speeches of Charles Dickens* (Oxford University Press, 1960)

FIELDS, JAMES T. *In and Out of Doors with Charles Dickens* (1876)

FITZGERALD, PERCY. *John Forster by one of his Friends* (1903)

—— *The Life of Charles Dickens as Revealed in his Writings* (1905)

—— *Memories of Charles Dickens* (1913)

FORD, GEORGE H. *Dickens and his Readers* (Princeton, 1955)

—— ed. *The Dickens Critics* (Cornell University Press, 1961) with Lauriat Lane, Jr.

FORSTER, JOHN. *The Life of Charles Dickens*, edited and annotated by J. W. T. Ley, (Doubleday, 1928); also Everyman's Library Edition, edited by A. J. Hoppé (Dent 1966)

GARIS, ROBERT. *The Dickens Theatre: A Reassessment of the Novels* (Clarendon Press, Oxford, 1965)

GISSING, GEORGE. *The Immortal Dickens* (1925)

GREENE, GRAHAM. 'The Young Dickens', in *The Lost Childhood and other Essays* (Viking, 1952)

GROSS, JOHN and PEARSON, GABRIEL, eds. *Dickens and the 20th Century* (Routledge and Kegan Paul, 1962); also John Gross's essay on *A Tale of Two Cities* in this.

HALL, SAMUEL CARTER. *A Book of Memories* (1877)

—— *Retrospect of a Long Life* (1883)

HOUSE, HUMPHRY. *The Dickens World* (Oxford University Press, 1941, Oxford Paperbacks, 1960)

—— Introduction to *Oliver Twist* in Oxford Illustrated Dickens.

—— *All in Due Time* (1955)

HOUSE, MADELINE and STOREY, GRAHAM, eds. *The Pilgrim Edition of the Letters of Charles Dickens*, vol. I, 1820–1839 (Clarendon Press, Oxford, 1965)

HUMPHREYS, ARTHUR L. *Charles Dickens and his First Schoolmaster* (1926)

JACKSON, THOMAS A. *Charles Dickens: The Progress of a Radical* (1938)

JOHNSON, EDGAR. *Charles Dickens. His Tragedy and Triumph* (Simon and Schuster, 1952)

KETTLE, ARNOLD. Essays on *Oliver Twist* in *An Introduction to the English*

Novel (1951) and on *Our Mutual Friend* in *Dickens and the 20th Century* (ed. John Gross and Gabriel Pearson, 1962)

KILLHAM, JOHN. Essay on *Pickwick* in *Dickens and the 20th Century* (1962)

KINGSMILL, HUGH. *The Sentimental Journey* (Morrow, 1935)

KITTON, FREDERICK G. *Charles Dickens by Pen and Pencil* (1890)

—— *The Dickens Country* (1905)

—— *The Minor Writings of Charles Dickens* (1900)

—— *The Novels of Charles Dickens* (1897)

LANE, LAURIAT. *See* Ford

LANE, MARGARET. Introduction to *Christmas Stories* in Oxford Illustrated Dickens

—— *Purely for Pleasure* (Hamish Hamilton, 1966)

LANGTON, ROBERT. *The Childhood and Youth of Charles Dickens* (1891)

LEAVIS, F. R. Essay on *Hard Times* in *The Great Tradition* (1948)

LEY, J. W. T. *The Dickens Circle* (1919). See also Forster and Dexter

LINDSAY, JACK. *Dickens: A Biographical and Critical Study* (1950)

MARCUS, STEVEN. *Dickens: From Pickwick to Dombey* (Basic Books, 1965)

MAUROIS, ANDRÉ. *Charles Dickens* (Harper, 1935)

MILLER, J. HILLIS. *Charles Dickens: The World of His Novels* (Harvard University Press, 1959)

MOYNAHAN, JULIAN. Essay on *Dombey and Son* in *Dickens and the 20th Century* (ed. John Gross and Gabriel Pearson, 1962).

—— *Essays in Criticism* (000)

NISBET, ADA. *Dickens and Ellen Ternan* (University of California Press, 1962)

ORWELL, GEORGE. 'Charles Dickens' in *Inside the Whale* (1940); reprinted in *Decline of the English Murder and Other Essays* (Penguin, 1965)

PEARSON, GABRIEL. Essay on *The Old Curiosity Shop* in *Dickens and the 20th Century* (ed. John Gross and Gabriel Pearson, Routledge and Kegan Paul, 1962)

PEARSON, HESKETH. *His Character, Comedy and Career* (Harper, 1949)

PERUGINI, KATE DICKENS. 'Edwin Drood and the Last Days of Charles Dickens', *Pall Mall Magazine* (June, 1906)

POPE-HENNESSY, UNA. *Charles Dickens* (1946)

PRIESTLEY, J. B. *Charles Dickens* (Studio, 1962)

PRITCHETT, V. S. Essays on *Oliver Twist* in *Books in General* (1953) and on 'The Comic World of Dickens' in *The Dickens Critics* (1961)

—— *The Living Novel* (1946)

PUGH, EDWIN. *The Dickens Originals* (1912)

QUENNELL, PETER. Essay on *Our Mutual Friend* in *The Singular Preference* (1952)

RAY, GORDON N. *The Letters and Private Papers of William Makepeace Thackeray* (1945–1946)

REDESDALE, LORD. *Memories* (1916)

REID, J. C. *The Hidden World of Charles Dickens* (1962)

RENTON, RICHARD. *John Forster and his Friendships* (1913)

RICHARDSON, JOANNA. Essay on *Hard Times* in Everyman's Library edition (Dent, 1954)

RICKS, CHRISTOPHER. Essay on *Great Expectations* in *Dickens and the 20th Century* (ed. John Gross and Gabriel Pearson, 1962)

SHAW, GEORGE BERNARD. Essays on *Hard Times* (1912) and on *Great Expectations* in *Majority, 1931–1952* (1952)

STOREY, GLADYS. *Dickens and Daughter* (Saunders, 1939)

STOREY, GRAHAM—see House

STRAUSS, RALPH. *Dickens: A Portrait in Pencil* (1928)

SYMONS, JULIAN. *Charles Dickens* (Roy, 1951)

TILLOTSON, KATHLEEN. *Novels of the 1840's* (Oxford, 1954)—see also Butt and Clarendon edition of *Oliver Twist* (1966)

TOYNBEE, WILLIAM, ed. *The Diaries of William Charles Macready* (1912)

TRILLING, LIONEL. Introduction to *Little Dorrit* in Oxford Illustrated Dickens

TROLLOPE, T. A. *What I Remember* (1887)

VAN GHENT, DOROTHY. Essay on 'The Dickens World: A View from Todger's' in *The Dickens Critics* (1961)

WAGENKNECHT, EDWARD. *The Man Charles Dickens* (University of Oklahoma Press, 1966)

WAIN, JOHN. Essay on *Little Dorrit* in *Dickens and the 20th Century* (ed. John Gross and Gabriel Pearson, 1962)

WILSON, ANGUS. 'Charles Dickens: A Haunting' in *The Dickens Critics* (1961) and 'The Heroes and Heroines of Dickens' in *Dickens and the 20th Century* (ed. John Gross and Gabriel Pearson, 1962) reprinted from the *Review of English Literature*

WILSON, EDMUND. 'Dickens: The Two Scrooges', in *The Wound and the Bow; Seven Studies in Literature* (Houghton, 1941)

WRIGHT, THOMAS. *The Life of Charles Dickens* (Scribner, 1926)

YATES, EDMUND. *Recollections and Experiences* (1884)

YOUNG, G. M., ed. *Early Victorian England* (Oxford, 1934)

Index

Adrian, Arthur A., 287
Ainsworth, William Harrison (1805–82), 206, 224; and C.D., 158, 183; Macrone asks him for advice, 180; editor of *Bentley's Miscellany*, 217
Alphington, 229
American Notes, see Works of Charles Dickens
Austin, Henry, 161, 206, 230

Barnaby Rudge, see Works of Charles Dickens
Barrow, Charles, 4
Barrow, John Henry, 128, 152
Barrow, Mary ('Aunt Fanny'), 6, 22, 23
Barrow, Thomas, 40–1
Battle of Life, The, see Works of Charles Dickens
Bayley, John, 77–8
Beadnell, Anne, 126, 138; engaged to Henry Kolle, 139; C.D. and, 161
Beadnell, George, 125, 126, 127, 285
Beadnell, Mrs George, 126, 127
Beadnell, Margaret, 126
Beadnell, Maria (later Mrs Henry Winter), 156, 161, 165, 251, 260; C.D. in love with, 125–7; sent to Paris, 129–30; encourages C.D., 130, 139; returns from Paris, 136; cruel to C.D., 138; Mary Anne Leigh makes trouble between C.D. and, 140–1; and C.D. in middle age, 144, 146–7, 285
Beard, Frank, 266, 267, 269
Beard, Thomas, 183, 189, 223; C.D. friendly with, 130, 206; recommends C.D. to *Morning Chronicle*, 152; lends money to C.D., 161; John Dickens and, 161; C.D.'s best man, 170
Bentley, Richard (1794–1871), 184, 229; and C.D., 179, 188, 206, 210, 212, 215–18; and John Forster, 181; character and appearance, 217–18
Bergonzi, Bernard, 74
Blackmore, Edward, 93–4, 103
Bleak House, see Works of Charles Dickens
Blessington, Marguerite, Countess of (1789–1849), 213, 214, 226
Bonny, Jane, 6
Boulogne, 143
Bowes Academy, Greta Bridge, 209
Boyle, Mary, 238

'Boz', origin of pseudonym, 156; most famous author in London, 178; Giles names C.D. 'The Inimitable Boz', 184
Bradbury and Evans, 242, 252, 258–9
Braham, John, 178
Brain, Walter Russell, Lord (1895–1966), xiv; on C.D.'s attacks of 'spasm', 273; on C.D.'s probable cyclothymia, 302
Brighton, 88, 200, 207
British Museum, 187; C.D. in Reading Room of, 127; Mrs Dickens gives C.D.'s letters to, 299
Broadstairs, 210, 223; C.D. able to work at, 136, 207; C.D. visits his children at, 200; C.D. on the delights of, 207; C.D.'s mock love-affair at, 227, 232; C.D.'s parents at, 228, 229
Brother–sister relationship, 193–5, 198–9, 291
Browne, Hablot Knight ('Phiz', 1815–82), 206; to illustrate Pickwick, 176; travels with C.D., 208–9, 210, 224
Browning, Robert (1812–89), 74, 180, 181
Bulwer, Edward, see Lytton, Edward Bulwer-
Burnett, Henry, 187–8
Buss, Robert William, 176
Butt, John, and Tillotson, Kathleen, *Dickens at Work*, 284–5, 291; on C.D.'s social criticism, 300–1

Canning, George, xiv, 4
Carlton, William J., 271, 276; quoted, on chambers at 5 Holborn Court, 97; on John Dickens, 284
Carlyle, Jane Welsh (1801–66), does not accompany her husband to Holland House, 214; on C.D., 245–6, 293; on dining with the Dickenses, 297
Carlyle, Thomas (1795–1881), 181; on Samuel Rogers, 213; on C.D.s' face, 225–6
Cattermole, George (1800–68), 224
Cecil, Lord David, 301
Chalk, Kent, C.D.'s honeymoon spent at, 173; Dickenses and Mary Hogarth at, 184, 187
Chapman and Hall, 217, 226; ask C.D. to write a serial, 168; C.D. gets his own way with, 169; *Pickwick* not an